BROWN AT 50

THE UNFINISHED LEGACY

Defending Liberty
Pursuing Justice

BROWN AT 50

THE UNFINISHED LEGACY

A COLLECTION OF ESSAYS

Edited by

Deborah L. Rhode and Charles J. Ogletree, Jr.

Cover art: Jacob Lawrence
(Photograph Courtesy of Gwendolyn Knight Lawrence / Art Resource, NY)

Cover design: Karen Gill

Printed in the United States of America.

Book design: Pinckard Gill Creative

Library of Congress Cataloging-in-Publication Data
Brown at 50: The Unfinished Legacy. Edited by Deborah L. Rhode and Charles J. Ogletree, Jr. Library of Congress Cataloging-in-Publication Data is on file.

ISBN Number: 1-59031-410-7 (hard bound)
ISBN Number: 1-59031-411-5 (soft bound)

The American Bar Association's Commission on the 50th Anniversary of *Brown v. Board of Education* acknowledges the generous support of our sponsors.

PLATINUM

General Motors

GOLD
SBC
BellSouth

SILVER
Coca-Cola Company
MGM Mirage
Microsoft Corporation
UPS

BRONZE
DuPont
Harvard Law School
Honigman Miller Schwartz & Cohn LLP
Ikon Office Solutions
Johnson Controls, Inc.
Kirkland & Ellis LLP
Meijer
Moore & Van Allen, PLLC
Sidley Austin Brown & Wood LLP
Starbucks Coffee Co.
Weil, Gotshal & Manges Foundation, Inc.

SUPPORTER
Detroit Lions
Detroit Pistons
Bingham McCutchen
Carlton Fields
Foley & Lardner LLP
Kilpatrick Stockton LLP
King & Spalding LLP

Mayer Brown Rowe & Maw LLP
National Bar Institute
Reed Smith LLP
Sonnenschein Nath & Rosenthal LLP
Vinson & Elkins LLP
VISA International
Wilmer Cutler Pickering LLP

SUSTAINER
Ave Maria School of Law
Barris, Sott, Denn & Driker, PLLC
Brigham Young University, J. Reuben Clark
Law School
Butzel Long
Catholic University of America, Columbus
School of Law
Indiana University Foundation
Lewis & Clark Law School
Edward J. Littlejohn
Pillsbury Winthrop LLP
Robins, Kaplan, Miller & Ciresi LLP
Shefsky & Froelich Partnership
South Texas College of Law
Stanford University
Texas Southern University
University of Alabama Law School Foundation
University of Memphis Humphrey School of Law
University of Pittsburgh
Venable, Baetjer and Howard Foundation
Karen Hastie Williams

CONTRIBUTOR
Honorable Avern Cohn
Greene and Letts
Howard University

Dedicated to all
who worked and sacrificed
for equality and justice
and to those who continue the struggle.

Preface

A half century ago, a unanimous Supreme Court issued its landmark decision in *Brown v. Board of Education*, holding that "separate educational facilities are inherently unequal." This collection of essays explores the unfinished legacy of that decision. Brown *at Fifty: The Unfinished Legacy* also marks another historic moment; the essays are published by the American Bar Association during the presidency of Dennis Archer, the first African American ever to lead the Association.

Contributors to this volume come from diverse backgrounds; they include Supreme Court justices, lawyers involved in the *Brown* litigation, and leading legal scholars, historians, and social scientists. Although they offer contrasting, complementary, and sometimes conflicting views of *Brown's* legacy, they share a passionate commitment to its underlying principles. Taken together, their essays remind us both of the progress that we have made over the last half century, and of the progress that remains to be made. From the standpoint of race, our nation remains in many respects still separate and unequal. This collection helps us understand why, and identifies crucial strategies for change.

The first section of the volume explores the role of the lawyers and courts involved in *Brown*. The opening essay by Dennis Archer focuses on the civil rights attorneys who struggled "to win equality by law." His nuanced portrait places that struggle in social context. It grew out of seventy-five years of the indignities of Jim Crow, and a corresponding history of courageous resistance by civil rights lawyers that is not yet over.

United States District Court Judge Robert L. Carter, one of the lawyers in *Brown*, offers a moving account of his involvement in the litigation and the early personal encounters with racism that motivated his commitment to the early civil rights movement. From his early legal training with Charles Hamilton Houston to his work with the NAACP lawyers litigating *Brown*, Judge Carter was convinced that equal education had to become a national priority. As we travel the road to *Brown* through his experiences, it is clear how school segregation came to symbolize a broader system of subordination. *Brown* was a way station in a struggle that Carter urges us to continue.

Professor Genna Rae McNeil chronicles the contributions of Charles Hamilton Houston, the dean of Howard Law School and architect of the early civil rights campaign. Her detailed narrative makes clear why then Supreme Court Justice Thurgood Marshall had it right in a tribute he paid to his former teacher: "We wouldn't have been any place if Charlie hadn't laid the groundwork for it."

At the heart of Stanford University Professor Deborah L. Rhode's piece is Thurgood Marshall, both because he led the legal campaign that culminated in *Brown v. Board of Education*, and because his subsequent career on the bench reflected the same principles underpinning that decision. Marshall's conviction that you "do what you think is right and let the law catch up" can continue to inspire the current struggle for social justice.

Supreme Court Chief Justice William H. Rehnquist shifts the focus to the courts. His essay centers on the role of former Chief Justice Earl Warren. Although Warren is most often remembered for the Court's decisions concerning the rights of criminal defendants, his most enduring contribution may have been *Brown*, which came during his very first year on the bench. As Chief Justice Rehnquist notes, Warren's success in ensuring a unanimous decision gave the ruling a legitimacy and influence that was crucial during the years of southern resistance that followed.

Part II of the collection evaluates *Brown*'s legacy in historical context. New York University Law Professor Derrick A. Bell, Jr., offers the most critical perspective. In his view, what is most striking is that a decision that promised so much has in fact accomplished so little in ending segregation and subordination. The reason, he suggests, is that the ruling allowed courts to avoid "issues of race with which the nation would rather not wrestle, much less try seriously to resolve." To bring that point home, he crafts a hypothetical alternative opinion that makes clear the limitations of the *Brown* holding. If the Warren Court had upheld *Plessy v. Ferguson*'s doctrine of separate but equal, but insisted that it be fully enforced, might African Americans today have better quality education? Perhaps what is now needed, Professor Bell suggests, is a commitment to the equal resources that *Plessy* envisioned but never accomplished.

Robert J. Grey, Jr., the president-elect of the American Bar Association, presents the experience of Prince Edward County, Virginia, as a case history of *Brown*'s significance. This county was a leader in the southern campaign of massive resistance that followed the Supreme Court's ruling. One measure of *Brown*'s accomplishments is that it is now "almost impossible to imagine" what then occurred in Virginia: "an entire county clos[ed] its public schools rather than admit a child of color." But, as Grey notes, the struggle for racial justice is far from over. We continue to need the courage and commitment of attorneys like those in the Prince Edward campaign, who struggled to make *Brown*'s promise a reality.

Harvard Law Professor Lani Guinier begins her essay with an observation echoed throughout the volume: Despite its "exalted status in the constitutional canon," *Brown*'s legacy now seems "more complicated and ambiguous." Part of the reason, she suggests, is that the decision, and those that followed in its wake, allowed integration to become the goal, rather than the means to securing the broader objective of educational equity. As a consequence, "many of the social, political, and economic problems that [lawyers] thought the Court had addressed through *Brown* are still deeply embedded in our society." Significant progress, Guinier argues, will require a fundamental recasting of legal strategies and doctrine.

Anthony Lewis, noted author and former *New York Times* editorialist, reminds us that *Brown* was "more than a decision about school segregation—more, indeed, than a landmark in the law. It was the beginning of a social and political revolution in this country." The virulent backlash that the decision provoked showed "racism for what it was." And the country didn't like what it saw. The result was to help enlist Congress and the federal government on the "side of equal rights" and to transform the racial landscape of the nation.

University of Chicago Law School Professor Cass R. Sunstein opens his essay with the reminder that "on the fiftieth anniversary of the fabled desegregation case, not everyone is celebrating." His analysis suggests why. By distilling insights from recent leading books on *Brown*, Sunstein highlights the decision's continuing contributions and constraints.

The assessment of Professor Mark Tushnet of Georgetown Law School is that *Brown* was an ambiguous holding because its objective was "legally simple but politically problematic." The ruling fudged the critical issue of what role race can ever legitimately play in governmental decision making. That issue remains divisive, as recent affirmative action cases reflect. In Tushnet's view, the nation's extended history of racial subordination has left a legacy of inequality that race-neutral measures cannot remedy. Achieving progress in the next fifty years will require grappling with *Brown*'s unresolved tensions concerning the legitimacy of race-based responses to race-based inequalities.

Part III of the volume focuses on the future. The first essay, by Supreme Court Justice Stephen G. Breyer, identifies two central legacies of *Brown v. Board of Education*, one fulfilled and one unfulfilled. The success of the decision was in establishing the "commitment of the Court and the Nation to the rule of law over prejudice." Implementation of *Brown* required federal troops, but the result was to affirm the supremacy of legal principle in the face of massive resistance. *Brown*'s other objective, however, remains unfulfilled: that of "equal quality education irrespective of race." As Justice Breyer notes, more than 70 percent of African Americans and more than 75 percent of Hispanics now attend schools in which racial minorities predominate. And the resources and performance of those schools are, by all conventional measures, unequal to those in which white students constitute the majority. In short, the "effects of centuries of inequality are painfully evident." And in Breyer's view, adequate responses must come more from policy leaders than from courts.

Columbia Law Professor and former *Brown* lawyer Jack Greenberg looks forward by first looking back. He begins his essay with a key episode in the desegregation of higher education: the admission of James Meredith to the University of Mississippi, eight years after the Court's landmark ruling. The account is a sobering reminder of the courage of those involved in early civil rights campaigns. The second part of Greenberg's essay is an equally sobering assessment of the distance we still need to travel to realize the equal rights that the campaigns envisioned. Our educational system has achieved neither integration nor equality, and no single or simple solutions can meet the complex challenges that remain.

The essay by Harvard Law Professor Charles J. Ogletree, Jr., argues that *Brown I* and *II*, for all their clear vision of the need to end segregation, in effect embraced full integration only gradually and grudgingly. Subsequent courts do not even seem to recognize integration as an imperative. And, according to Ogletree, perhaps the greatest limitation of *Brown* and its progeny is their blind faith in the inevitably of progress and their failure to anticipate how readily those of a different mind could not only resist, but in some cases reverse, our halting progress toward a fully integrated society. The essay concludes with a review of proposals, both radical and incremental, that might bring us closer to the racial equality that *Brown* envisioned but could not realize.

The essay by Harvard social scientists Gary Orfield and Erica Frankenberg summarizes extensive research on school desegregation and resegregation over the last half century. They conclude by identifying concrete remedial strategies involving metropolitan education and housing policies that will be necessary to realize *Brown*'s vision.

In the final analysis, one of *Brown*'s most important legacies is to refocus attention on the gap between our aspirations and achievements on matters of race. Despite enormous progress over the last half century, racial inequalities remain profound, not just in education but on virtually every other measure of social welfare, including health, income, employment, and incarceration. Too many children of color remain trapped in schools that are still separate and still starved for resources. And what is worse, too many adults fail to make these issues a social priority. Massive resistance to integration is behind us, but passive indifference to inequity is not. This volume, like the anniversary it commemorates, is an occasion to celebrate our progress, confront our failures, and reassess our strategies. Most of all, it is an opportunity to reaffirm our commitment to *Brown*'s vision of justice, and the struggle still necessary to achieve it.

Deborah L. Rhode, Stanford Law School
Charles J. Ogletree, Jr., Harvard Law School

Contents

PART III ✂ THE FUTURE

PART I
THE CASE

Bettmann/CORBIS

Demonstration against "Jim Crow" segregation laws. (1944)

Overcoming All Obstacles:
The Lawyers in *Brown v. Board*

Dennis W. Archer

When I became President of the American Bar Association in August of 2003, I decided to dedicate a major portion of my term to promoting a national dialogue about the 1954 Supreme Court decision in *Brown v. Board of Education*. Because issues of race and equality and law are so central to our experience as a nation, I believed that a national reflection on the history and legacy of *Brown* was vital. To advance that vision, I established the ABA Commission on the 50th Anniversary of *Brown v. Board of Education*.

The Commission, headed by Professor Charles J. Ogletree, Jr., of Harvard Law School, has conducted many activities, each designed to help illuminate *Brown*'s place in American history and its legacy in civil rights jurisprudence. This book is the capstone of the Commission's activities.

As my contribution to the book, I'd like to focus briefly on the lawyers involved in the struggle "to win equality by law," to use Thurgood Marshall's eloquent phrase. The *Brown* case did not occur in a vacuum, of course. Behind it were more than 75 years of the indignities of Jim Crow, and a history of legal resistance nearly as long.

The reign of Jim Crow wasn't ended by bullets or ballots. Winning equality didn't come about through violence, and, because of the disenfranchisement of so many African American voters, it couldn't take place through the political process. Instead, it came about through our courts and our Constitution.

Think of the plight of the men and women who strove against the Jim Crow regime. The removal of federal troops from the South in 1877, and subsequent developments, meant that they couldn't count on any help from the national government. It was even more futile to approach the state legislatures or city councils and ask for a repeal of the unjust laws of segregation. Without the vote, minorities had no real opportunity to influence the political process.

All that they had, really, was the fact that the courts were open to them and the Constitution afforded certain guarantees, most notably that no state shall "deny to any person within its jurisdiction the equal protection of the laws."

The first attempts to win equality through the law did not go well. By the 1890s, laws throughout the South separated the races almost everywhere—in restaurants, hotels, theaters, parks, and, of course, in schools. These laws would seem, on their face, to deny the "equal protection of the laws" commanded by the Fourteenth Amendment. In 1896, the case of *Plessy v. Ferguson* challenged one such law—providing for separate railroad cars for each race—before the U.S. Supreme Court.

The Court held 8-1 that separate facilities did not violate the Fourteenth Amendment, as long as the facilities provided for blacks were equal to those provided for whites.

Justice Henry Billings Brown's majority opinion distinguished between legal and social equality.

> *"The object of the [Fourteenth] amendment was undoubtedly to enforce the absolute equality of the two races before the law, but in the nature of things it could not have been intended to abolish distinctions based upon color, or to enforce social, as distinguished from political, equality. . . . If one race be inferior to the other socially, the Constitution of the United States cannot put them upon the same plane."*

Justice John Marshall Harlan was the sole dissenter, writing "Our Constitution is color-blind, and neither knows nor tolerates classes among citizens."

Less than fifteen years after the Supreme Court upheld "separate but equal" facilities in *Plessy*, a group of individuals committed to fighting against the brutalities of Jim Crow formed the National Association for the Advancement of Colored People (NAACP). It was the NAACP that was ultimately to lead the legal struggle against discrimination.

In its early years, under the leadership of a white attorney, Moorfield Storey, the NAACP had a role in several Supreme Court cases, and scored some victories. Shortly after the founding of the NAACP, Storey filed an amicus brief for the NAACP in *Guinn v. United States* (238 U.S. 347, 1915). The case involved a provision of the Oklahoma Constitution with a "grandfather clause" that said that no one lineally descended from a voter qualified as of 1866 could be excluded from voting, even if he were illiterate. The Court unanimously struck this down as contravening the

Fifteenth Amendment. A few years later, Storey argued the case of *Buchanan v. Warley* (245 U.S. 60, 1917), in which the Court unanimously struck down a Louisville statute that segregated housing in the city. The Court determined that the statute violated the Fourteenth Amendment as well as civil rights statutes of the Reconstruction Era.

The greatest part of the legal struggle, however, had to wait until a great lawyer and teacher put together an all-star team of litigators. Charles Hamilton Houston, the son of a Washington, D.C., lawyer, was a Phi Beta Kappa student at Amherst and was class valedictorian. At Harvard Law School, he was the first African American elected to the *Harvard Law Review*. After graduating, he earned a graduate degree from Harvard as Doctor of Juridical Science, then returned to the District to practice law with his father. His dream, however, was to use the law to lift his race from second-class citizenship.

He got his opportunity in 1929, when he was named dean of the all-black Howard University Law School. Under his leadership, the faculty at Howard included such eminent scholars and future civil rights litigators as George Hayes, William Henry Hastie, and James M. Nabrit, Jr. Together they produced some of the greatest legal talents America has seen. This group of black attorneys included Robert L. Carter, Oliver Hill, Spottswood W. Robinson III, and—perhaps

most famous of all—Thurgood Marshall. Working individually and through the NAACP, and along with such colleagues as William T. Coleman, Louis Redding, and Constance Baker Motley, these lawyers would change the course of American law and society.

In 1935, Houston left Howard to become special counsel to the NAACP. In the '30s and '40s, the NAACP and the lawyers Houston trained chipped away at the legal structure supporting segregation. They successfully challenged all-white jury pools, covenants that restricted ownership of property in certain neighborhoods by race, and laws disenfranchising black voters.

Howard University Law School
1943–1956

At the NAACP, Houston refined a legal strategy to end school segregation. According to Richard Kruger in his masterful book *Simple Justice*, Houston reasoned as follows:

> *The black attack [on school segregation] ought to begin in an area where the whites were most vulnerable and least likely to respond with anger. That segregation had produced blatantly discriminatory and unequal school systems, Houston calculated, was most obvious at the level of graduate and professional schools.... There*

were [only two] graduate or professional schools at any black college in the South....Here was an area where the educational facilities for blacks were neither separate nor equal but non-existent...[Through legal action] the South would either have to build and operate separate graduate schools for blacks or admit them to white ones.

One of the first successful tests of this strategy was *Murray v. Maryland* (182 A. 590, 1936), which is also notable for being Thurgood Marshall's first civil rights case. Marshall and Houston worked on the case together, but Marshall's recollections leave no doubt as to who was the lead counsel.

I worked on the case on the ground and I drew the pleadings since there was some intricate old Maryland common law involved, but outside the legwork, I did very little. The court presentation was his [Houston's] doing. The fact is, I never was chief counsel in a case that Charlie took part in.

Maryland refused to admit Mr. Murray, an African American, to its law school. No law or school charter commanded this result—it was the school's custom. Noting that there was no in-state alternative institution through which Murray might receive a legal education, Marshall and Houston argued that he must be admitted to the law school. The trial court agreed, issuing a writ of mandamus to that effect. The Maryland Court of Appeals upheld that ruling, noting "Compliance with the Constitution cannot be deferred at the will of the state. Whatever system is adopted for legal education now must furnish equality of treatment."

Charles H. Houston
Chief Counsel for the National Association for the Advancement of Colored People Charles Hamilton Houston was nominated by the United Government Workers to be appointed to the U.S. Supreme Court by President Roosevelt. (1939)

Even though Houston resigned as a staff member of the NAACP in 1939, he remained active in the organization and in its legal struggles. The strategy he outlined guided a number of cases and produced notable victories. In *Missouri ex rel. Gaines v. Canada* (305 U.S. 337, 1938), Missouri had offered to pay the black plaintiff's tuition at an out-of-state law school. The U.S. Supreme Court held that this denied him equal protection and ordered his admission to the school. In *Sweatt v. Painter* (399 U.S. 629, 1950), the Court held that a hastily created law school for blacks in Texas was in no way equal to the University of Texas Law School, and ordered that the black plaintiff be admitted to the state's formerly all-white school. In *McLaurin v. Oklahoma State Regents for Higher Education* (339 U.S. 637, 1950) the Court struck down the practice of admitting a black student but keeping him physically separated from his white counterparts.

Houston didn't quite live to see these last two victories. He died earlier in 1950, at the age of 55. His colleague William Hastie wrote this tribute:

> *He guided us through the legal wilderness of second-class citizenship. He was truly the Moses of the journey. He lived to see us close to the promised land of true equality under the law, closer than even he dared hope when he set out on that journey and so much closer than would have been possible without his genius and his leadership.*

Houston's original strategy had envisioned beginning the assault on segregated education on the graduate level and eventually bringing it to the elementary and secondary schools. Both *Sweatt* and *McLaurin* were unanimous decisions, in which the Court's opinions were blunt and forceful. It seemed to many observers that statutory school segregation was on its last legs, and Thurgood Marshall, then the NAACP's legal counsel, urged the organization to deliver a frontal attack by directly challenging "separate but equal" in cases from the public schools.

The strategy was not without risk. James Nabrit, soon to become Howard Law School's dean, acknowledged that fact but argued:

> *I thought it was fallacy to say, as some were saying, that if we lost before the Court on overturning segregation per se, we'd be set back a generation. Separate-but-equal was still there, and if we lost we could come back into court the next day arguing [equalizing facilities under]* Plessy.

The NAACP pursued several school desegregation cases in the early 1950s. The general pattern was that each case would be handled jointly by a local lawyer and a lawyer from the NAACP's national headquarters. The extent of inequality in the various school systems varied, with segregated schools occasionally equal in regard to some measures, such as money spent per student. In all instances, however, the schools were segregated by law, and the NAACP's position was that real equality could not be achieved until segregation was brought to an end.

The case known as *Brown v. Board of Education of Topeka, Kansas,* actually included appeals from decisions in four separate states: Kansas, Delaware, South Carolina, and Virginia. Two of the cases came from states that were not part of the Confederacy, in keeping with the NAACP's general strategy of not bringing test cases from the Deep South.

The *Brown* case itself came from one of the few segregated schools in Kansas. Kansas law permitted cities of 15,000 or more to segregate schools under the high school level. Parents of 13 black elementary-age students tried to enroll their children in one of the city's "white only" elementary schools. In 1951, the parents filed suit in federal district court to enforce their right to equal protection of the law. On this case, Topeka lawyer Charles Scott teamed with a young protégé of Thurgood Marshall, Robert L. Carter, another Howard Law graduate.

The district court found that the facilities provided for black and white students were substantially equal to those provided for white students. Under *Plessy*, the court felt that it was bound by precedent to deny that segregation violated the students' equal protection rights. The court did issue a finding of fact that "segregation of white and colored children in public schools has a detrimental effect upon the colored children," and that "the impact is greater when it has the sanction of law."

The Delaware case, *Gebhard v. Belton*, was jointly argued by Jack Greenberg from NAACP headquarters and a Wilmington lawyer, Louis Redding, for whom this case was one of many outstanding contributions to cause of equal justice. It gave the NAACP a taste of the victory to come when Chancellor Collins Seitz of the Delaware Court of Chancery ruled that two "white only" schools had to admit black students who had proved that the education they were offered at segregated schools was substantially unequal to the education white students received. The Delaware Supreme Court affirmed, noting that a decision that segregation per se violated the Constitution would have to come from the United States Supreme Court. Nonetheless, the victory in *Gebhard* was such that it was the only one of the consolidated cases brought on appeal to the U.S. Supreme Court by the defendants, not the plaintiffs.

Bettmann/CORBIS

Thurgood Marshall, chief counsel NAACP Legal Defense Fund, with James M. Nabrit, Jr., dean of Howard University Law School (center) and Jack Greenberg, assistant counsel NAACP Legal Defense Fund. (1960)

The two other test cases were from the South. In Virginia, the test case (*Davis v. County School Board of Prince Edward County*) came from a bastion of segregation that, after *Brown*, closed down its public school system rather than desegregate. The lawyers in charge were Spottswood W. Robinson III from the NAACP office, teaming with another Howard Law graduate, Oliver Hill, a Richmond lawyer and member of that locality's city council.

The case arose after black students protested the inadequate conditions at their high school and got nowhere. They sought the NAACP's help, leading to the federal lawsuit asking the court to declare invalid the provision of Virginia's state constitution that required segregation of schools by race. State officials scrambled to "equalize"—and thus preserve—the segregated high school, approving the building of a new school. A three-member panel of federal judges ordered school authorities to continue to equalize educational opportunities for black students, but declined to rule segregation unconstitutional.

In South Carolina, the test case (*Briggs v. Elliott*) came from a poor rural county in which white children had 30 school buses to transport them, and black children none. White schools were modern brick buildings; black schools were wooden shacks without running water. Spending per black pupil was less than a quarter of spending for white students. Even though the inequalities were easy to demonstrate, co-counsels Thurgood Marshall and Harold Boulware, a local attorney who was also a product of Howard Law School, offered expert testimony by social scientists on the detrimental effects of legally enforced segregation.

The three-judge federal panel split 2-1, with the majority holding that the state must equalize the segregated black facilities, but refusing to invalidate segregation itself. Judge Julius Waties Waring dissented from the opinion of his two colleagues, declaring that "*segregation is per se inequality.*"

The four cases were argued on appeal to the United States Supreme Court, along with a fifth companion case, *Bolling v. Sharpe*, from the District of Columbia. (Because the Fourteenth Amendment applies only to the states, the D.C. case was argued separately as a violation of Fifth Amendment liberty guarantees; the lawyers were James Nabrit and Howard Law School faculty member George Hayes).

The chief justice's article in this book discusses what happened next—the arguments and the rearguments, culminating in a unanimous decision that declared, "We conclude that in the field of public education the doctrine of separate but equal has no place. Separate educational facilities are inherently unequal." Not only did *Brown* strike down schools segregated by law, it sparked demands for justice in other contexts, in areas like voting rights, gender equality, and protections for disabled Americans. The spirit of *Brown* deserves much of the credit for the country's achievement in social justice, and it continues to inspire the push for progress.

In many ways, *Brown v. Board of Education* was a triumph of law and of a band of dedicated and incredibly talented lawyers. But I don't want to leave the story there.

We can't forget the plaintiffs in these and the other cases that accomplished so much on the march toward equality. Each case represented individual acts of courage by families willing to face local resistance—even hostility—to bring an end to segregation. Plaintiffs were threatened; some lost their jobs. By persevering against pressure, they made these cases possible.

Conspicuously missing from this honor roll, I'm sorry to say, is the organized bar. The ABA itself was segregated until the 1940s and took no part in any of the cases consolidated in *Brown*. It filed no amicus brief in *Brown*, and none of its committees or other entities seems to have taken any role. Ironically, the association receives some reflected glory from an earlier period. Moorfield Storey, the white NAACP president who won a Supreme Court case during World War I, was a former ABA president.

Of course, many state bar associations remained segregated even longer than the ABA, and they too took no role in the NAACP's quest for justice. This was a serious problem. As James Nabrit described the early years:

> *The real problem in those days was that we didn't have the facilities to argue these cases as well as we might have. We didn't have the lawbooks, we didn't have the precedent cases, we didn't have the sample briefs and records of procedure, and we couldn't use the facilities or contacts of the bar associations since they wouldn't let us belong.*

As the ABA enters its 127th year, in August, 2004, I cannot help but think about the likes of William Hastie, Leon Higgenbotham, Charles Hamilton Houston, Damon J. Keith, Constance Baker Motley, Wade McCree, and Mr. Justice Thurgood Marshall. And there are so many others. I wonder how the legal profession might have advanced if they could have, as young lawyers, been involved in the great debates that took place in our association and how much further we might have been in the area of race relations, and how much better our country might have been.

Of course, the situation is far different now, and I believe we have a bright future: I think my having the privilege to serve as ABA president, and Robert Grey, Jr., of Virginia being president-elect, is a major statement and bodes well for the future of our association. For example, at the 2004 ABA Annual Meeting, Steven Zack, a Cuban American, will become chair of the ABA House of Delegates, and Armando Lasa Ferrer, a Latino American, will become secretary of the American Bar Association.

If you look at the world, the majority of people happen to be people of color. And if we are to be competitive in the global marketplace, to work with one another and cause the world to be a better place in which to live, it is important that we have respect for one another and for the rule of law.

The bar associations can and do have a significant role to play in this process. The ABA is involved in myriad issues, fully debated by our diverse membership. On many of the pressing questions, the ABA contributes to the national debate, through such means as congressional testimony and the filing of amicus briefs, such as our brief in favor of the University of Michigan's affirmative action policies in *Grutter v. Bollinger*.

Demographers have told us that "minorities" will be the majority in this country by 2056. Coincidently, this will be right around the time of the 100th anniversary of *Brown*. The tides of change are sweeping across America now, just as they were in the years before and after *Brown*. This time, I trust, the American Bar Association and the legion of state and local bars are ready to participate fully, and to lend the weight of the collective wisdom of our diverse members to the ongoing process of achieving equality under law.

Dennis W. Archer, former Detroit mayor and Michigan Supreme Court justice, is the president of the American Bar Association. Mr. Archer is the first person of color elected to the highest office of the association. He served two four-year terms as mayor of the city of Detroit, and was president of the National League of Cities. After leaving the mayor's office, Mr. Archer was elected chairman of Dickinson Wright PLLC law firm, and he sits on the boards of several corporations. Mr. Archer was appointed an associate justice of the Michigan Supreme Court in 1985. He was elected to an eight-year term the following year. He has served as president of the Wolverine Bar Association, the National Bar Association, and the State Bar of Michigan. He is a Life Member of the Fellows of the American Bar Foundation and the National Bar Association; a Fellow of the International Society of Barristers; and Life Member of the Sixth Circuit Judicial Conference. He has also been recognized for his leadership by several organizations and publications. He earned a bachelor of science degree in education from Western Michigan University, and a Juris Doctor degree from Detroit College of Law.

African American Student Sits Outside of Classroom
G. E. McLaurin, a 54-year-old African American, sits in an anteroom, apart from the other students, as he attends class at the University of Oklahoma. The university insisted he be segregated within the school after a federal district court ruling forced the institution to accept McLaurin as a student. (1948)

The Road to *Brown*

Robert L. Carter

The road to *Brown* runs through me. I was born in Florida on March 11, 1917. The rest of the family had gone to Newark, New Jersey, where my father was relocating the family after having accepted a job working in a factory in Newark. I believe I was told it was a supervisory position, but I am not certain of that. My mother was left in Careyville to await my birth. Six weeks after I said hello to the world my mother and I joined the rest of the family in Newark. We were part of the initial wave of black migration from rural South to urban North.

My father and mother were residents of Wilmington, North Carolina. I do not know why my mother was in such a rural location awaiting my appearance. My initial thought was that my mother and father were itinerant sharecroppers, but my mother had an above-average education for a first-generation black woman to be born free. She could read and write and until her death at 98 years of age she kept abreast of the news by reading the local newspapers augmented by radio and later television news reports. Her role as my father's wife was to make a home for him and their children.

I had no interest in any of this until about a year ago when I decided to put to paper my own history. By then unfortunately the people who could enlighten me had all gone—mother, father, aunts, uncles, and older siblings whom might know more. I have no idea what my father did. My mother did not expect to work but my father died suddenly when I was a year old. Having no marketable skills and being black, she had to try to make a living washing clothes for white people. Until I was about eleven years old, we lived on the second- and third-floor flat on Boyden

Street, which was reported to have become one of the worst black slums in the country. (Newark is now undergoing a slum clearance and rebuilding program that may remove Boyden Street from its "worst black slum" category.)

There was no indoor heating at the Boydon Street address. There was a wood-burning stove in the kitchen and an outhouse about 20 yards from the back of the building available not only for my family's use but for the public at large. We were poor, of course, but poverty then seems to have been far different from poverty now. Entrance to our quarters was up a flight of stairs on the side of the building about 25 feet from the street. There was a kitchen, a good-sized living room, and two decent-sized bedrooms. The upper floor was an open attic where I slept. I bathed once a week in a tin tub filled with water heated on the kitchen stove.

When my father died suddenly in 1918, my mother was immobilized with grief until her sister Aunt Lena came from North Carolina and forced her to face the reality that my father was gone from her life and that she had three small children to care for and five adolescents to steer to maturity. Being an indifferent cook, the only employment available for her was washing clothes for one or more white families. When I was about six years old, another devastating tragedy struck. My oldest brother and second oldest sister, both the beauties of the family, and my oldest sister, who was in an unhappy marriage, fell ill and died within a span of eighteen months. At the time, I thought their deaths were from tuberculosis and that we were all doomed to sicken and be felled by that disease. The probability was that some more lethal and fast debilitating virus was the culprit, since tuberculosis is a longer lingering disease than the one that took my three oldest siblings. But we were spared further deaths in the family until 1943 when my then oldest brother and oldest sister died, leaving only the three youngest alive. My mother and oldest sister died circa the mid-1970s, leaving only my sister and me. She will be 90 in October 2004, and I turned 87 in March 2004.

Although the correlation is now being questioned, I was a skilled test taker, which was then taken as evidence of gifted intellectual capability. I do not know how intellectually gifted I was, but I knew how to take tests so I was regarded as being gifted and was skipped over several grades in my K to 8th grade grammar school. The teachers in the Burnet Street elementary school I attended kept an eye on me and reported home when they thought I was getting too involved with anyone whom they regarded as bad company.

During my childhood and young adult years in the state, New Jersey in race relations mirrored the South more closely than any of the other northeastern seaboard states. It was firmly committed to white supremacy and black subordination. Employment discrimination was severe. Blacks were barred from hotels and restaurants except in some service capacity. While the schools were not segregated, interracial social intercourse was virtually nonexistent. This is one of the reasons the memory of a black girl and a white girl in my sixth grade class is still retained after all these years.

The white girl had straight brown hair, which she wore long, and had to constantly toss her head to keep the hair away from her eyes. The black girl mimicked her friend's head tossing activity, although her hair was in braids tightly pinned to the top of her head and not falling over her eyes obscuring her vision. At one point the two had a falling out and the white girl complained to the teacher about something the black girl had done to her. The teacher offered no sympathy and told the white girl, "It serves you right. You should stay with your own kind." I have never forgotten that incident. Even if the actual words spoken differ from what I recollect, the message would be the same. Nonetheless there was no open hostility to the presence of blacks.

I enrolled in a college preparatory course in Barringer High School in Newark, one of the most select public high schools in the state, highly regarded for the quality of its college preparatory curriculum and attended largely by middle-class whites. I was the only black enrolled in the college preparatory program. There had been no black teachers in my elementary grades and none thus far in high school. Until I reached high school, all my teachers had been white women except for the physical education instructor. Barringer High's Latin and French teachers were white men. As was true of the Newark elementary school I attended, there did not appear to be any open hostility to blacks but social relationships across race lines almost never happened.

Even though I had straight A's in my two-and-a-half year attendance at Barringer, no teacher or school official advised me about scholarships to Rutgers, a state university, or even discussed the possibility of college. I am reasonably certain that today a student of color whom teachers considered intellectually gifted would receive help and assistance in getting to college. We moved to East Orange, requiring me to complete the secondary school curriculum at East Orange High School. Racism was virulent in East Orange. Faculty and school officials made no attempt to dissemble their distaste for having blacks in attendance at the school. In that hostile atmosphere my grades fell from A's to mostly D's, and I almost flunked out. That near disaster appears to have given me the mental toughness to never again allow a hostile environment in which I was forced to work adversely effect the quality of my professional performance. Because I had done so well previously, even with the scholastic disaster at East Orange High, I might have secured some kind of work scholarship at Rutgers. But no one I knew had that kind of information and no school official with the information supplied it. As I reflect on my experience it seems that none of the white teachers or school officials put forth any effort to help even those black students they believed possessed gifted intellectual potential to go on to the university. Today, it seems, help, encouragement, and assistance would be forthcoming—a major advance from my elementary and secondary school days.

When I reached the 7th grade in elementary school, my family's economic resources improved to allow us to adopt a middle-class lifestyle. We moved to dwellings recessed from the street, fronted with a lawn and hedges, with indoor heating, bathrooms, and a bedroom for myself. This more comfortable lifestyle was fine, but I knew for me to survive it had to be capped with at least a college education. An alumnus of Lincoln University, and $500 my family somehow managed to produce, saw me off to Lincoln University in September 1933 at age 16.

In 1933 Lincoln was on the cusp of change. It began as a missionary-type institution run by former Princeton University professors and alumni seeking to lift up poor blacks by providing educational benefits enabling them to help bring civilization to their people. My class rebelled against this "white man's burden" ethos—the perceived duty of white Christians to bring civilization to what they regarded as near-savage blacks.

We demanded that more blacks be hired on the faculty and in administrative positions. Our class began the process of putting African Americans in control of the institution. The school is sited in a beautiful bucolic setting between Baltimore and Philadelphia. In this semi-isolated environment, one tends to bond closely with fellow students and devote more time to one's books without the many distractions of an urban environment. I made friendships there that lasted for a lifetime and I flourished academically. My chief academic interests were history and political science.

I wanted to pursue either of those subjects in graduate school. However, in my senior year the dean of Howard University Law School came to Lincoln recruiting, offered me a scholarship, and off to law school I went in September 1937. Charles Houston had graduated from Harvard Law school and became Howard's law dean in 1928. At the time Howard had a night school and was geared chiefly to getting its students equipped to pass the D.C. bar exam. As dean, Houston abolished the night school, put in place a curriculum fashioned on Harvard's, secured accreditation for the school and attracted some outstanding scholars to join Howard's law faculty.

Houston looked upon the 14th Amendment as the black Magna Charta, and declared Howard's primary mission to be the training of a cadre of well-qualified black lawyers who would return to their hometowns and commence a variety of test case litigation challenging on 14th Amendment grounds the validity of racial discrimination in various areas of American life. This was in effect civil rights litigation. Until then no mainline law school offered such a course. Now civil rights is part of the curriculum of every major law school in the country.

Test case litigation was key to freeing blacks from government-enforced segregation and racial discrimination. Segregation was enforced through the so-called separate but equal doctrine—segregation was valid if black facilities were the substantial equivalent of facilities provided for whites. Houston's idea was to have qualified blacks apply for acceptance to all the state colleges where graduate facilities available to whites were not available in the black state facilities—the theory being that maintenance of the system would become too costly and would be abandoned. When I finished Howard, I was awarded a Rosenwald Fellowship and enrolled in Columbia University to pursue what was then called a doctorate in juridical science. My dissertation was a probe of the relevance and correlation between preservation of the First Amendment and maintenance of our democratic society. Under my program at Columbia, approval of the partially completed dissertation by my faculty advisor authorized award of a masters in law degree. I received my advisor's approval but too late for the award in the 1941 school year. It was given in February 1942. At that point I was a draftee in the Army Air Force and had been in the service for about seven months.

Before becoming a draftee in the Army Air Force I had, of course, experienced race discrimination and had been subjected to segregation and dismissal by whites because of my race and color. What black person then or now has not had that experience? Racism encountered in the army, however, was so raw, crude and virulent, so spawned by hatred, that you were completely engulfed by its venom. Before my exposure to this racist indoctrination of the armed forces, my plan, although not set, was to complete my dissertation and secure a teaching position in the academy.

The arbitrariness and harm inflicted by the racism I encountered in the army, however, made me discard all thought of academia as a career. I was determined to use my talents on return to civilian life to fight racism. In 1945, I had never heard of the NAACP and did not know who Thurgood Marshall or Walter White were. I had achieved an outstanding scholastic record at Howard. Marshall was

Robert L. Carter, a lawyer for the national NAACP, defends Daisy Bates, State President of the Arkansas NAACP, in a Little Rock courtroom. (1958)

looking for someone with my credentials. Thus I joined the NAACP legal staff as a legal research assistant since I had not yet been admitted to the bar. I took one of those bar review courses and took the bar exam in July or October and was notified in December that I had passed.

In or about 1952 we were about to institute litigation challenging grade and secondary school segregation in South Carolina and Kansas. I was reading anything that I thought had relevance, and I came across a study by Otto Klineberg showing that the longer black children migrating from segregated schools in the South to unsegregated schools in Philadelphia stayed in the Philadelphia school system, the higher they scored on IQ and intelligence achievement tests. What the study told me was that segregation adversely affected the ability of the black child to learn.

This was the controlling thesis of the school segregation cases decided under the rubric *Brown v. Board of Education*, as briefed, argued, and adopted by the Court in its 1954 decision on the merits. It is regarded as the most important law holding of the twentieth century and it changed American life. It is gratifying to have participated in something that has had such momentous impact for good.

Robert L. Carter is U.S. district judge for the Southern District of New York and a pillar of the civil rights movement. Born in Florida and raised in New Jersey, Judge Carter earned his bachelor's degree from Lincoln University and his law degree from Howard University. He studied further at Columbia University as a Rosenwald Fellow. He served in the United States Army Air Corps as second lieutenant from 1941 to 1944. Judge Carter began his twenty-four-year career with the National Association for the Advancement of Colored People (NAACP) in 1944 as a legal assistant. He became assistant special counsel (NAACP) and assistant counsel (NAACP Legal Defense Fund) in 1945, and NAACP general counsel in 1956. While counsel for the NAACP and assistant counsel for the Legal Defense Fund, Judge Carter was part of the legal team that planned the strategies and argued the landmark case of *Brown v. Board of Education*, which outlawed segregation in public education. Judge Carter won an unprecedented twenty-one of twenty-two cases before the United States Supreme Court.

Bettmann/CORBIS

Charles Houston Voicing His Protest

Charles H. Houston (standing) protests to the Washington, D.C., school board concerning its decision against allowing African American singer Marian Anderson to sing in the Central High School Auditorium. Anderson had already been barred from Constitution Hall by the Daughters of the American Revolution. (1939)

Groundwork

Genna Rae McNeil

Excerpted from
Groundwork: Charles Hamilton Houston and the Struggle for Civil Rights[1]
(University of Pennsylvania Press, 1983)

W e wouldn't have been anyplace if Charlie hadn't laid the groundwork for it," Thurgood Marshall, associate justice of the Supreme Court of the United States, told an audience of blacks and whites assembled to pay tribute to his former teacher and friend, Charles Hamilton Houston.[2] Encountering some puzzled faces following such a sweeping testimonial, Marshall, with his inimitable directness, added:

> *You have a large number of people who never heard of Charlie Houston. But you're going to hear about him, because he left us such important items.... When Brown against the Board of Education was being argued in the Supreme Court ... [t]here were some two dozen lawyers on the side of the Negroes fighting for their schools.... [O]f those ... lawyers only two hadn't been touched by Charlie Houston.... [T]hat man was the engineer of all of it.... I can tell you this, ... if you do it legally, Charlie Houston made it possible....This is what I think ... Charlie Houston means to us.*[3]

Marshall, Charles Houston's best-known student, has always been generous with his praise concerning Houston. Some have listened and dismissed Marshall's assessment as the adoration of an admiring student. Others have discounted it as an aspect of the dutiful modesty of a student who surpassed his teacher. Nevertheless, Marshall's words serve to remind African Americans and white Americans who are insistent about equal and just distribution of civil rights and liberties that they are recipients of Houston's legacy.

Twenty years after *Brown v. Board of Education* and *Bolling v. Sharpe*, Justice William O. Douglas joined Marshall in directing attention to Houston as a civil rights lawyer and litigator. "I knew Charles H. Houston, and I sincerely believe he was one of the top ten advocates to appear before this court in my 35 years." In a later autobiography, *The Court Years, 1939–1975*, Douglas vividly recalled that Houston "was a veritable dynamo of energy guided by a mind that had as sharp a cutting edge as any I have known."

When Houston decided to study law so that he could influence American government and protect African American citizens in the exercise of their rights, he joined three traditions. Kenneth Tollett has noted the historical relationship of the legal profession to government and the enunciation of civil liberties.

> *Traditionally, lawyers have played a critically important role in the political and economic development of the United States. Twenty-five of the fifty-six signers of the Declaration of Independence were lawyers. Thirty-one of the fifty-five members of the Constitutional Convention were lawyers. The United States House of Representatives and Senate … and legislative bodies across the country have had a larger proportion of officials and members from the legal profession than from any other profession.*[4]

Houston's choice of career placed him in this one tradition, while his principles and race placed him in two other traditions. Since John S. Rock's admission to practice before the U.S. Supreme Court on February 7, 1865, black lawyers have been attempting to win equal rights for citizens of African descent in the Court. Moreover, since Africans' and African Americans' petitions and resolutions to colonial ruling powers, blacks in North America have been protesting denials of liberty and justice in not only courts but also in legislative assemblies. Regarding this third tradition, of which Houston became a part, Derrick A. Bell, Jr., legal scholar, has offered critical insights. "The history of black people's reliance on the law in their centuries-long struggle for freedom and equality is a story … of slow, painful ascent from slavery … and virtually no attention is given to just how little even some of the major events changed or improved [African Americans'] status."[5]

Charles Houston's life and work elucidate the stark reality of the second-class status of African Americans between 1895 and 1950. As an attorney, Houston found that the truths labeled "self-evident" and the rights labeled "natural" became arguable issues when he presented claims for African Americans. The basis for this was historical.

The "all men are created equal" of the 1776 Declaration of Independence and the "We the people of the United States" of the 1787 Constitution were not obviously inclusive. The first phrase generally proclaimed a new normative system, while the other described the citizenry, but both were framed by whites with whites only in mind. The generality of the eighteenth-century language provided options to consider or not to consider the humanity of blacks. However, the political and economic affairs of a burgeoning nineteenth-century slave system eroded the options. Because so few challenged either slavery or the racism it bred, in 1857 Justice Roger Taney confidently claimed, for the majority of the Supreme Court, that in early American history a black "had no rights which the white man was bound to respect."[6] As Judge A. Leon Higginbotham, Jr., has said, there was an "early failure of the nation's founders and their constitutional heirs to share the legacy of freedom with black Americans."[7]

Only after blacks seized liberty and demanded rights during a time of civil strife did lawmaking bodies delineate clearly the citizenship rights of African Americans. The U.S. Supreme Court's *Dred Scott* decision on black citizenship in 1857 was nullified by the collective language of the Thirteenth Amendment abolishing slavery (1865), the Civil Rights Act of 1866, and the Fourteenth (1868) and Fifteenth (1870) Amendments. The 1866 statute specified that "all persons born in the United States and not subject to any foreign power" were citizens who, regardless of "race and color," were entitled to "make and enforce contracts, to sue, be parties, and give evidence; to inherit, purchase, lease, sell, hold and convey real and personal property," and to enjoy the "full and equal benefits of all laws and proceedings for the security of persons and property as is enjoyed by white persons."[8] The Fourteenth Amendment not only affirmed the national and state citizenship of African Americans, but also prohibited any state's action to "make or enforce any law which shall abridge the privileges or immunities of citizens … deprive any person of life, liberty, or property, without due process of law … [or] deny to any person within its jurisdiction the equal protection of the laws." Finally, the Fifteenth Amendment provided that interference with voting on account of race color was illegal. By 1870, African Americans were citizens with equal rights on paper. The laws of the land conceded their personhood and citizenship.

In less than four decades, the "gains made by blacks—political, legal and social—were erased … [and] the Supreme Court and the lower courts confirmed in their decisions … that the citizenship [blacks] had been granted, which they believed they had earned through the blood of thousands of black men who had died fighting on the Union side during the [Civil] War, was citizenship in name only.["]9 Unless they were acting on behalf of a state, white Americans could discriminate against blacks, and forced separation of people on the basis of race and color became perfectly legal. The Civil Rights Cases of 1883 and the *Plessy v. Ferguson* case of 1896, respectively, permitted state and private discrimination and segregation.[10] White racist force, wealth, and power effectively disfranchised blacks in the southern states, where over 75 percent of the African American population lived, and the federal government failed to invoke its considerable legal powers to prevent violation of black people or their rights. Likening the United States to the Republic of South Africa, the late William H. Hastie, Jr., the first black appointed to a federal judgeship, summarized the status of African Americans, and the conditions under which they lived in the early twentieth century: "The effective institutionalization of racism was the common experience of most Negroes.…[A]partheid seemed as irradicable and almost as pervasive a feature of the American legal order as it appears to be in South Africa."[11]

Because of institutionalized racism in America, two of the consequences of Houston's choice to complete law school and become a practicing attorney were his double exclusion and double minority. As a black man, he was excluded from full participation in American society, and as a black lawyer he was excluded from full participation in the predominantly white American bar and the legal process. As a black man, he was part of a group that constituted only 10 percent of the American population, and as a black lawyer he was part of a group that constituted less than 1 percent of the American legal profession.

❖ ❖ ❖

Howard Law School

Charles Houston is remembered best by those students who encountered him during the formative period of the modern accredited Howard Law School. Few of them were without mixed emotions while going through Howard as its first accredited classes, because Dean Houston was ferocious in his insistence that no one be a mediocre Howard Law graduate. As these students recalled, he "ran Howard the same way Harvard was run," and was quite at ease telling first-year students, "Look to your left and look to your right . . . next year one of you won't be here." He never seemed to be at a loss for sobering tenets or alarming witticisms as he "worked the students without mercy." His favorite expression was, "No tea for the feeble, no crepe for the dead." He also reminded them with shocking regularity that "doctors could bury their mistakes, but lawyers couldn't." Thurgood Marshall, Houston's student and later his colleague, remembered that

"Houston's drive earned for him the affectionate nickname, 'Iron Shoes.' " Houston simply "rejected out of hand all complaints that work was too difficult or assignments too long." And he had no tolerance of carelessness, laziness, or lack of attention to detail. Oliver Hill, distinguished Richmond, Virginia, attorney, loves to tell the story of Houston (whose office was on the second floor) sending to the homes of his students (who all generally studied and attended classes on the first floor of the law school) special delivery registered letters with return receipts in order to be certain that they were advised of his desire to meet with them in his office. (Although to his students it seemed at best an idiosyncrasy, it was certainly an unmistakable lesson on documentation.)

Nor did Dean Houston's intolerance of mediocrity and laziness change after the first three-year day school class's graduation…. Dean Houston was painfully conscious of the need for black lawyers to be "not only good but superior, and just as superior in all respects as time, energy, money and ability permit." This viewpoint transformed itself into demands that could become hardships on some of the students who, while serious about the law and law school, had to work at night. One such student was William Bryant, who was to become a partner in the Houston firm and the first black chief judge of the U.S. District Court for Washington, D.C. "How many of you work?" was the question that preceded Houston's survey of the freshmen class when Bryant began law school in 1933. Eventually reaching Bryant, as he was called on to answer questions about work, "How long do you work?" inquired Houston. "Twelve A.M. to eight A.M.," Bryant replied. "You can't work and go to law school. Don't get any notion that you can," Houston told Bryant. Bryant, who had already worked a full year doing manual labor in order to save money to attend Howard Law School, wanted clarification because he did not intend to waste his time or hard-earned money in a no-win situation. "Are you telling me I can't work and go to law school or are you telling me I can't work and get the law?" he asked, and then quickly announced, "I'm not asking for any favors." Houston went on to the next student. After class, fellow students warned that one just did not "cross the dean." Everyone was so adamant about it that Bryant began to wonder if his law school career would come to a quick, inglorious end. In reflection, Bryant remarked that what Houston did not know was that the job Bryant held was at a Howard University dormitory switchboard where, after about forty minutes to an hour, there

Charles Houston, Clarence Darrow, and Mordecai W. Johnson, president of Howard University, meet at Howard Law School. (1931)

ceased to be any telephone calls. "I wasn't a whiz kid that defied Charles Houston. I studied, read, and had no interruptions." At first Bryant was "a little paranoid." What William Bryant and his classmates did not know initially but would learn was that Charles Houston was not unfair or vindictive. He was just a perfectionist who believed the law was "a jealous mistress." There was "no place in his mind for the law accommodating any weakness." Nevertheless, William Bryant got "some of [his] best grades from Charles Houston" in such courses as "legal bibliography," "history of law," and "common law pleading." Houston remained a demanding teacher, but Bryant "got the law, graduating first in his class."

Most of Houston's students came to know him outside the classroom as both "sociable and humane." "His purse was never very full, if only because he so often emptied it to tide a student over an emergency." Nor could Mag [Charles's wife, Gladys Houston] count all the times Charles called to let her know the students would be coming over so she should prepare something. Marshall recalled, "He was a sweet man once you saw what he was up to. He was absolutely fair and the door to his office was always open."

Charles Houston was much more than a good teacher and dean. He was a man possessed by his vision and confident of the nature of his special mission. With as much fervor as his grandfather had preached the Christian's duty of loving God and neighbors as self, Houston preached the lawyer's basic duty of social engineering. Required courses included trips to the Federal Bureau of Investigation and penitentiaries. No student left Howard during Houston's tenure without a considerable understanding of the workings of the government with respect to race and justice. And why? "There was a social engineering job which they could not avoid."

Not for a moment did Houston equivocate. "A lawyer's either a social engineer or he's a parasite on society," he told all students. "What is a social engineer?" was a question that was answered before any could ask. A social engineer was a highly skilled, perceptive, sensitive lawyer who understood the Constitution and knew how to explore its uses in the solving of "problems of … local communities" and in "bettering conditions of the underprivileged citizens." As he explained to his students, discrimination, injustice, and the denial of full citizenship rights and opportunities on the basis of race and a background of slavery could be challenged within the context of the Constitution if it were creatively, innovatively interpreted and used. The "written constitution and inertia against … amendment give the lawyer wide room for experimentation … and enable [black people] to force reforms where they could have no chance through politics."

In his writings he was even more specific about the task of social engineering. It entailed duties to "guide … antagonistic and group forces into channels where they will not clash" and ensure that "the course of change is … orderly with a minimum of human loss and suffering." A social engineer by definition was to be "the mouthpiece of the weak and a sentinel guarding against wrong." The black social engineer further was called on not only to "use … the law as an instrument available to [the] minority unable to adopt direct action to achieve its place in the community and nation," but also consistently and competently to interpret the race's rights, grievances, and aspirations. Preeminently, Charles Houston's presence was synonymous with this conviction about the moral obligation of black lawyers, and emanating from Houston was an intensity that inspired serious commitment to freedom and justice from his students and associates. And he knew well, as he taught those around him, that the struggle for fundamental change should not be deferred.…

* * *

The NAACP Campaign

From 1935 to 1940, Charles Houston established himself as the "architect and dominant force of [this] legal program of the NAACP." He devised the legal strategy, chartered the course, began a program of political education for the masses, and handled the civil rights cases. He called on former students to accept the challenge of civil rights law and brought into the campaign eager, alert, and astute lawyers. He advised and directed black lawyers throughout the nation about their local campaigns against discrimination in education, transportation, jury exclusion, and denial of the vote.

With his philosophy of social engineering, Houston was confident of his cause, his strategy, and of his ability and that of his cohorts to engage in meaningful and successful struggles against segregation and inequality. Houston's commitment to the NAACP campaign against racial discrimination was inextricably bound to a deeply personal disquietude about society and the relationships of human beings to one another. His commitment to this legal struggle was a commitment to the larger struggle for freedom and was fundamentally rooted in respect for human life. In the final analysis, slavery, exploitation, and oppression were morally wrong. But law, Houston believed, should be an "aspect of civilization which had as its chief purpose reconcil[ing] conflicting human interests and controll[ing] the antagonistic individual and group forces operating in the community, state, and nation." Given an immoral America, the NAACP campaign required that lawyer–social engineers use the Constitution, statutes, and "whatever science demonstrates or imagination invents" both to foster and to order social change for a more humane society....

Charles Houston introduced his 1935 special appeal for support of the NAACP's legal work against discrimination in education with the words of Frederick Douglass, a central figure in the nineteenth-century struggle for the liberation of black people, who had died in the year of Houston's birth:

> *To make a contented slave you must make a thoughtless one ... darken his moral and mental vision, and ... annihilate his power of reason. He must be able to detect no inconsistencies in slavery ... It must not depend upon mere force; the slave must know no higher law than his master's will.*[12]

It seemed to Houston that a new form of slavery still existed in the South and that greater oppression would await blacks throughout the nation if they did not ceaselessly protest discrimination and fight for identical quality and quantity of educational opportunity [for] all citizens regardless of race, color or creed." Democracy and ignorance cannot "endure side by side," Houston insisted. If ignorance prevails among masses, among any race, they become "the tools of a small exploiting class."

Houston was persuaded that failure to eradicate inequality in the education of black youth would condemn the entire race to an inferior position within American society in perpetuity. The white man claims black American slowness, backwardness, and lesser intelligence to justify "poorer teachers, wretched schools, shorter terms, and an inferior type of education" for blacks, Houston declared, but the reason for such treatment has nothing to do with alleged black inferiority.

> *Discrimination in education is symbolic of all the more drastic discriminations which Negroes suffer in American life. And these apparent senseless discriminations in education against Negroes have a very definite objective on the part of the ruling white to curb the young [blacks] and prepare them to accept an inferior position in American life without protest or struggle. In the United States the Negro is economically exploited, politically ignored and socially ostr[a]cized. His education reflects his condition; the discriminations practiced against him are no accident.*[13]

This assessment of American conditions and the black American reality informed Houston as he sought to determine limited objectives and the ultimate goal of the NAACP campaign against unequal, discriminatory, segregated public education. Clearly, he asserted, "equality of education is not enough. There can be no true equality under a segregated system. No segregation operates fairly on a minority group unless it is a dominant minority … The American Negro is not a dominant minority; therefore he must fight for complete elimination of segregation as his ultimate goal."

Having set this goal, the special counsel, understanding that the "law [is]… effective … always with its limitations," selected as his second task devising "positionary tactics" or "the steps [one] takes to move from one position to another"—and clearly articulating the rationale for these tactics. Houston had accepted the position on the condition that the program of litigation be conducted as a protracted legal struggle based on the planned, deliberate prosecution of test cases to secure favorable legal precedents, and thereby lay a foundation for subsequent frontal attacks against racial discrimination and segregation. He developed a plan of attack in accordance with this view.

After a great deal of thought and study, Houston committed himself to this action, for he was very aware of the degree to which it differed from ideas of other civil rights/civil liberties lawyers. His white predecessor, Nathan Margold, had suggested in his "Preliminary Report to the Joint Committee" that an immediate and direct attack on segregation be made, since it was unconstitutional when it involved inequality.

Nevertheless, Houston believed the step-by-step process would have greater long-range effects, first because it would take into account the lack of tradition for equality within the American system. Addressing the National Bar Association, Houston said that it was not realistic to expect that an immediate, direct attack on segregation would be sympathetically heard by judges.

> *We must never forget that the public officers, elective or appointive, are servants of the classes, which places them in office and maintains them there. It is too much to expect the court to go against the established and crystallized social customs, when to do would mean professional and political suicide … We cannot depend upon the judges to fight … our battles.*[14]

Second, Houston preferred the protracted struggle because he did not view the campaign as an exercise in "legal hand[i]work." An effective program must involve the masses of blacks, with their role being the initiation of action against inequalities and discrimination in education subsequent to the exposure of the evils. Yet in the course of his work Houston found many black people fearful of militant action within their own communities, and others, who were not directly fac-

NAACP Parade Float (ca. 1944)

ing debilitating discrimination, seemed apathetic about struggle. "This means that we have to … slow down until we have developed a sustaining mass interest behind the programs … The social and public factors must be developed at least along with and, if possible, before the actual litigation commences," Houston reported to the Joint Committee.[15]

Third, Houston sought to proceed slowly, building precedents to support equality, because to his mind it was also important to neutralize the poor-white masses and persuade them of the logic and justice of the NAACP position. There would be no true educational equality until racial discrimination in mixed schools was also attacked and eliminated, for it was racial prejudice bolstered by inequalities which in part caused poor whites to be blinded to mutual interests with blacks. It was Houston's position that the achievement of democracy, equality, and justice in education, as in other areas, required the recognition that poor whites and most blacks were in the same economic condition and that unified action could advance their common interests. Pursuant to these views, Houston determined that any program put forward, any case presented, any "proposition … for public action, should be interpreted not simply as a Negro proposition, but as a proposition affecting the majority of the people: all the poor people of this country, white and black alike."[16]

The concurrent recognition, by Houston, of the NAACP's limited funds and personnel, the segregated schools in a large section of the nation, and racial discrimination in educational systems throughout the entire United States, led Houston to make specific choices regarding the objectives and tactics of the NAACP's attack on discrimination in education and transportation. There were three possible objectives. First, the direct, immediate result, such as a court-ordered admission of a student or equalization of salaries in a school system, could be the object of litigation. Second, the NAACP could go to court realizing the high probability of losing but making use of the case to achieve beneficial by-products, such as calling attention to the evil, using the court as a forum, building public sentiment around the case, and creating a sufficiently strong threat for some temporary ameliorative action to be taken: for example, suing for admission of a student to a university and losing, but having legislation for out-of-state scholarships put on the state's books.[17] Third, the NAACP could use the court as a laboratory to extract information. For example, explained Houston:

We have very little money, very few trained investigators. But all we need is about $10.00. Then we can file a case in court. Five dollars more and we can bring the whole state education department into court with all its records, put each official on the stand under oath and wring him dry of information."[18]

The "positionary tactics" devised by Houston—within the context of a basic strategy of judicial precedent-building for the erosion of the "separate but equal" principle and establishment of the unconstitutionality of segregation—constituted the program of the NAACP for the legal struggle against educational discrimination for the period of Houston's special counselship and subsequent years. He selected

three glaring and typical discriminations as focal points for legal action…;[(1)] differentials in teachers' pay between white and Negro teachers having the same qualifications, holding the same certificate, and doing the same work; [(2)] inequalities in transportation facilities which lie at the basis of all problems of consolidation of rural schools; [(3)] inequalities in graduate and professional education usually offered white students in universities supported by state funds, while Negro education is cut off with the undergraduate work in college.[19]

Houston selected the differential in teachers' salaries because the salary scale was generally regulated by law and it presented a definite concrete issue. On the teachers' salary cases Houston framed three litigation alternatives: First, a suit by the teacher who is still in service, with a mandamus to equalize his or her pay, or a suit by the teacher, after he or she has left service, for the differential in back pay; second, a parent's and student's suit to equalize salaries on the ground that equal education with regard to teaching cannot be obtained on the inferior pay scale for black teachers; and third, a taxpayers' suit alleging that the state can obtain adequate public teaching service on the black teachers' salary scale and therefore it is a waste of taxpayers' money to pay white teachers more than blacks. With respect to the third alternative, Houston explained that the NAACP intended not to bring the pay scale down, but to "shock" the white teachers into serious consideration of raising the salaries of black teachers.…

Houston wanted to focus some attention on discrimination in transportation for two reasons. First, as he understood it, the success of the consolidation of rural schools is dependent on getting children to and from school within a reasonable amount of time. Second, "there is psychological aspect to white children being transported to school in buses while Negro children plod along the road. An inferiority complex is installed in the Negro children without one word being said about the difference between the races. It does not have to be said to either white children or Negro children who have ridden to a consolidated brick school for eight years, clean and dry, in buses furnished by the county while the Negro children have trudged along the road ... to a little ramshackled, wooden, one-room schoolhouse." With cases such as *Dameron v. Bayliss* holding that black children having to walk further than white children in order to attend school did not constitute a sufficient reason for abolishing segregated schools, the difficulty of successful litigation relative to transportation was apparent. However, Houston indicated that a lawsuit to compel transportation for black children at public expense was most likely to produce beneficial results.[20]

The court attack on graduate and professional schools of state universities was selected because of the general failure of states to furnish to blacks either professional education or graduate education and because of the urgent need for blacks to have access to professional and graduate training for personal development and for leadership positions. "There was not a single state-supported institution of higher learning in any one of the 17 out of 19 states, requiring separation by law," Houston noted, "where a Negro might pursue professional or graduate training at public expense," in 1935. Three "southern" or "border" states—West Virginia, Missouri, and Maryland—by this same time were making a pretext of equalizing the graduate and professional studies for blacks by providing so-called out-of-state scholarships that covered tuition but not travel or maintenance outside the state. To Houston's mind, this meant whites were taxing blacks "to educate the future white leaders who are supposed to rule over" blacks. Houston insisted, "We must break this up or perish."

In 1935, the NAACP launched its legal campaign against the policy of the southern and border states to provide fully at state expense professional or graduate training for white college graduates only. The first case was filed against the University of Maryland on behalf of Donald Gaines Murray, a black Marylander, grandson of a prominent African Methodist Episcopal bishop, Abraham Gaines, and graduate of Amherst College (1934), seeking acceptance of his application to the law school of the University of Maryland and examination of his credentials.

Not only did Donald Murray have a good college record and the desire to fight for his right as a state citizen to attend the University of Maryland Law School, but, also, his situation met the NAACP's requirements for a test case. The situation represented a "sharply defined issue," which could be "supported by demonstrable evidence." It presented "key discrimination" while it both provided an opportunity for enforcement through "auxiliary legal proceedings" and "furnished a focus or springboard for extending the attacks on a larger front." The case first came to the attention of Thurgood Marshall, who was practicing in his hometown of Baltimore. He recommended the case to Houston who believed it "a chance to develop under oath by examination of witnesses and ... documents, the discriminations from which Maryland Negroes suffer."

The groundwork having been flawlessly laid by Marshall, the NAACP, aided by William I. Gosnell, filed a petition without reference to race and color which asked that the court compel the university authorities to receive Murray's application, consider in regular order Murray's application, and admit him if he met the general standards. *Murray v. The University of Maryland* was heard on 18 June 1935 in a relatively empty courtroom. After all testimony had been taken and the arguments heard, the presiding judge directed the university to admit Murray—in accordance with his constitutional right—pending appeal. The appeal was argued on 5 November 1935 after Murray had been attending the university for over a month. Holding that the out-of-state institution scholarship provisions made by Maryland for Negroes did not afford Murray equal protection as guaranteed by the Fourteenth Amendment, the Maryland Court of Appeals affirmed the writ of mandamus on 15 January 1936. Murray's case set a significant legal precedent; further state actions regarding the graduate or professional education of blacks might be judged by the Maryland court's decision. Donald Murray's attendance at the university law school without racial incident would become a key social precedent in a later law school case, *Sweatt v. Painter*.[21]

After the court of appeals affirmed the decision for Murray, Charles Houston was as much concerned about his people's understanding the victory as he was about the future cases of the NAACP's campaign against discrimination in education. He decided to air his views through the official magazine of the NAACP, *Crisis*. In an article entitled "Don't Shout Too Soon," he warned that the fight was just beginning:

> *Law suits mean little unless supported by public opinion. Nobody needs to explain to a Negro the difference between the law in books and the law in action. In theory the cases are simple; the state cannot tax the entire population for the exclusive benefit of a single class. The really baffling problem is how to create the proper kind of public opinion. The truth is there are millions of white people who have no real knowledge of the Negro's problems and who never give the Negro a serious thought. They take him for granted and spend their time and energy on their own affairs."*[22]

Houston's suggested remedy for this problem was that black people, their friends, and civil libertarians seek opportunities to state their case to the white public since the old channels of publicity were inadequate and the radio was not customarily open for discussions or speeches promoting the concept of racial equality. Houston also encouraged blacks to "cooperate in public forums ... agitate for more truth about the Negro [in educational institutions and] ... along with the educational process ... be prepared to fight, if necessary, every step of the way." Finally, Houston reminded the readers, "This fight for equality of educational opportunity [is] not an isolated struggle. All our struggles must tie in together and support one another ... we must remain on the alert and push the struggle farther with all our might."

* * *

Education

Part of the discrimination on a national level that disturbed Charles Houston most was discrimination that interfered with the education of blacks. He still maintained that exploitation and oppression were directly related to the denial of education and equal opportunities. He continued the battle for enlarged educational opportunities in conjunction with the NAACP and the NAACP Legal Defense and Educational Fund, Inc. (the Inc. Fund). Houston was chairman of the National Legal Committee and a member of the NAACP's board of directors. His most satisfying work, however, was advising the lawyers of the NAACP's Legal Defense Fund as they built on the foundation of [*Missouri ex rel. Gaines v. Canada*].[23]

The NAACP's lawyers and the Inc. Fund lawyers were "one and the same." The Inc. Fund had been separately incorporated to facilitate tax-exempt contributions as of 1939. The NAACP, however, sometimes paid the salaries of Inc. Fund lawyers, especially Marshall (who was occasionally needed to represent the NAACP) and the two organizations "spoke with one voice." (In fact, there was virtually "no separation until 1956," when the tax-exempt status of the Inc. Fund was in jeopardy.) ... After Houston successfully argued [*Steele v. Louisville & Nashville Railroad et al.*[24]] in the U.S. Supreme Court, he met on weekends with Marshall and sometimes the entire staff to discuss matters of tactics and strategy, such as what to include in complaints, cases on which to focus, and witnesses to be used in cases.... Houston had to earn an independent living by means of his private practice, but he was as anxious as Marshall and his first assistant, Robert L. Carter, to push the NAACP's legal campaign to achieve its original goal—the elimination of legal segregation. Despite the eventually prohibitive costs of separate and equal facilities, racist southerners were determined to resist at all costs. It seemed the better part of wisdom to take full advantage of the *Gaines* decision and the increasing militancy of the post-World War II black population. Marshall, Carter, and other staff members saw no compelling reason to wait for segregation to topple under its own weight. Carter regularly argued that it was time to attack the *Plessy* doctrine of "separate but equal." Charles Houston looked at how far the NAACP had come since 1935 and heartily supported a direct attack on segregation both in the NAACP-Inc. Fund meetings and in public. A 1947 article in the *Afro-American* included Houston's affirmation of the escalated struggle. "The NAACP lawyers in order to get the campaign underway accepted the doctrine that the state could segregate … provided equal accommodations were afforded…. Now the NAACP is making a direct, open, all-out fight against segregation…. There is no such thing as 'separate but equal.' Segregation itself imports inequality."

Sometimes the demands of the Inc. Fund's caseload were such that Houston was needed to litigate at the trial level and teach by example. *McCready v. Byrd*, the suit of Ester McCready for admission to the University of Maryland's school of nursing, was a case in point. Constance Baker Motley, chief judge of the U.S. District Court in New York, recalls that she came in 1945 to the Inc. Fund to work as a clerk but found the work and the cause so much to her liking that she stayed on as a staff lawyer. Before she was permitted to argue an Inc. Fund case, however, Marshall directed her to go to Baltimore, where "Charlie Houston" was chief counsel in *McCready*, and "watch the case being tried." This man, who "could design strategy" and whom "everyone regarded as a legal scholar," was considered by most the "best trial lawyer—white or black." Forceful but not flamboyant," Charles Houston handled this case so that it could be readily appealed. As was his custom, he had a notebook in hand "with every question written out." When his heart condition forced him to turn the case over to Marshall, Houston left an impeccable record, and all that remained was for Marshall to handle what black lawyers always encountered, racist chicanery of opposing counsel.

Mrs. Ada Lois Sipuel, applying for admission to the University of Oklahoma School of Law, after a long legal struggle culminating in a U.S. Supreme Court decision ordering the school to accept her. Reading the transcript of her record at Langston University is J. E. Fellows of the university office of admission and records. In rear are D. H. Williams of the Oklahoma NAACP; Thurgood Marshall, attorney for the national NAACP; and Amos Hall, state representative from Tulsa. (1948)

By 1948 a more solid foundation was laid when the U.S. Supreme Court handed down its opinion [in *Sipuel v. Oklahoma State Board of Regents*] that Oklahoma must not only provide Ada Sipuel with a legal education but also "provide it as soon as it does for applicants of any other group."[25] Charles Houston was also available to advise on and participate in cases concerning other matters of racial discrimination such as voting rights (*Rice v. Elmore*) and public transportation (*Morgan v. Virginia* and *Boynton v. Virginia*). After the restrictive covenant cases and the Sipuel victory against Oklahoma, however, Houston participated primarily in the higher education cases, such as *McCready*, *Sweatt v. Painter*, and *McLaurin v. Oklahoma State Regents*, as time and energy permitted.[26]

By August 1949, when Houston had first begun to feel that something other than fatigue was a problem, he had not confided in Henrietta [his second wife] but he had made a firm decision. He had coordinated programs and assisted with NAACP litigation for nearly fifteen years. Houston knew that he had dangerously overextended himself. With no regrets, Houston wrote to assure Robert L. Carter, first assistant special counsel: "These education cases are now sufficiently tight so that anyone familiar with the course of the decisions should be able to guide the cases through. You and Thurgood can proceed without any fear of crossing any plans I might have." (By mid-1950 the NAACP and its Inc. Fund won two more Supreme Court victories in *Sweatt v. Painter* and *McLaurin v. Oklahoma State Regents*, providing—as Houston had planned—a foundation of precedents beginning with *Missouri ex rel. Gaines v. Canada* to eviscerate the "separate but equal" doctrine of *Plessy v. Ferguson* and to "re-interpret equal protection under the fourteenth amendment." The NAACP's victory of 1954 in *Brown v. Board of Education* was simultaneously the culmination of the legal campaign based on Charles Houston's modified strategy carried forward by the NAACP's cadre of lawyers and a watershed decision in constitutional law with respect to equal protection of the laws.)[27]

✿ ✿ ✿

Social Engineer

Challenging the government to give credence to constitutional guarantees of full citizenship, Charles Houston's contribution to civil rights advocacy, in particular, and the black struggle against oppression, in general, was theoretical and practical. He was a legal scholar-teacher-practitioner who became so involved in struggle that he wrote neither treatises nor lengthy law review articles. He, however, expounded a theory of "social engineering" to the black bar and black law students. The term fell into disuse, but his concepts of social engineering continued beyond his lifetime, as they became part of the legal training for Howard University students and the NAACP's lawyers of the National Legal Committee and the Inc. Fund.

Houston understood from his law school education that the principal professional task was knowing the law and understanding the legal process, so that one could capably advise and represent lay people in "legal matters revolving around their problems with family or community." As a law professor he was called everything from "insensitive" to "a machine" because of his unyielding attachment to the goal of graduating *only* first-rate lawyers from Howard, no matter how many students began the three-year course of study. Beyond this, however, Houston felt a social-moral obligation to produce cadres of socially alert black lawyers for the struggle. The values transmitted from one oppressed generation to the next, in combination with Houston's liberal arts educational background and his Harvard encounter with Roscoe Pound's sociological jurisprudence, were evident in the premises of the theory that Houston posited about law, lawyers, and the United States. He accepted as given that "every group must justify and interpret itself in terms of the general welfare … i.e., doing a distinct, necessary work for the social good" and that "lawyers serve as reinforcement units in the social structure."

In light of this, Houston insisted that black lawyers could not afford the luxury of merely being capable lawyers handling ordinary professional tasks. "The black lawyer must be trained as a social engineer," Houston argued, "in contrast to the traditionalists' view of the lawyer's role." Thereafter he variously described between 1929 and 1948 the role and the functions of the social engineer. Houstonian social engineering entailed five obligations for black lawyers: (1) to be "prepared to anticipate, guide and interpret group advancement"; (2) to be the "mouthpiece of the weak and a sentinel guarding against wrong"; (3) to ensure that "the course of change is … orderly with a minimum of human loss and suffering," when possible "guiding … antagonistic and group forces into channels where they would not clash"; (4) to recognize that the written constitution and inertia against its amendment give lawyers room for social experimentation and therefore, to "use … the law as an instrument available to the minority unable to adopt direct action to achieve its place in the community and nation"; (5) to engage in "a carefully planned program to secure decisions, rulings and public opinion on … broad principles while arousing and strengthening the local will to struggle." Of these obligations, Houston taught that the second and third were basic, regardless of race. This also distinguished Howard's legal education from elsewhere.

Undoubtedly, Pound's view that judicial and legislative functions, while separate, at times ran together in the "judicial ascertainment of the common law by analogical application of decided cases," was a catalyst as Houston urged black social engineers to prepare for arguments in the U.S. Supreme Court. In the Court a black man could "compel a white man to listen," and reforms could be forced when blacks had no chance through politics. So convinced was Charles Houston of the correctness of his theory of social engineering and its potential to prompt a nondiscriminatory interpretation of the Constitution or federal statutes that he taught students a lawyer was "either a social engineer or a parasite on society." Moreover, in a 1935 article, he declared that the "primary social justification" for the black lawyer in the United States was the "social service he could render the race as an interpreter and proponent of its rights and aspirations."

In its reliance on resort to courts for gaining recognition of their constitutional rights, social engineering was consistent with the traditional faith of African Americans in the possibility of changing their subordinate status not only through resistance but also through protests and appeals based on the expressed fundamental principles of the U.S. government. The influence of social engineering on the black jurisprudential matrix was significant and novel in its exposition of the duties of black American lawyers and its presentation of the rationale for use of the law by blacks. Finally, Houston's emphasis on experimentation with the Constitution and on planning and affinity with the local community of blacks in struggle provided the basis both for black law studies and for action on behalf of the masses of black people.

Bettmann/CORBIS

Optimistic over Anti-Segregation Ruling William Gordon (right), managing editor of the *Atlantic Daily World*, a black newspaper, checks a copy of the *Memphis World* carrying the story of the Supreme Court's May 17 decision to end segregation in the public schools. (1954)

Charles Houston's entire career as a civil rights lawyer exemplified the belief that the law could be used to promote fundamental social change and that it was an instrument available to a minority even when that minority was without access to the ordinary weapons of democracy. His reputation is indelibly linked with the NAACP against racial discrimination in education that ultimately led to the watershed public school segregation decisions of 1954, *Brown v. Board of Education* and *Bolling v. Sharpe*.[28] His place in history has been principally established by his role as either chief counsel and key strategist or adviser-strategist for precedent-setting cases in three areas of law: education, labor, and housing. As a constitutional lawyer and litigator—in the graduate public education "equal protection" case of *Missouri ex rel. Gaines v. Canada* (1938), the fair-representation cases of *Steele v. Louisville & Nashville Railroad*

Company and *Turnstall v. Brotherhood of Locomotive Firemen and Enginemen* (1944), and the anti-restrictive-covenant cases of *Hurd v. Hodge* and *Shelley v. Kraemer* (1948) — Charles Houston demonstrated that demands could be made on the system's courts with the result being changes in the common law.[29] The U.S. Supreme Court in *Gaines*, *Steele*, *Turnstall*, *Hurd*, and *Shelley* rendered decisions supportive of the protection of the civil rights of African Americans, sometimes relying on constitutional interpretations of federal statutes, and other times reaching adjudication of constitutional issues per se.

Houston engaged in planned litigation campaigns with what Brazilian social theorist Paulo Freire has described as "critical consciousness." This critical consciousness incorporated both understanding and rejecting the oppressor's models and behavioral traits, and identifying the system (or aspects of the system) as a collective endeavor, the strategies of which were to be developed through dialogue across class lines. Although after the defenses of George Crawford and Bernard Ades, Houston exhibited a naiveté about the dominant majority and the legal process, his consciousness was raised as he confronted leftist condemnations and reflected both on the criticisms and on the black experience in the United States. Even when they were overzealous, Communists, socialists, and LLD members influenced Houston by directing his attention to the analysis that assumed class antagonism, while stressing not only mass resistance and militant struggle but also the class ties of the judiciary. For all three litigation programs — education, labor, and housing — Houston's assumption was that public officials were servants of the class that placed them there and that blacks could not depend upon judges to fight their battles. A critical consciousness also prompted Houston to extract from his legal training those aspects of the judicial process that were likely to have the greatest impact on the black struggle. In planning his activity, he took into account *stare decisis*, judicial self-restraint, the step-by-step process, and the requirement of reasonable predictability of legal consequences. The result was a three-pronged strategy: selecting cases that presented clear legal issues and building strong records in those cases; overturning negative legal decisions by invalidating gradually or attacking directly the controlling precedents; and developing a sustaining community or mass interest in each case.

The relation between Houston's critical consciousness and planning effectiveness has been examined by Jesse McNeil, Jr., in a study of the Houston-directed NAACP campaign against discrimination in education. Characteristic of each program of litigation handled by Houston was a well-conceived and well-executed plan of preparation and litigation. Houston's high level of competence in planning was indicated by his consistent pattern of defining the problem, setting a goal, analyzing the situation, assessing the available options, developing the appropriate strategy and tactics, and implementing the planned strategy. In addition, the legal campaign was characterized by collaborative activity among lawyers, scholars, and concerned lay people, responsive leadership with communication across traditional class and social boundaries, and the use of the media and public forums to raise community consciousness and to mobilize community support.

During the early 1930s, Charles Houston criticized the NAACP—as did Du Bois. In contrast to Du Bois, who at the time counseled "voluntary segregation," Houston stressed another criticism of the NAACP's leadership and its relationship to the masses. In his view, an effective assault on racial discrimination was essential during this era. Such an attack on racism required black self-determination and consciousness-raising appeals to blacks and whites of the society. Although the NAACP never had the mass support of the Garvey movement, substantial numbers of blacks were branch members. They knew and articulated their local concerns and identified with such general issues as the right to vote, the right to have blacks serve on juries, equal schools, and equal pay for teachers' equal work. Houston devoted resources to such clearly relevant issues with the hope that even greater interest would arise, and, when necessary, he slowed down the litigation campaign until factors generating mass support were developed.

Outside the NAACP structure, Houston consistently planned civil rights litigation in response to client-identified grievances. Effective work in the areas of labor, housing, and public education resulted in the precedent-setting *Steele* doctrine, the *Hurd* ruling, and predecessor cases of the District of Columbia's 1954 decision against segregated public education. Collaboration and cooperation across class, social, and racial boundaries again proved indispensable to court victories, while Houston's warnings about the limitations of the judicial system proved indispensable to the larger civil rights struggle.

Charles Houston held a respected position of leadership among blacks during the 1930s and 1940s. His ability to educate and inspire lawyers and lay people, respectively, to work as social engineers and to pool their resources to seek enforcement of rights through the courts was of particular historical significance. His legal successes, especially in the U.S. Supreme Court, were key collective victories that laid the groundwork for subsequent civil rights laws supporting equality of educational opportunity, fair housing, and fair representation. These Court victories had far-reaching significance for the future progress of blacks, while most of Houston's efforts in the African American struggle had an immediate impact on opportunities for blacks to exercise rights in some areas of American life. His work was also instrumental in creating a climate for more militant direct action.

Houston's commitment to the use of the law for social change was prudent because blacks, even if a "subordinate minority," had rights through the "Thirteenth, Fourteenth and Fifteenth Amendments … in theory and in law," and one problem was enforcement. However, there were other systemic problems that required Houston to maintain a flexible posture toward the American legal process; despite his Supreme Court victories, realism dictated that he perceive himself as a technician probing in the courts how far the existing system would permit the exercise of freedom before it clamped down. In 1935, while some cheered his saving of Jess Hollins from execution as a triumph for the NAACP's first black appellate team, Houston wrote about being struck by the relationship between miscarriages of justice, race, and poverty. A few

years later, when Odell Waller (the sharecropper convicted of first-degree murder after fatally shooting a white farmer in self-defense), who had not sufficiently able counsel to defend him and was scheduled for execution in spite of a conviction by an unconstitutional jury, Houston gave short shrift to the legal process. In response to the request of Pauli Murray and Morris Milgram of the Workers Defense League, Houston communicated with the governor of Virginia: The violation of fundamental American civil liberties required commutation "regardless of the merits of … the case."

Rejection of any position that might hold the legal code absolutely sacred also marked Houston's approach to the American legal process in general. Flawed in its ability to protect a subordinate racial minority and hold in check the immoral conduct of the majority, Houston sometimes found the legal system and its enumerated civil liberties inadequate as a basis for protest. Whereas he acted within the system to publish a brief condemning the Tuscaloosa lynchings and the complicity of officials, he immediately advised an NAACP official that it was "not a matter of free speech and free press … but a fundamental matter of human life and orderly government." For Houston it was evident that a

Blacks March Against Lynching
Some of more than 3,000 blacks who took part in the protest parade in the streets of the Capital. Federal intervention was sought so that the series of hangings and killings of blacks by whites would be curbed. (1922)

government's obligation to protect its citizens' lives, regardless of race, took priority over arguments for free speech and press. This belief had a simple origin: Houston never questioned the moral superiority of a society governed by laws that guaranteed basic human rights. Repeated incidents of blatant disregard for the lives of black people pushed Houston away from the standpoint that the "goodwill of the dominant majority" might be a determining factor in devising civil rights protests tactics. By 1935 he asserted that "real amicable race relations could not be purchased by the surrender of … rights."

As an NAACP official, political appointee, publicist, and concerned black American, Houston regularly attempted to use the legislative and executive branches to direct attention to pervasive racism with respect to lynchings, jury exclusion, "railroading" of blacks to jail, the need for a federal agency with power to enforce fair employment policies, discrimination in the armed forces, racially segregated public accommodations, and black disfranchisement. Regarding the latter, Houston was adamant that, in the United States, voting—the ability to put in and take out of office particular officials in relationship to their representation of one's interests—was of paramount importance. However, the disfranchisement of overwhelming numbers of blacks in the South—where the majority lived—rendered the race virtually ineffectual in the political-legal process. Moral suasion seemed to fail consistently when presidents, senators, and members of the House weighed support of the rights of nonvoting blacks against other political considerations.

Logically, Houston refused to place his faith entirely in the three branches of the American legal system, but encouraged and participated in direct action to secure African Americans' rights. Peaceful assembly, petitioning, and extra-legal demonstrations as well escalated the black struggle that could not achieve all its aims within the legal process. Not only did he conclude that law had value always within its limitations, he also joined other black people whom he had challenged to "do their own fighting and more of it by extra-legal means." As he promoted this extensive fight against oppression, he realistically urged that some grievances not be presented as special pleading for blacks alone, but when possible as propositions for the relief of the oppressed masses to support a greater public good. As a racial minority in the United States, blacks needed allies among the citizens of the nation. Simultaneously, he stressed the potential alliance of blacks in the United States with the nonwhite majority of the rest of the world. He was certain that the struggle against oppression was indivisible.

From 1935 to 1950, Charles Hamilton Houston played a principal role in defining and pacing the legal phase of the struggle of African Americans for freedom, justice, equality, and a right to the pursuit of happiness. His role was definitive because, in the context of this struggle, he operated primarily within the arena of the courts. Houston did recognize that use of the other branches of the legal system might result in more speedy remedies. But with little power to compel congressional or presidential concessions and with violent racism ever a possible consequence of direct action, blacks were in a better position to seek redress of grievances through the courts, Houston reasoned. The usually high chances for reversals of court decisions favorably affecting the legal status of African Americans were minimized by the strategy of Charles Houston. His own legal accomplishments were the consequence of carefully considered, well-developed legal strategies and skillful arguments. More important, many civil rights lawyers throughout the nation accepted Houston's philosophy of social engineering. Their use of the law to secure fundamental social change for the protection of African Americans and the improvement of society placed pressure on the judicial system, to which it yielded. Supreme Court decisions handed down and civil rights statutes enacted after Houston's death in 1950 specify rights for which he effectively argued in courts, and black lawyers continue to use the law as a weapon in the struggle against racial discrimination. As Derrick Bell concluded in *Race, Racism, and American Law*, "decisions, particularly since World War II ... seemed to support an argument that reliance by blacks on courts was not misplaced."

Nonetheless, in a nation where wealth, privilege, and power were vested in the dominant majority of a different race, where racism was the prevailing attitude, and where a racist, exploitative ruling class governed with discriminatory laws so pervasive as to have established apartheid in the United States, the adoption of legalism could neither eradicate oppression nor guarantee freedom, justice, and equality. This understanding—reached after years of struggle within the framework of the American system—obliged Charles Houston to see himself in the late 1940s as a technician probing *not if* the system would clamp down on the exercise of freedom, *but when* it would.

Charles Houston's groundwork extends beyond contributions to the American law and the improvement of African Americans' legal status. In historical perspective, it becomes clear that Houston's life is especially instructive because of his open-mindedness and ideological integrity. Houston always struggled so that his people might have freedom, self-determination, justice, equality of rights, and equality of opportunity. Yet in struggling, he openly entertained a wide range of views pertaining to the means to create a society in which such conditions were guaranteed by law. As most blacks of his era, Houston sought to exhaust every option within the existing system. He was, however, so fundamentally opposed to injustice and laws that contravened morality that, when moved to criticism of the existing system, he did not equivocate. His concern and his commitment to struggle were so great that—at the time he felt he might not survive his first heart attack—he decided to cheat death of any opportunity to obscure his most highly developed critical views. The tape-recorded message that resulted from this resolve (and his desire to have his son more clearly understand his father's sacrifice) stands as Charles Houston's final word on the struggle. His paramount concern was "that the Negro shall not be content simply with demanding an equal share in the existing system." Thus, Houston's groundwork was also the grim reminder that "there's no particular honor in being invited to take a front seat at one's own funeral." In the final analysis, Houston believed that it was the task of all black people in the United States "to make sure that the system, which shall survive in the United States of America … guarantees justice and freedom for everyone."

Charles Hamilton Houston cut through the bitterness that racism and the absence of authentic freedom in the United States might have made a permanent malady for African Americans and affirmed his own values. The price exacted by American society was great. Relentless struggle brought him to his death at the age of fifty-four. Yet, as he told his son, "in any fight some fall." Charles Houston laid the groundwork for part of the continuing black struggle in an effort to keep faith with his ancestors, to create a better society, and to offer hope to the children. The cost was not nearly as important as the cause. He emerged in history insisting that the United States must use the Constitution and its laws to reform itself and to assure black people human rights. He turned the Constitution, the laws, and the legal process into weapons in the cause of his people, but finally, he challenged black people to fight for their rights even as the system threatened to "clamp down." This too was Charles Houston's legacy: that there should be no end to struggling, no immobilizing weariness until full human rights were won.

[1] The footnotes accompanying the excerpts selected for this publication have themselves been excerpted and renumbered. The complete endnotes can be found in McNeil, *Groundwork: Charles Hamilton Houston and the Struggle for Civil Rights* (University of Pennsylvania Press, 1985).

[2] "College Honors Charles Houston '15," *Amherst Magazine*, Spring 1978, p. 14.

[3] Ibid., pp. 12, 14.

[4] Kenneth S. Tollett, "Black Lawyers, Their Education, and Their Community," *Howard Law Journal* 17 (1972): 326–27.

[5] Derrick A. Bell, Jr., "Black Faith in a Racist Land," in *From the Black Bar*, ed. Gilbert Ware (New York: G.P. Putnam's Sons, 1976), pp. 11–12.

[6] *Dred Scott v. Sandford*, 60 U.S. (19 How.) 393 (1857).

[7] A. Leon Higginbotham, Jr., "Racism and the Early American Legal Process, 1619–1896," *Annals of the American Academy of Political and Social Science* 407 (May 1973): 15.

[8] 14 Stat. 27 (1866).

[9] Bell, "Black Faith in a Racist Land," p. 12.

[10] 109 U.S. 3 (1883) and 163 U.S. 537 (1896).

[11] William H. Hastie, Jr., "Toward an Equalitarian Legal Order," *Annals of the American Academy of Political and Social Science* 407 (May 1973): 19–20 passim.

[12] CHH, "A Program Against Discrimination in Public Education," ms., n.d. [c. December 1935], p. 2, Fraternities and Sororities, 1935, AFPS, Adm. files, C1999 NAACP Records.

[13] CHH, "Proposed Legal Attacks on Educational Discrimination," typescript summary of address delivered to the National Bar Association, 1 August 1935, p. 2, CHH folder, Speeches, Adm. files C429, NAACP Records.

[14] CHH, "Proposed Legal Attacks on Educational Discrimination," p. 8, C429, NAACP Records.

[15] CHH, "Memorandum to the Joint Committee American Fund for Public Service, Inc. – NAACP," 14 November 1935, p. 4, C199, NAACP Records.

[16] CHH, "Proposed Legal Attacks on Educational Discrimination," pp. 2–3.

[17] Ibid., pp. 3–4.

[18] Ibid., p. 6.

[19] CHH, "Tentative Statement Concerning Policy of N.A.A.C.P.," 12 July 1935, p. 11, AFPS, Adm. files, C197, NAACP Records. See *Plessy v. Ferguson*, 163 U.S. 537 (1896).

[20] CHH, "Proposed Legal Attacks on Educational Discrimination," p. 7. See *Dameron v. Bayliss*, 14 Ariz. 180 (1912).

[21] *Pearson et al. v. Murray*, 169 Md. 478 (1936). See also *Sweatt v. Painter*, 339 U.S. 629 (1950).

[22] CHH, "Don't Shout Too Soon," *Crisis* 43 (March 1936): 79.

[23] 305 U.S. 337 (1938).

[24] 323 U.S. 192 (1944).

[25] *Sipuel*, 332 U.S. 631 (1948).

[26] *Sweatt*, 339 U.S. 629 (1950); *McLaurin*, 339 U.S. 639 (1950); *McCready*, 195 Md. 131 (1950).

[27] *Brown*, 347 U.S. 483 (1954).

[28] 347 U.S. 483 and 347 U.S. 427 (1954).

[29] 305 U.S. 337 (1938); 323 U.S. 192 and 323 U.S. 210 (1944); 334 U.S. 24 and 334 U.S. 1 (1948).

Robert Lawson

Genna Rae McNeil is author of the definitive biography of Charles Hamilton Houston, mentor of Thurgood Marshall and architect of the litigation strategy that culminated in *Brown v. Board of Education*. A professor of history at the University of North Carolina in Chapel Hill, Professor McNeil specializes in African American history and twentieth-century United States history with an emphasis upon race, law, and social movements. Her publications include scholarly articles and four books: *Historical Judgments Reconsidered*, co-edited with Michael R. Winston; *Groundwork: Charles Hamilton Houston and the Struggle for Civil Rights*, which was awarded the distinguished Silver Gavel Award of the American Bar Association; *African Americans and the Living Constitution*, co-edited with John Hope Franklin; and *African Americans and Jews in the Twentieth Century*, co-edited with V. P. Franklin and others. She is currently completing a book-length study of *State v. Joan Little*.

The Warren Court
From left to right and on the bottom row, are Justices Felix Frankfurter, Hugo L. Black, Chief Justice Earl Warren, Stanley F. Reed, and William O. Douglas. Left to right in the rear row are Tom C. Clark, Robert H. Jackson, Harold H. Burton, and Sherman Minton. (1953)

Chief Justice Warren's Role in
Brown v. Board of Education

William H. Rehnquist

In 1896, the Supreme Court of the United States ruled in *Plessy v. Ferguson* that the Equal Protection Clause of the Fourteenth Amendment was not violated if a State provided separate facilities for whites and blacks so long as they were equal. That decision ratified the Jim Crow regime in the South and stood for almost sixty years, until it was overruled by *Brown v. Board of Education* fifty years ago. In *Brown*, the Court issued a unanimous decision outlawing segregation in public schools and striking down the "separate but equal" doctrine of *Plessy*.

Chief Justice Earl Warren wrote the opinion in *Brown* and due to his efforts the opinion was unanimous. Warren joined the Court in October 1953, at the beginning of the Term in which *Brown* was decided. Just before the start of the 1953 Term, on September 8, 1953, Chief Justice Vinson died of a heart attack. On Wednesday, September 30, President Eisenhower called Warren, who was then the governor of California, and asked him to accept a recess appointment as Chief Justice and to be in Washington for the opening of the Court's Term the following Monday. Warren accepted the appointment.

When Chief Justice Warren joined the Court, it was sharply divided over the issue of racial segregation in schools. *Brown* was originally argued in the 1952 Term, but the Court was so deeply split on the issue that the case was put over for reargument the following Term. Warren understood the magnitude of the issue and the importance of framing the Court's opinion to maximize the public's acceptance of it. If the opinion were not unanimous, it would be much more vulnerable to attack. In Warren's first Term as Chief Justice, getting the entire Court to agree on such a contentious issue was a very tall order.

Chief Justice Earl Warren

Brown was reargued over three days, on December 7, 8, and 9, 1953. The case was discussed at the conference of the Justices on December 12. As Chief Justice, Warren spoke first. Warren announced that he believed the "separate but equal" doctrine of *Plessy* could not be sustained, and acknowledged that any decree ending segregation would have to be very carefully crafted in order not to "inflame more than necessary." Based upon the positions taken by the other Justices after *Brown* originally had been argued, Warren had a majority—including Hugo Black, William Douglas, Harold Burton, and Sherman Minton—in favor of overturning *Plessy*. But Warren suggested that no vote be taken until further discussions took place.

The Justices discussed the case informally throughout the Term until, by early May, every member of the Court save one agreed to overrule *Plessy*. Even so, both Justices Frankfurter and Jackson had indicated an intention to write separate, concurring opinions. Warren, however, was still intent on convincing his colleagues that, for the good of the country and the Court, the Court should speak with one voice. In the memorandum circulating his draft opinion, Chief Justice Warren noted that he tried to make the opinion "short, readable by the lay public, non-rhetorical, unemotional and, above all, non-accusatory." Frankfurter and Jackson agreed to sign onto Warren's opinion without writing separate concurrences. Finally, the ninth Justice, Stanley Reed, agreed to join the majority. The unanimous decision was released 50 years ago, on May 17, 1954.

On that day, Justice Frankfurter wrote a note to Chief Justice Warren congratulating him:

> *Dear Chief: This is a day that will live in glory. It is also a great day in the history of the Court, and not in the least for the course of deliberation which brought about the result. I congratulate you.*

Justice Burton also wrote to the Chief Justice:

> *To you goes the credit for the character of the opinions which produced the all important unanimity. Congratulations.*

The Court's decision in *Brown* was criticized by many, but the fact that it was unanimous undercut those who questioned its legitimacy. Chief Justice Warren is most often remembered for the Court's decisions during his tenure relating to the rights of criminal defendants. Yet, perhaps Earl Warren's most lasting legacy as Chief Justice came during his very first year on the bench with his success in ensuring that the Court's decision in *Brown* was unanimous.

William H. Rehnquist is Chief Justice of the United States. He was born in Milwaukee, Wisconsin, October 1, 1924. He married Natalie Cornell, now deceased, and has three children—James, Janet, and Nancy. From 1943–1946 he served in the U.S. Army Air Forces. He received a B.A., M.A., and LL.B. from Stanford University and an M.A. from Harvard University. He served as a law clerk for Justice Robert H. Jackson of the Supreme Court of the United States during the 1951 and 1952 Terms, and practiced law in Phoenix, Arizona, from 1953–1969. He served as Assistant Attorney General, Office of Legal Counsel, from 1969–1971. President Nixon nominated him to the Supreme Court, and he took his seat as an Associate Justice on January 7, 1972. Nominated as Chief Justice by President Reagan, he assumed that office on September 26, 1986.

Deborah L. Rhode

Justice Thurgood Marshall in Supreme Court chambers
(1979)

Letting the Law Catch Up

Deborah L. Rhode

By the time I clerked for Justice Marshall in the late 1970s, an established Supreme Court tradition was that each Justice would preside over a lunch for all of the law clerks once during the term. On these occasions, the Justice would offer a few inspirational thoughts and respond to questions. At Justice Marshall's lunch, a clerk asked him to describe his judicial philosophy. From most Justices, it was the sort of question that prompted vacuous homilies, stale leftovers from the judicial confirmation process. Justice Marshall, who had little patience for such platitudes, actually answered the question. "You do what you think is right and let the law catch up."

He did. And in some important areas it has, in part because of his efforts on and off the bench. The fiftieth anniversary of *Brown v. Board of Education* is a particularly appropriate moment to reflect on the legacy not only of that decision, but also of the attorneys like Marshall who fought so courageously to achieve it. At a time of widespread concern about lawyers' ethics, it is fitting to reflect on those whose careers embody all that is best in our profession.

The lawyers who litigated *Brown* and its progeny lived in the gap between constitutional principles and social practices. That experience left them with a personal understanding of injustice and a passion to combat it that is too often missing today. My focus here is on Thurgood Marshall, both because he led the legal campaign that culminated in *Brown*, and because his subsequent career on the bench exemplified the same commitment to equal opportunity that underpinned that decision.

Marshall's own experience of racism inspired his philosophy, first as a litigator, and then as a Supreme Court Justice. He grew up in segregated Baltimore. As the son of a Pullman railroad porter and elementary school teacher, Marshall was among the better off blacks of that era. But that still meant education in a highly overcrowded "separate but equal" Colored High and Training School with no library, cafeteria, or gymnasium. The salaries for black teachers were substantially lower than those of the white janitors.

In his early years, Marshall witnessed all the gross injustices and petty indignities of racism: riots in nearby Washington, D.C., epithets from white students, and segregated seating in buses and movie theaters. Ironically, Marshall noted, black domestic workers were deemed unfit to sit next to the white children they fed, bathed, and clothed. And if "enforcement hadn't been such a problem," Marshall speculated that the theaters would have had a rule that "white folks got to laugh first." Marshall ended up at Howard Law School because the University of Maryland would not admit blacks. And when he graduated, he entered a profession that was 99 percent white.

Marshall's early experiences as a lawyer kept him ever mindful of the gap between formal rights and social practices. He often recalled southern court proceedings in which all three stages—arraignment, trial, and sentencing—could be completed in less than a half hour. He had been appellate counsel after robbery trials that observed the formalities, but lasted less than fifteen minutes; the proof was presented so swiftly that no one ever even learned what had been stolen. The best a defense lawyer could often do was to make sure that the defendant had a pregnant wife and several needy children in the courtroom (borrowed if necessary).

"...With All Deliberate Speed"

THURGOOD

NAACP'S DESEGREGATION SPECIAL

That gap between procedural and substantive justice was what Marshall dedicated his life to change, most notably as a litigator for the NAACP. And what bears particular emphasis here is the personal risks involved in litigating early race discrimination cases in the Deep South. During trials, Marshall was sometimes moved several times a night to avoid lynch mobs, and was once warned by local police to be on a 4 P.M. train because the "sun was never going down on a live nigger in this town." When told by state troopers that they were present in courtrooms for "his protection," Marshall sometimes wondered if he "had to take their word for it."

There were petty indignities as well. One was the inconvenience for black lawyers who were litigating where all the downtown lunch facilities were "for whites only." On the first day of a trial challenging the University of

Oklahoma's refusal to admit black law students, Marshall treated himself and his young female client to a meal of peanuts from the courthouse vending machine. He then served notice that "I'm gonna try this case for you, but as of tomorrow, you're in charge of bologna sandwiches." Although Marshall won that case, he remained acutely aware that victories in legal principle were not easily translated into social practices. The plaintiffs who won in court often paid a heavy price in the world outside it. The black student who gained admission to Oklahoma Law School had to sit in the back of class in a chair marked "colored." She could neither participate in discussion nor eat with others in the law school cafeteria. Developing a taste for one's own bologna sandwiches was plainly a useful survival skill for early civil rights litigants.

Despite their personal toll on lawyers and clients, these cases also brought enormous satisfactions. Never were the rewards greater than when Marshall righted some of the wrongs that he had personally witnessed or experienced, like challenging unequal pay scales for black Maryland teachers, or forcing integration of the law school that had excluded him. The public recognition that came with his victory in *Brown v. Board of Education* also had its appeal, although Marshall was characteristically wry in his reaction. When his picture ran on the front page of the *New York Times*, he remembered wondering if it was the first time that a black man had ever gained such notoriety for "something other than raping a white woman." Needless to say, not all of this celebrity was favorable. When Marshall appeared on an NBC interview shortly after *Brown*, Georgia television stations replaced the segment with a statement by segregationist Governor Herman Talmadge.

Marshall's personal history of racism and poverty enabled him to see the world from the bottom up. From that vantage, he could assess the value of formal entitlements with unique clarity. In neither overstating nor overlooking the importance of legal guarantees, he left a legacy not only for civil rights but also for all movements toward equal justice

Marshall's insistent focus on the nation's substantive commitments to equality encompassed nondoctrinal issues as well. The most vivid example occurred during the bicentennial celebration of the U.S. Constitution. To Marshall, the pomp and ceremony of the event threatened to obscure its central significance. The lofty ideals on which the celebration focused overlooked the social practices on which the nation's commitments foundered. As Marshall noted, when the founding fathers spoke of "we the people" they were not in fact using the term generically, nor did they have in mind the majority of the nation's people. Racial minorities and women of all colors were originally excluded from the Constitution's protections, uninvited in its formulation, denied a

Deborah L. Rhode

Justices Marshall and Brennan
Justices walking to a conference during Supreme Court's spring 1979 term.

voice in its ratification, and until the last decade, largely absent in its interpretation. Marshall was determined that these omissions not recur in bicentennial events. In a well-publicized speech, he gave voice to those marginalized by the celebration. He reminded us that while " 'we the people' no longer enslave or disenfranchise the majority of our residents," the credit does not belong to the framers. It belongs rather to those who refused to acquiesce in the Founders' original intent and in their restrictive notions of liberty, justice, and equality. Marshall also challenged the Chief Justice's plans for an historical pageant in which members of the Court would reenact the original signing of the Constitution. Marshall was willing to participate, but only on terms that would be faithful to the nation's racial history; he would appear in livery and kneebritches, carrying trays.

The reenactment never happened. But in other ceremonies in which he participated, Marshall sounded similar themes, reminding the nation of the distance between its ideals and institutions. In receiving the Liberty Medal in Philadelphia, Marshall noted: "I wish that I could say that racism and prejudice were only distant memories. I wish I could say that this Nation had traveled far along the road to social justice and that liberty and equality were just around the bend. But as I look around, I see not a nation of unity, but of division. . . .The legal system can force open doors and sometimes even knock down walls But it cannot build bridges. That job belongs to you and me."

David Weintraub

Deborah L. Rhode is the Ernest W. McFarland Professor of Law and Director of the Stanford Center on Ethics. She graduated Phi Beta Kappa and summa cum laude from Yale College and received her legal training from Yale Law School. After clerking for Supreme Court Justice Thurgood Marshall, she joined the Stanford faculty. She is the former chair of the American Bar Association's Commission on Women in the Profession and the former president of the Association of American Law Schools, and the author or editor of thirteen books. She has received the American Bar Foundation's W. M. Keck Foundation Award for Distinguished Scholarship on Legal Ethics and Professional Responsibility, and the American Bar Association's Pro Bono Publico Award for her work on expanding public service opportunities in law schools.

PART II
THE FIRST 50 YEARS

Bettmann/CORBIS

Thurgood Marshall and John Davis
John Davis (left) and Thurgood Marshall argued for and against (respectively) school segregation before the Supreme Court in *Brown v. Board of Education*. Marshall's arguments succeeded, and he went on to become a Supreme Court justice. (1952)

Brown Reconceived:
An Alternative Scenario

Derrick A. Bell, Jr.

Considered within the context of American political, economic, and cultural life, the *Brown* decision is a long-running racial melodrama. As with a film or play, the decision stimulated varying feelings. It energized the law, encouraged most black people, enraged a great many white people, and, like so many other racial policies, served the nation's short-term, but not its long-term interests. Generating an emotionally charged concoction of commendations and condemnations, the *Brown* decision recreated the nineteenth century's post-Civil War Reconstruction/Redemption pattern of progress followed by retrogression. It stirred confusion and conflict into the always vexing question of race in a society that, despite denials and a frustratingly flexible amnesia, owes much of its growth, development, and success to the ability of those who dominate the society to use race to both control and exploit most people, black and white.

Over the decades, the *Brown* decision, like other landmark cases, has gained a life quite apart from the legal questions it was intended to settle. The passage of time has calmed both the ardor of its admirers and the ire of its detractors. Today, of little use as legal precedent, it has gained in reputation as a measure of what law and society might be. That noble image, dulled by long-term resistance and now the resegregation of even those school systems that were found to be in compliance, has transformed *Brown* into a magnificent mirage, the legal equivalent of that city on a hill to which all aspire without any serious thought that it will ever be attained.

As had happened in the past, the law employing the vehicle of a major judicial decision offered symbolic encouragement to the black dispossessed. The substantive losses so feared by its white adversaries evolved almost unnoticed into advances greater for whites than those gained by the black beneficiaries. And, as now must be apparent to all, the nation's racial dilemma—*modernized* and, one might say, *colorized*—a half-century later has become more complex rather than resolved. The racial disparities, wide and widening in every measure of well-being, overshadow the gains in status achieved by those black Americans who, through varying combinations of hard work and good fortune, are viewed as having "made it." Indeed, although it did not achieve what its supporters hoped for, historians and other social scientists, safely removed from the fray, may come to view *Brown* as the Perfect Precedent. As a dictionary would define perfect, it was: "pure, total; lacking in no essential detail; complete, sane, absolute, unequivocal, unmitigated, an act of perfection."

They will have a point. In law, perfection in the social reform area is a legal precedent that resolves issues in a manner that: (1) initially or over time gains acceptance from broad segments of the populace; (2) protects vested property in all its forms through sanctions against generally recognized wrongdoers; (3) encourages investment, confidence, and security through a general upholding of the status quo; and (4) while recognizing severe injustices, does not disrupt the reasonable expectations of those not directly responsible for the wrongs. Such reform, of seeming necessity, is arranged within the context of a silent covenant. That is, the policymakers who approve the policy do so with the knowledge, unspoken but clearly understood, that they or those who follow them stand ready to modify or even withdraw the reforms where adverse reactions or changed circumstances threaten any of the first three components.

Arguably, the *Brown* decision eventually met each of these standards. The question is whether an approach other than the one embraced by the Supreme Court might have been more effective and less disruptive in the always contentious racial arena. The claim that the perfect is the enemy of the good sounds like a bureaucratic excuse for failing to do what needed to be done. At least in the first *Brown* decision, the Supreme Court did not settle for the pragmatic approach. Overcoming fears of predictable resistance, the Court sought to change society with one swift blow. A year later, the Court in *Brown II*, reacting to the outraged cries of "never" coming from the South, and the absence of support from the executive and legislative branches, backed away from its earlier commitment. In evident response to the resistance, the Court issued a fall-back decision that became a prelude to its fifteen-year-long refusal to issue orders requiring any meaningful school desegregation.

Long-time friend and Harvard University professor, Frank Michelman, asked: "Was there any way that they, as a Court acting subject to certain public expectations about the differences among courts, legislatures, and constitutional conventions, could have framed their intervention differently from, and better than, the way they actually chose?"

The answer, I think, is yes. Despite decades of efforts to reverse *Plessy v. Ferguson* and the NAACP lawyers' well-researched legal arguments, supported by reams of social science testimony, the Court might have determined to adhere to existing precedents. Suppose that, while expressing sympathy for Negroes' plight, the Court had decided that *Plessy v. Ferguson* was still the law of the land? Suppose, moreover, that they understood then what is so much clearer now: that the edifice of segregation was built not simply on a troubling judicial precedent, but on an unspoken covenant that committed the nation to guaranteeing whites a superior status to blacks?

On this understanding, could the Court have written a decision that disappointed the hopes of most civil rights lawyers and those they represented while opening up opportunities for effective schooling capable of turning constitutional defeat into a major educational victory? Again, I think the answer is, yes. And I have imagined such an alternative.[1]

Student Protests Integration
In Tennessee, a high school student carries a sign outside the school protesting racial integration as the school opened its first session in which blacks attended classes with white students. (1956)

The Supreme Court of the United States
May 17, 1954

Today, we uphold our six-decades-old decision in Plessy v. Ferguson, *163 U.S. 537 (1896). We do so with some reluctance and in the face of the arguments by the petitioners that segregation in the public schools is unconstitutional and a manifestation of the desire for dominance whose depths and pervasiveness this Court can neither ignore nor easily divine. Giving full weight to these arguments, a decision overturning* Plessy, *while it might be viewed as a triumph by Negro petitioners and the class they represent, will be condemned by many whites. Their predictable outraged resistance could undermine and eventually negate even the most determined judicial enforcement efforts.*

No less a personage than Justice Oliver Wendell Holmes acknowledged the limits of judicial authority when, speaking for the Court in a 1903 voting rights case from Alabama, he denied the relief sought by black voters because if, as the black petitioners alleged, the great mass of the white population intends to keep the blacks from voting, it would do little good to give black voters an order that would be ignored at the local level.

**Supreme Court Justice
Oliver Wendell Holmes**

"Apart from damages to the individual," Holmes explained, "relief from a great political wrong, if done, as alleged, by the people of a state and the state itself, must be given by them or by the legislative and political department of the Government of the United States." [2]

While giving racial discrimination the sanction of law, Justice Holmes refused either to interfere with or to acknowledge the status-affirming role for whites reflected in their refusal to grant blacks even the basic citizenship right to vote. The Court in Plessy v. Ferguson *had done the same seven years earlier when, by distinguishing between the denial of political rights and the separation of the races on a social basis, the Court rejected Homer Plessy's argument that this law-enforced separation branded blacks with a "badge of inferiority."* [3]

Respondents' counsel, John W. Davis, a highly respected advocate, urges this Court to uphold "separate but equal" as the constitutionally correct measure of racial status because, as he put it so elegantly: "somewhere, sometime to every principle comes a moment of repose when it has been so often announced, so confidently relied upon, so long continued, that it passes the limits of judicial discretion and disturbance."

Elegance, though, must not be allowed to trample long-suppressed truth. The "separate" in the "separate but equal" standard has been rigorously enforced. The "equal" has served as a total refutation of equality. Within the limits of judicial authority, the Court recognizes these cases as an opportunity to test legal legitimacy of the "separate but equal" standard, not as petitioners urge by overturning Plessy, *but by ordering for the first time its strict enforcement.*

Counsel for the Negro children have gone to great lengths to prove what must be obvious to every person who gives the matter even cursory attention: With some notable exceptions, schools provided for Negroes in segregated systems are unequal in facilities—often obscenely so. Unfortunately, this Court, in violation of Plessy's *"separate but equal" standard, rejected challenges to state-run schools that were both segregated and ruinously unequal.*

Hardly three years after setting the "separate but equal" standard, this Court diluted the equal prong with "practical considerations." When black parents sought to enjoin a Georgia school board from collecting school tax levies from them for a black high school it had closed, while continuing to operate the white high school, Justice Harlan, speaking for the Court, reasoned that enjoining the board from operating a high school for whites would deprive whites of a high school education without regaining the black high school that had served sixty, and that had been turned into a primary school for 300 children. Given the board's limited resources, he found their decision reasonable. [4]

Justice Harlan returned to his dissenting role in race cases when the Court upheld a Kentucky statute subjecting to a heavy fine Berea College, a private college that admitted both white and black students. [5] *Because* the state had chartered the private school and could revoke the charter, it could also amend it to prohibit instruction of the two races at the same time and in the same place. Harlan pointed out that the precedent could bar minority association with whites in churches, markets, and other public places, a warning that by 1908 had become fact in many jurisdictions.[6]

In recent years, this Court, acknowledging the flouting of the "separate but equal" standard at the graduate school level, ordered black plaintiffs into previously all-white graduate programs. In Sweatt v. Painter,[7] the most significant of these cases, Texas denied admission to a black law school applicant, Herman Marion Sweatt. When Sweatt filed suit, the state sought to meet the separate but equal standard by setting up a small law school in three basement rooms eight blocks from the University of Texas School of Law. It would have no regular faculty or library and was not accredited. This Court, in ordering Sweatt's admission, considered

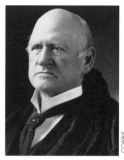

Supreme Court Justice John Marshall Harlan

both its inadequate facilities and the intangible assets of the white law school, including its reputation, the value of interaction with its faculty, student body, and alumni that include most of the state's lawyers and judges.

Encouraged by those decisions, petitioners now urge that we extend those holdings to encompass segregation in literally thousands of public school districts. In support, their counsel speak eloquently both of the great disparities in resources, and of the damage segregation does to Negro children's hearts and minds. We recognize and do not wish to reject petitioner's evidence of this psychological damage. Indeed, these findings suggest that segregation perpetuates the sense of white children that their privileged status as whites is deserved in fact, rather than bestowed by law and tradition. Racial segregation, thus, afflicts white children with a lifelong mental and emotional handicap that is as destructive to whites as the required strictures of segregation are damaging to Negroes.

It would seem appropriate to declare wrong what is clearly wrong. And, given the history of segregation and the substantial reliance placed on our decisions as to its constitutionality, a finding by this Court that state-supported racial segregation is an obsolete artifact of a bygone age, one that no longer conforms to the Constitution, will likely be the holding in cases seeking the desegregation of state-operated public transportation railroad or street cars or facilities open to the public.

The desegregation of public schools, though, is a special matter, the complexity of which is not adequately addressed in the petitioners' arguments. In urging this Court to strike down state-mandated segregation in the public schools, the petitioners ignore two important concerns. First, there is good reason to predict that immediate desegregation will set the stage not for compliance, but for levels of defiance that will prove the antithesis of the equal educational opportunity. Second, the petitioners fail to consider the admonishment of W.E.B. DuBois, one of the nation's finest thinkers. Commenting on the separate school, integrated school

African American children at a segregated school in Uno, Virginia, just a few years before *Brown* was decided. (1947)

debate back in 1935, Dr. DuBois observed that: *"Negro children need neither segregated schools nor mixed schools. What they need is education."*[8]

We are aware that despite the tremendous barriers to good schools posed by the Plessy *"separate but equal"* standard, some black schools, through great and dedicated effort by teachers and parents, achieved academic distinction. Many of the most successful blacks today are products of segregated schools and colleges. In urging what they hope will be a brighter tomorrow, petitioners need not cast aside the miracles of achievement attained in the face of monumental obstacles. While truly harmed by racial segregation, there is far too much contrary evidence for this Court to find that Negroes are a damaged race.

We conclude that Dr. DuBois is right as an educational matter and that as a legal matter his still accurate admonition can be given meaning within the structure of the Plessy v. Ferguson *holding. The three phases of relief that we will describe below focus attention on what is needed now by the children of both races. It is the only way to avoid a generation or more of strife over an ideal that, while worthwhile, will not provide the effective education petitioners' children need and that existing constitutional standards, stripped of their racist understandings, should safeguard.*

While declaring racial segregation harmful to Negro children, the unhappy fact is that, as the nation's racial history makes clear, racial division has been a source of much underserved benefit to whites and a great deal of misery to Negroes. And, as is always the case, oppression is harmful to the oppressor as well as the oppressed. We accept the expert testimony submitted in this case that a great many white as well as Negro children have been harmed by segregation.

Pressured by this litigation, the school boards assure this Court that they are taking admittedly tardy steps to equalize facilities in Negro schools. We find these measures worthwhile, but woefully inadequate to remedy injustices carried on for most of a century. This being the case, more important than striking down Plessy v. Ferguson *is the need to reveal its hypocritical underpinnings by requiring its full enforcement for all children, white as well as black. Full enforcement requires more than either equalizing facilities or, as in the case of Delaware, one of the five cases before the Court, ordering plaintiffs to be admitted into the white schools because of the inadequacy of the Negro schools.*

Realistic rather than symbolic relief for segregated schools will require a specific, judicially monitored plan designed primarily to provide the educational equity long denied under the separate but equal rhetoric. This Court finds that it has the authority to grant such relief under the precedent of Plessy v. Ferguson. *As a* primary step toward the disestablishment of the dual school system, this Court will order relief that must be provided all children in racially segregated districts in the following components.

1. Equalization. *Effective immediately on receipt of this Court's mandate, lower courts will order school officials of the respondent school districts to:*

> *(A) Ascertain through appropriate measures the academic standing of each school district as compared to nationwide norms for school systems of comparable size and financial resources. These data, gathered under the direction and supervision of the district courts, will be published and made available to all patrons of the district, white as well as black.*

> *(B) All schools within the district must be fully equalized in resources, physical facilities, teacher-pupil ratios, teacher training, experience, and salary with the goal of each district, as a whole, measuring up to national norms within three years. School districts will report progress to the court annually.*

2. Representation. *The battle cry of those who fought and died to bring this country into existence was "taxation without representation is tyranny." Effective relief in segregated school districts requires no less than the immediate restructuring of school boards and other policy-making bodies to insure that those formally excluded by race from representation have persons selected by them in accordance with the percentage of their children in the school system. This restructuring must take effect no later than the start of the 1955–56 school year.*

3. Judicial oversight. *To effectuate the efficient implementation of these orders, federal district judges will establish three-person monitoring committees, with the Negro and white communities each selecting a monitor and a third person with educational expertise selected by an appropriate federal agency. The monitoring committees will work with school officials to prepare the necessary plans and procedures to enable the school districts' compliance with phases one and two. The district courts will give compliance oversight priority attention and will address firmly any actions intended to subvert or hinder the compliance program.*

School districts that fail to move promptly to comply with the equalization standards set out above will be deemed in noncompliance and, following a judicial determination to this effect, courts will determine whether such noncompliance with the "separate but equal" standard justifies relief such as we have ordered in the graduate school cases, including orders to promptly desegregate their schools by racially balancing the student, faculty, and populations in each school.

Given orders that depart so substantially from those urged by both petitioners and respondents, some further explanation may prove helpful. In this Court's view, the petitioners' goal—the disestablishment of the dual school system—will be more effectively achieved for students, parents, teachers, administrators, and *other individuals connected directly or indirectly with the school system by the procedures set forth above. Our expectations in this regard are strengthened by the experience in the Delaware case, where school officials unable to finance the equalization of separate schools opted to desegregate those schools.*

We recognize that this decision neither comports with the hopes for orders requiring immediate desegregation by petitioners nor the states' contentions that we should simply reject those petitions and retain the racial status quo. Our goal, though, is not to determine winners and losers. It is, rather, our obligation to unravel the nation's greatest contradiction as it pertains to the public schools. Justice John Marshall Harlan, while dissenting in Plessy, *perhaps unwittingly articulated this contradiction in definitive fashion when he observed:*

> *"The white race deems itself to be the dominant race in this country. And so it is, in prestige, in achievements, in education, in wealth and in power. So, I doubt not, it will continue to be for all time, if it remains true to its great heritage and holds fast to the principles of constitutional liberty. But in view of the Constitution, in the eye of the law, there is in this country no superior, dominant, ruling class of citizens. There is no caste here. Our Constitution is color-blind, and neither knows nor tolerates classes among citizens."* [9]

The existence of a dominant white race and the concept of color blindness are polar opposites. The Fourteenth Amendment's Equal Protection Clause cannot easily ferret out the racial injustice masquerading in seemingly neutral terms like "separate but equal" and "color blindness." It has proven barely adequate as a shield against some of the most pernicious modes of racial violence and economic domination. The Clause, perhaps unfortunately given its origins, most comfortably serves to adjudicate relationships between legally recognized categories of business or other entities, rather than squarely addressing the validity of the state's exercise of coercion against a whole group.

This Court does not ignore the value of simply recognizing the evil of segregation, an evil Negroes have experienced first-hand for too long. There is, we also agree, a place for symbols in law for a people abandoned by law for much of the nation's history. We recognize and hail the impressive manner in which Negroes have taken symbolic gains and given them meaning by the sheer force of their belief in the freedoms this country guarantees to all. Is it not precisely because of their unstinting faith in this country's ideals that they deserve better than a well-intended, but empty and likely unenforceable expression of equality no matter how well meant? Such a decision will serve as sad substitute for the needed empathy of action called for when a history of racial subordination is to be undone.

The racial reform-retrenchment pattern so evident in this Court's racial decisions enables a prediction that when the tides of white resentment rise and again swamp the expectations of Negroes in a flood of racial hostility, this Court and likely the country will vacillate and then, as with the Emancipation Proclamation and the Civil War Amendments, rationalize its inability and—let us be honest—its unwillingness to give real meaning to the rights we declare so readily and so willingly sacrifice when our interests turn to new issues, more pressing concerns.

It is to avoid still another instance of this by now predictable outcome that we reject the petitioners' plea that the Court overturn Plessy *forthwith. Doing so would systematically gloss over the extent to which* Plessy's *simplistic "separate but equal" form served as a legal adhesive in the consolidation of white supremacy in America. Rather than critically engaging American racism's complexities, this Court would substitute one mantra for another: where "separate" was once equal, "separate" would be now categorically unequal. Rewiring the rhetoric of equality (rather than laying bare* Plessy's *white supremacy underpinnings and consequences) constructs state-supported racial segregation as an eminently fixable aberration. And yet, by doing nothing more than rewiring the rhetoric of equality, this Court would foreclose the possibility of recognizing racism as a broadly shared cultural condition.*

Imagining racism as a fixable aberration, moreover, obfuscates the way in which racism functions as an ideological lens through which Americans perceive themselves, their nation, and their nation's Other. In addition, the vision of racism as an unhappy accident of history immunizes "the law" (as a logical system) from anti-racist critique. That is to say, the Court would position the law as that which fixes racism rather than that which participates in its consolidation. By dismissing Plessy *without dismantling it, the Court might unintentionally predict, if not underwrite, eventual failure. Negroes, who despite all, are perhaps the nation's most faithful citizens, deserve better.*

Orders in conformance with this decision will be issued promptly and transmitted to lower courts for immediate implementation.

Had this been the decision handed down in 1954, both civil rights and school board lawyers would likely have, for differing reasons, condemned it. Yet it makes sense today. As Duke Law Professor Jerome Culp has suggested, "A gradualist approach would have been less acrimonious and would have avoided the emergence of political forces in both political parties—forces that have helped to elect every nonincumbent Republican president since that time, and have created a minor political force inside the Democratic Party for cutting back the requirement of racial justice."[10]

Yet later in the same article, Professor Culp acknowledges that the *Brown* opinion's non-gradualist approach "did challenge the fundamental assumption of inferiority that underlay the *Plessy* regime and had supported the racial status quo."[11]

There is no doubt that the *Brown* decision brought about a major change in the nation's racial framework. And like most policies claiming to advance racial justice, the major beneficiaries were white. Professor Michael Seidman explains how *Brown* brought about a transformation without real change. He reminds us that the Court in *Brown* faced a massive contradiction between the nation's oft-cited commitment to equality and the great value whites placed on the racial preferences and priorities given tacit approval by the Court in *Plessy v. Ferguson*,[12] the decision that approved segregation. Given their lack of political and economic power, it appeared that the black demand for equality could never be satisfied. As Seidman puts it, though, the contradictions in the ideology of the separate-but-equal doctrine were permanently destabilizing and threatened any equilibrium.

By purporting to resolve those contradictions, *Brown* served to end their destabilizing potential. The Court, Seidman claims, "resolved the contradictions by definitional fiat: Separate facilities were now simply proclaimed to be inherently unequal. But the flip side of this aphorism was that once white society was willing to make facilities legally non-separate, the demand for equality had been satisfied and blacks no longer had just cause for complaint. The mere existence of *Brown* thus served [to] legitimate current arrangements. True, many blacks remained poor and disempowered. But their status was no longer a result of the denial of equality. Instead, it marked a personal failure to take advantage of one's definitionally equal status."[13]

Brown, then, served to reinforce the fiction that, by the decisions' rejection of racial barriers posed by segregation, the path of progress would be clear. Everyone can and should make it through individual ability and effort. One would have thought that this reinforcement of the status quo would placate, if not please, even the strongest supporters of segregation. To the contrary, the *Brown* decision provided politicians with a racial issue through which to enrage and upset large groups of white people, initially in the South, but far more generally as efforts to implement the decision moved across the country.

If nothing else, the half-century of law under the *Brown* decision has taught us that the landscape for meaningful racial reform is neither smooth nor easily traveled. History's lessons have not been learned and even, at this late date, may not be teachable. Racial reforms that blacks view as important, many whites oppose as a threat to their status, an unfair effort to make them pay for wrongs committed by neither they nor theirs. Color blindness, now as a century ago, is adopted as the easy resolution of issues of race with which the nation would rather not wrestle, much less try seriously to resolve. It is all too easy to opt for an attractive veneer that obscures flaws in the society that do not correct themselves by being hidden from view. *Brown v. Board of Education* was a dramatic instance of a remedy that promised to correct deficiencies in justice far deeper than the Court was able to understand. Understanding those deficiencies more fully and suggesting how we should address them is the challenge racial justice advocates face today and will likely continue to face as far into the future as we dare to look.

[1]   The opinion that follows is modeled on an imagined dissent published in *What* Brown v. Board of Education *Should Have Said*, Jack M. Balkin, editor (New York University Press, 2001).

[2]   *Giles v. Harris*, 189 U.S. 475, 488 (1903).

[3]   *Plessy v. Ferguson*, 163 U.S. 537, 552 (1896).

[4]   *Cumming v. Richmond Co. Board of Education*, 175 U.S. 528 (1899).

[5]   *Berea College v. Kentucky*, 211 U.S. 45 (1908). See also, *Gong Lum v. Rice*, 275 U.S. 78.
(1927) (the Court rejected the challenge of Chinese parents whose child was assigned to a Negro school).

[6]   C. Vann Woodward, *The Strange Career of Jim Crow* (New York, Oxford University Press, 2d rev. ed. 1966).

[7]   *Sweatt v. Painter*, 339 U.S. 629 (1950). See also, *McLaurin v. Oklahoma State Regents*, 339 U.S. 637 (1950); *Sipuel v. Oklahoma*, 332 U.S. 631 (1948); *Missouri ex rel. Gaines v. Canada*, 305 U.S. 337 (1938).

[8]   W.E.B. DuBois, "Does the Negro Need Separate Schools?" 4 J. Negro Educ. 328 (1935); See generally Bell, "The Legacy of W.E.B. DuBois: A Rational Model for Achieving Public School Equity for America's Black Children," 11 *Creighton L. Rev.* 409 (1977).

[9]   163 U.S. 537, 559.

[10]   Jerome McCristal Culp, "An Open Letter from One Black Scholar to Justice Ruth Bader Ginsburg: Or How Not to Become Justice Sandra Day O'Connor," 1 *Duke J. of Gender L. & Policy* 21, 27 (1994).

[11]   Id. at 28.

[12]   163 U.S. 537 (1896).

[13]   Michael Seidman, "Brown and Miranda," 80 *Calif. L. Rev.* 673, 717 (1992).

Derrick A. Bell, Jr., a visiting professor at the New York University School of Law, has spent his 45-year career in every aspect of civil rights as a litigator, administrator, law teacher, and scholar. During the early 1960s, he represented literally hundreds of children and their parents in school desegregation law suits. His writings include both legal texts, including *Race, Racism and American Law*, now in its 5th edition, and books for the general public including *Faces at the Bottom of the Well: The Permanence of Racism* and *Ethical Ambition: Living a Life of Meaning and Worth*. His latest book is *Silent Covenants:* Brown v. Board of Education *and the Unfulfilled Hopes for Racial Reform*.

Bettmann/CORBIS

Segregated drinking fountain in use in the American South.

Side by Side, Brick for Brick, Room for Room: Oliver Hill, *Brown v. Board*, and Prince Edward County, Virginia

Robert J. Grey, Jr.

The broad strokes of *Brown v. Board* are familiar to most of us—the courage of Linda Brown and her family, Thurgood Marshall's towering presence and skillful lawyering, the landmark decision of the Warren Court. Like other great theoretical and constitutional achievements, the *Brown* decision illuminated what in retrospect is obvious but at the time was unclear: There is no equality in separation.

Time and distance are necessary for any understanding and evaluation of *Brown*. Now, marking half a century since the decision, we pause to reflect on the decision's weight, to evaluate its place in our society's legal and social evolution, and to pay homage to the people who sacrificed, in little ways and in large, to make *Brown* not simply a decree, but a reality.

Of course, vital to the success of *Brown* was the work of the NAACP's Legal Defense Fund team, led by Marshall and including the towering legal talents and intellect of Robert Carter, James Nabrit, George Hayes, Louis Redding, Jack Greenberg, and Oliver Hill. Of similar significance was the willingness of all those they represented—not only Linda Brown, but also the black children from the other communities that formed the core of the cases that became over time known through *Brown*. This work—gathering and piecing together legal suits and actions over time, first to enforce the "equal" in the separate doctrine and finally to discredit it as a legal principle and undo *Plessy*—represents the full fabric of the *Brown* decision. In a way, the lawyers of the NAACP Legal Defense Fund each became a master weaver, pulling together his own section of the *Brown* "tapestry."

In Virginia, Oliver Hill, and his partners, Martin A. Martin and Spottswood Robinson, were the advance guard, marshaling the weapons to defeat *Plessy* and later to counter the effects of "massive resistance," the Virginia strategy devised to attack the *Brown* victory and undermine any efforts toward desegregation of the Virginia public schools. Die-hard segregationists were committed to closing public schools rather than integrating these, so, as a consequence, countless black children were effectively deprived of an education, or forced to relocate to gain access to one.

But this was the aftermath of *Brown*. To get to *Brown*, Hill and his compatriots first had to find the perfect case for Virginia, one that would not simply push for "equal" facilities, but that would challenge the legitimacy of the very notion of separate. In 1951, Hill found his case—or more accurately, the case found him.

Attorneys Arriving at Federal Court for Desegregation Case

Attorneys Spottswood Robinson (left) and Oliver W. Hill arrive at federal court. They were pleading for an order to allow 30 African American children to attend traditionally all-white schools in Arlington, Virginia. (1958)

Prince Edward County lies in the heart of Virginia, just south of the center, in an area of the state known as "Southside." The county's history is rich, as is that of the state. The county seat, Farmville, was home to Barbara Johns, a senior at the Negro Robert Moton High School, who led her entire class on a strike to protest the dismal conditions of their segregated school and—at first—to secure "equal" facilities. For years the school district had promised but not delivered adequate facilities to the black students. The students managed, somehow, in an overcrowded building, augmented by three temporary tarpaper-covered structures, with leaking roofs, two working water fountains, and inadequate heat. As is so often the case, one voice—Johns'—said, enough; she organized the student strike.

Johns was a niece of the then-influential Reverend Vernon Johns, a nationally recognized minister and civil rights activist. She contacted Hill. Hill was familiar with the dismal conditions of Moton High School, and he initially urged Johns to end the strike: She had brought attention to her cause, and what, he asked, was the benefit of continued agitation for separate institutions?

Prince Edward County in 1951 was typical of its time. Like much of the South, it was largely rural, with the bulk of its economy still based on agriculture. Power and wealth were concentrated in the hands—

white—of but a few. Hill, a Virginian born in Richmond in 1907 and educated in the segregated South before attending Howard University to earn his undergraduate and law degrees, knew well the devastating effects of court-sanctioned and socially demanded racism. Absolute power, after all, will corrupt absolutely. Hill turned his considerable legal skill to undoing the legal support structure for unequal treatment and tyranny, starting with education, the bedrock of access and achievement in America. Hill recalls that:

> *Even though we initially sought enforcement of the separate but equal rule, I once argued before the court of appeals that if a school board built two schools side by side, brick for brick, room for room, with identical materials, curricula, and furnishings and limited Negro children to attending one school and white children to attending the other, I would still say it was discriminatory against the Negroes. As long as Negroes are excluded from the societal mainstream, they will continue to be relegated to a form of second-class citizenship. When the government excludes a person through segregation laws, and the general society by custom, that exclusion places the excluded person in a position where there are too many things that happen that the person doesn't know anything about. White children going to school have parents who are involved in various functions in the political, business and social affairs of the community. Those children bring experiences, perspectives, and other things to the schools that black children have had no opportunity to become familiar with. (Oliver Hill, The Big Bang, 148)*

Opportunity and access are impossible without equality—a tenet so basic that people fight to obtain it, and also to withhold it. Hill and his compatriots knew that the time was at hand to challenge the "separate but equal" doctrine enshrined in *Plessy* and bring an end to legalized segregation. But such a battle would require will and courage, as well as a commitment not to settle for any illusion of separate but equal. Johns' courage and will impressed Hill. And so he and his partners agreed to talk to Johns and her family, as well as some of the other students. Hill remembers:

> *On our way to Farmville, we had anticipated telling the class to go back to school. When we arrived we found these students had such fine morale and were so well disciplined that we didn't have the heart to break their spirit. We said to them that we were going to Christiansburg and we would return on Thursday night. We told them that there had been a change in NAACP policy. We were no longer taking*

cases to make separate facilities equal. Now we sought to challenge segregation per se *and have the Court declare racial segregation in public schools unconstitutional. . . . [W]e instructed the students that they first needed to talk with their parents. If their parents agreed to support them in a suit challenging segregation* per se, *we would take the case.* (Hill, *The Big Bang*, 150.)

Students Hoisting American Flag
School doors in Farmville, Virginia, swung open for children of Prince Edward County. Public schools had been padlocked since 1959 in an effort to avoid court-ordered integration. (1963)

That Thursday, the parents agreed to stand behind their children in bringing a suit challenging *Plessy* and, recognizing the countywide importance of their decision, they pressed for a countywide meeting of students, parents, and community members. The following day, in a meeting room filled to capacity, the courage displayed by Johns and her fellow students coalesced among others in the county into a desire to see the fight through. It was not easy to come to such a united position, to take a stand for betterment of children throughout the country, and to demand lasting change for future generations. It was a leap of faith, away from the admittedly limited but familiar, into a potentially richer, more self-sufficient but unknown place and way of being. Some felt that seeking to make schools equal, rather than integrated, was a better strategy. Others feared the very real threat of white retribution. But as Billie Holiday's melancholy-tinged, bitter refrain reminds us, it is better to have your own.

That evening, after considerable debate, weighing of consequences, and measuring of risks and rewards, the community determined to seek an end to segregation. Soon after, Hill and his colleagues filed a petition with the school board, requesting relief for the students. When (as expected) relief was not granted, another petition was filed, this one challenging the constitutionality of *per se* segregation. This became the beginning of *Dorothy E. Davis, et al. v. County School Board of Prince Edward County, Virginia*, one of the five suits eventually consolidated and heard as a part of *Brown*.

✧ ✧ ✧

Frederick Douglass is famous for saying, "power concedes nothing without a demand. It never did, and it never will." This was absolutely the situation Hill faced in Virginia. Even before the *Brown* decision was reached, lawmakers in the state began to manufacture ways to maintain the status quo of white supremacy and to further legitimize separation of the races. Ironically, the Prince Edward County suit, had Hill been given his druthers, was not the one that he would have chosen:

> *If we had any choice in the matter, we would have never picked Prince Edward as the community for a test case. If we were going to pick a case, we would have worked with parents who wanted to improve their children's educational opportunities by challenging public school segregation in Richmond, or Norfolk or some other metropolitan center. . . . I do not believe that local officials in Richmond or Norfolk would have closed their schools. . . .Only in the heartland of segregation, some place like Southside Virginia, would they have shut down all the public schools and let the children suffer rather than desegregate.* (Hill, *The Big Bang,* 160.)

In response to *Brown,* and with the lash of Senator Harry Byrd, Sr.'s segregationist rhetoric driving them, whites throughout the state entered into "massive resistance," a strategy that called on southerners to defy the Supreme Court's order to desegregate. In Virginia, the state closed its public schools rather than integrate, a situation that lasted until 1959 when supreme courts at the state and federal levels ruled the closings to be unconstitutional. However, white segregationists in Prince Edward County—with extensive support from across Virginia and around the South—immediately opened a private all-white academy, and the all-white board of supervisors kept their public schools closed until 1964. Prince Edward County's black children, as well as many low-income whites, in many circumstances went without education for five years.

During this volatile time, Hill risked his personal safety and well-being to ensure that the white power structure in his state did not succeed in its end-run around the Supreme Court. Like so many others engaged in the battle for civil rights, he met with threats and other acts of intimidation to deter him from his work. These tactics did not succeed. Hill remained a constant, vocal presence in leading the law to catch up. In 1965, Hill appeared before the Virginia General Assembly in an attempt to persuade its members of the importance of heeding the Supreme Court's direction, in *Brown II,* of "all deliberate speed." In his address to the General Assembly, Hill reminded its members:

> *Today, gentlemen, all loyal persons subject to the jurisdiction of the United States, irrespective of whether they reside in Oregon or Florida, Texas or Maine, California or Virginia, or even Mississippi, owe their primary allegiance to the United States. It is time that we pause and consider this fact and stop this*

irresponsible talking and irrational action now taking place in Virginia and else-where in the South. The Supreme Court simply gave recognition to the fact that all American citizens are entitled to be treated with the individual respect and dignity set forth in the Declaration of Independence, guaranteed by the Constitution of the United States, and consistent with the principles of a sovereign democratic power. (Hill, The Big Bang, 173.)

Hill's appeal to justice was to no avail, and white Virginians continued to perpetuate massive resistance to integration. The General Assembly even created a Pupil Placement Board, which usurped local school boards' authority to assign students to classrooms. The placement board became the single authority in the state to place local public school students. Black students who wanted to attend white schools had to apply through the board, which routinely denied their applications.

By today's standards, it is almost impossible to imagine an entire county closing its public schools rather than admit a child of color. Perhaps one of the most important legacies of *Brown* is that even the mere contemplation of such an act is viewed as outrageous and absurd. The challenge of *Brown* and of the lawyers who so courageously fought to end segregation in our public schools is with us still. Hill's appeal to Virginia's General Assembly nearly fifty years ago continues to call, a finger to tap us on our collective shoulders, to insist that we remain vigilant in our efforts to guarantee that all Americans, no matter where we live, how we look or sound, or what we believe, are treated with individual respect and dignity. Our nation's fundamental values and principles demand no less.

Thurgood Marshall noted that the true miracle of the Constitution is not its birth, but its life. Oliver Hill gave it life through his dedication to *Brown* and to equal rights and dignity for all Americans, particularly for blacks who had been systematically disenfranchised and relegated as second-class citizens. He was not content to let the law catch up; he used his own might, when-ever he could, to push it forward.

George Gilliam and William Thomas. *The Ground Beneath Our Feet. Episode 3: Massive Resistance* (video and Web site). www.vcdh.virginia.edu/vahistory/massive.resistance. 2000.

Oliver Hill. *The Big Bang:* Brown v. Board of Education *and Beyond, The Autobiography of Oliver W. Hill*, Edited by Jonathan K. Stubbs. Winter Park, Fla.: FOUR-G Publishers, Inc., 2000.

U.S. National Archives and Records Administration. *Frontiers in Civil Rights:* Dorothy E. Davis, et al. versus County School Board of Prince Edward County, Virginia. www.archives.gov

Virginia Commonwealth University Libraries, James Branch Cabell Library. *Separate But Not Equal: Race, Education and Prince Edward County, Virginia.* Online exhibit and documents. www.library.vcu.edu/jbc/speccoll/pec01.html

Chad Hunt

Robert J. Grey, Jr., a partner in the Richmond, Va., office of Hunton & Williams, is president-elect of the American Bar Association, and will become president in August 2004 at the association's annual meeting in Atlanta. Grey, former chair of the ABA House of Delegates, will be the second person of color to head the association. Grey's work at Hunton & Williams focuses on administrative matters before state and federal agencies. He works in mediation and other forms of dispute resolution on both state and national levels, and represents corporate and industry interests in the legislative arena. Grey earned his J.D. from Washington and Lee University in Virginia in 1976, and his B.S. from Virginia Commonwealth University in 1973. Prior to joining Hunton & Williams in 2002, Grey was a partner in several Virginia law firms, including LeClair Ryan, 1995–2002, Mays & Valentine, 1985–1995, and Grey & Wesley, 1978–1982.

Youths Protest Integration of Schools
White youths protest African American integration outside Rock Junior High School, Little Rock, Arkansas. (1950s)

From Racial Liberalism to Racial Literacy:
Brown v. Board of Education
and the Interest-Divergence Dilemma

Lani Guinier

On its fiftieth anniversary, *Brown v. Board of Education* no longer enjoys the unbridled admiration it once earned from academic commentators. Early on, the conventional wisdom was that the courageous social engineers from the National Association for the Advancement of Colored People Legal Defense and Educational Fund (NAACP LDEF), whose inventive lawyering brought the case to fruition, had caused a social revolution. Legal academics and lawyers still widely acclaim the *Brown* decision as one of the most important Supreme Court cases in the twentieth century, if not since the founding of our constitutional republic. *Brown*'s exalted status in the constitutional canon is unimpeachable, yet over time its legacy has become complicated and ambiguous.[1]

The fact is that fifty years later, many of the social, political, and economic problems that the legally trained social engineers thought the Court had addressed through *Brown* are still deeply embedded in our society. Blacks lag behind whites in multiple measures of educational achievement, and within the black community, boys are falling further behind than girls. In addition, the will to support public education from kindergarten through twelfth grade appears to be eroding despite growing awareness of education's importance in a knowledge-based society. In the Boston metropolitan area in 2003, poor people of color were at least three times more likely than poor whites to live in severely distressed, racially stratified urban neighborhoods. Whereas poor, working-class, and middle-income whites often lived together in economically stable suburban communities, black families with incomes above $50,000 were twice as likely as white households earning less than $20,000 to live in neighborhoods with high rates of crime and concentrations of poverty. Even in the so-called liberal North, race still segregates more than class. Gerald N. Rosenberg, emphasizing the limited roles courts can generally play, bluntly summed up his view of *Brown*'s legacy: "The Court ordered an end to segregation and segregation was not ended." If *Brown* was a decision about integration rather than constitutional principle, Mark Tushnet observed in 1994, it was a failure.[2]

Even as constitutional principle, the Court's analysis and the formal equality rule it yielded became more troubling in the intervening years. Presented with psychological evidence that separating black children from whites "solely because of their race generates a feeling of inferiority as to their status in the community that may affect their hearts and minds in a way unlikely ever to be undone," Chief Justice Earl Warren led the Court to declare segregation unconstitutional. *Brown*'s holding became the gold standard for defining the terms of formal equality: treating individuals differently based on the color of their skin was constitutionally wrong. However, once the Court's membership changed in the 1970s, advocates of color blindness used *Brown*'s formal equality principle to equate race-conscious government decisions that seek to develop an integrated society with the evils of de jure segregation. The new social engineers on the right adapted the Warren Court's rhetoric to create a late twentieth-century constitutional principle that forbids government actors to remediate societal discrimination. They changed *Brown* from a clarion call to an excuse not to act.[3]

The academy has produced a host of explanations for the discontinuity between *Brown*'s early promise and its present reality. Some scholars have challenged the Warren Court's motives; others have criticized its reasoning; still others have found fault with its method of implementation. For example, focusing on motivation, Derrick A. Bell, Jr., questioned the case's power to promote social justice because it was shaped, not by the intentional coalescing of a transforming social movement that reached across boundaries of race and economic class, but by the calculated convergence of interests between northern liberals, southern moderates, and blacks. The resulting alliance was temporary, lacked deep populist roots, and built on a tradition of treating black rights as expendable. For throughout United States history, Bell contended, the rights of blacks have regularly been sacrificed to preserve the greater interests of the whole society.[4]

In an influential article published in 1980 in the *Harvard Law Review*, Professor Bell concluded that the *Brown* decision represented the interest *convergence* between blacks and middle- and upper-class whites:

> *[The] principle of "interest convergence" provides: The interest of blacks in achieving racial equality will be accommodated only when it converges with the interests of whites. However, the fourteenth amendment, standing alone, will not authorize a judicial remedy providing effective racial equality for blacks where the remedy sought threatens the superior societal status of middle and upper-class whites. . . . Racial remedies may instead be the outward manifestations of unspoken and perhaps subconscious judicial conclusions that the remedies, if granted, will secure, advance, or at least not harm societal interests deemed important by middle and upper-class whites.[5]*

In the post–World War II period the alignment of interests of a biracial elite shifted to accommodate legal challenges to Jim Crow, Bell argued. The Court gave its imprimatur to the desegregation of public schools to add legitimacy to the U.S. struggle against Communism; to reassure blacks that precepts of equality heralded in World War II would be applied at home (and thus to quiet the resentment and anger of black veterans who returned from the war only to be denied equality); and to eliminate an important barrier to the industrialization of the South and the transition from a plantation to a modern economy. Consistent with Bell's interest-convergence thesis, Philip Elman, special assistant to the attorney general, filed a brief on behalf of the United States in which he framed the problem of racial discrimination "in the context of the present world struggle between freedom and tyranny."[6]

African American Army Unit at Embarkation Docks
Men of Unit 4505-C, 780th MP Battalion, before embarkation on USS *General.* (1944)

The ideals of racial liberalism helped fashion the legal strategy of the biracial elite. Racial liberalism emphasized the corrosive effect of individual prejudice and the importance of interracial contact in promoting tolerance. Racial liberals stressed the damaging effects of segregation on black personality development to secure legal victory as well as white middle-class sympathy. The attorneys in *Brown* and their liberal allies invited the justices to consider the effects of racial discrimination without fear of disrupting society as a whole. The Court responded by seeking to mollify southern whites even as it declared the end to the de jure separate but equal system. Yet, to the extent that *Brown* reflected the alliance of some blacks and some upper-class whites unthreatened by desegregation, it left out crucial constituencies for change, including southern black educators and poor rural blacks.[7]

Reservations also abound about the Court's reasoning, which was influenced by the litigation tactics of *Brown*'s advocates and allies. The lawyers wanted to dismantle segregation so that all black children would have access to resources presumptively enjoyed by all white children. The lawyers chose to achieve their goal by encouraging the Court to assume the role of protecting black children from the intangible effects of stigma and self-hate. This intangible damage thesis seemed to offer the best possible means of directly dismantling Jim Crow (de jure, formal inequality) and *indirectly* dismantling its effects. Unfortunately, in this court-centered universe, the tactic of desegregation became the ultimate goal, rather than the means to secure educational equity. The upshot of the inversion of means and end was to redefine equality, not as a fair and just distribution of resources, but as the absence of formal, legal barriers that separated the races.

Advocates for the NAACP made a conscious choice to abandon cases that demanded that states equalize the facilities, staff, and budgets of separate white and black schools to focus the Court's attention on segregation itself. As part of their litigation strategy, they appended studies by social scientists to their brief in *Brown*. The plaintiffs' attorneys successfully mobilized social scientists to support the fight against segregation, presenting racism as pathological because of the "toll it took on the black psyche." In a magisterial study, Daryl Michael Scott faulted the Court's dependence on psychological damage imagery to demonstrate the intangible costs of segregation. Segregation's evils had social and economic, not just psychological, ramifications. Even more, as others have pointed out, the psychology of segregation did not affect blacks alone; it convinced working-class whites that their interests lay in white solidarity rather than collective cross-racial mobilization around economic interests. Writing in 1935, W. E. B. Du Bois described the "public and psychological wage" paid to white workers, who came to depend upon their status and privileges as whites to compensate for low pay and harsh working conditions.[8]

The Court's reasoning suffered once it considered the caste system of Jim Crow narrowly, as a function of individual prejudice. The Court's minimalist analysis had legal, sociological, and psychological consequences. In legal terms, the focus on prejudice alone cast a long doctrinal shadow, allowing subsequent courts to limit constitutional relief to remedying acts of *intentional* discrimination by local entities or individuals. Absent evidence that local officials or state actors intentionally manipulated school boundaries *because of racial animus*, *Brown*'s principled conclusion ultimately excused inaction in the face of a gradual return to racially segregated schools that are unquestionably separate *and* unequal. The sociological ramifications—that de facto separation became invisible—were predictable, given the Court's lopsided psychological framing.

The Court's measure of segregation's psychological costs counted its apparent effect on black children without grappling with the way segregation also shaped the personality development of whites. This analytic asymmetry influenced the reaction of blue-collar whites and arguably restigmatized blacks. The decision modified but did not eliminate "the property interest in whiteness" that Du Bois earlier observed and that came to define the Court's equal protection jurisprudence. As Cheryl I. Harris has written, "*Brown I*'s dialectical contradiction was that it dismantled an old form of whiteness as property while simultaneously permitting its reemergence in a more subtle form" by failing to redress "inequalities in resources, power, and, ultimately, educational opportunity."[9]

Other scholars deplore the Court's remedial approach as overly deferential to southern whites; some also criticize integration efforts as benefiting very few poor blacks. What blacks won was not freedom, but tokenism. A cadre of middle-class blacks has enjoyed the privileges of upward mobility, but for the mass of blacks (and poor and working-class whites), educational opportunities remain beyond reach.[10]

A few scholars have sought to demonstrate that a bench-based, lawyer-crafted social justice initiative was ill equipped to address complex social problems. *Brown* actually had little effect on educational opportunity, Michael J. Klarman has argued, serving instead to reenergize white racial consciousness, while providing little in the way of integrated or improved educational facilities. Without executive and legislative branch leadership, the courts could not bring about the dynamic social change envisioned by the *Brown* lawyers. The federal judge John Minor Wisdom, renowned for his landmark decisions ordering desegregation in the wake of the Supreme Court's ruling in *Brown*, was candid about the lack of judicially inspired progress in the face of fierce white backlash. Like Wisdom, Rosenberg concluded that "the courts acting alone have failed." It was not until nonviolent and courageous civil rights activists were violently brutalized on national television that blacks won their "freedom" from state-sanctioned oppression. But they won through legislative action, which was after all the more democratic and sustaining force for change.[11]

John Minor Wisdom
(1957)

Beyond the academic debates, many black activists struggle to reconcile their early optimism and contemporary hopelessness. A sense of lost opportunity has sparked increasing cynicism among some. There is an eerie nostalgia for the feeling of community that was destroyed post-*Brown*. As Adam Fairclough has noted, school integration has long divided the black community. For a surprising number

Trio of Civil Rights Activists
An African American man and two African American women hold hands and try to brace themselves against the harsh spray of a fire hose during an anti-segregation protest in Birmingham, Alabama. Against the 3,000 protesters, police released dogs, attacked with electric cattle prods, and used water sprayed with the strength to rip bark off of trees. These images were televised across the nation. (1963)

of blacks, the question is not whether we mistook integration for the promised land. Confusion, even skepticism, reigns in some quarters over whether the promised land can exist in a United States that has yet to come to terms with the way slavery and the racialized compromises it produced shaped our original understanding of the nation as a republic.[12]

Racism—meaning the maintenance of, and acquiescence in, racialized hierarchies governing resource distribution—has not functioned simply through evil or irrational prejudice; it has been an artifact of geographic, political, and economic interests. In the United States racism was foundational, indeed constitutional. Mainstream historians are now busy tracing the constitutional legacy of the three-fifths clause that gave southern states, and most often southern plantation owners, disproportionate electoral clout at the national level. For roughly 50 of our country's first 72 years, the presidency was won by southern slave owners. Indeed, before and after the Civil War the social alliances between northern and southern elites encouraged both to suppress the ideological dissonance of a country "of free men" that "worshiped liberty while profiting from slavery" and "left the public arena to men of propertied independence." Such histories remind us that the northern "lords of the loom" and the southern "lords of the lash" were complicit in the maintenance of slavery and its aftermath. As David Brion Davis has explained, the South may have lost the Civil War battles, but it won the ideological civil war, propagating white acceptance nationwide of both "Negro inferiority" and white supremacy for most of the nineteenth and twentieth centuries.[13]

Under those circumstances, it is an open question whether any legal analysis, even one grounded in more rigorous social science research or employing a more balanced assessment of segregation's causes and effects, could have accomplished the goals of the *Brown* attorneys or could now accomplish the massive tasks that still await us: to extirpate a complex system of relationships that have tortured this country from its earliest beginnings and then to refashion a new social and economic order in its place. Formal legal equality granted through the courts could never guarantee economic, political, and social opportunity for the mass of blacks, for whom civil rights alone were not the measure of success. Their struggle was for "jobs and freedom" and encompassed many of the principles of self-government and property ownership that animated the early American revolutionaries.[14]

While Bell focused on interest *convergences* to explain the limited reach of the Court's initiative in *Brown*, geographic, racial, and class-based interest *divergences* were also at work ordering social, regional, and class conflict between northern and southern elites; between white elites and poor whites, North and South; between poor blacks and poor whites, whose concern was not unequal treatment, but the maldistribution of resources and opportunity; and between poor and middle-class blacks, who arguably benefited most. When *Brown* is read in light of these divisions, it is clear that the task confronting those who took on Jim Crow would prevent even the most ambitious policy-minded experts from challenging white supremacy as it reemerged in new garb. The social engineers in *Brown* identified state-sponsored segregation as the visible manifestation of American racism. This understandable preoccupation with de jure segregation disabled the plaintiffs' attorneys and their liberal allies from comprehending Jim Crow as the visible manifestation of a larger, constantly mutating racialized hierarchy. That hierarchy was racialized both by elites to consolidate their power and privilege and by poor whites to palliate their own debased circumstances.

Brown's legacy is clouded at least in part because post–World War II racial liberalism influenced the legal engineers to treat the symptoms of racism, not the disease. Their strategy was to eliminate desegregation, which they assumed would strike a fatal blow to racialized hierarchies. The lawyers' assumption and its corollary remedial emphasis were limited by the nature of their allies, who wanted to do good without sacrificing any of their own privileges, believing integration was possible without significant resource redistribution. The legal engineers failed to anticipate the down-sides of a singular preoccupation with desegregation because their analysis essentialized all white children, without identifying the regulatory role race and class played within the white community. The lawyers and their allies went to court to enforce a right without consciously considering the remedy, which ended up restigmatizing blacks, reinforcing white working-class fear of economic downward mobility, and reserving for a privileged few the resources they needed to learn. Finally, while dismantling Jim Crow was a noble imperative, the lawyers did not realize that the disease Jim Crow betokened could and did easily reappear in a new guise. Racism was not ended by the defeat of Jim Crow, even in school systems that achieved unitary status. As Judge Robert Carter, one of the NAACP LDEF lawyers in *Brown*, has since written, "Both northern and southern white liberals and blacks looked upon racial segregation by law as the *primary* race relations evil in this country. It was not until *Brown I* was decided that blacks were able to understand that the fundamental vice was not legally enforced *racial segregation* itself; that this was a mere by-product, a symptom of the greater and more pernicious disease—white supremacy."[15]

Even when race is no longer explicitly coded by appearance or ancestry, the allocation of seats in a classroom, the use of buses to transport schoolchildren, or the hue of the dolls with which those children play, race is, and was, about the distribution of power. Race in the United States is a by-product of economic conflict that has been converted into a tool of division and distraction. It is not just an outgrowth of hatred or ill will. Racism has had psychological, sociological, and economic consequences that created the separate spheres inhabited by blacks and whites in 1954 but extended well beyond them.

To address the full range of racialized inequities in this country, racial justice advocates need to move beyond the early tenets of racial liberalism to treat the disease and not just its symptoms. A first step would be to make legible racism's ever shifting yet ever present structure. The oppressive conditions that most blacks still confront must not be ignored, but the continuing puzzle is how to address the complex ways race adapts its syntax to mask class and code geography. Racism is a structural phenomenon that fabricates interdependent yet paradoxical relationships between race, class, and geography—what I am calling the interest-divergence dilemma. It is the interest-divergence dilemma that requires a new racial literacy, meaning the capacity to decipher the durable racial grammar that structures racialized hierarchies and frames the narrative of our republic. To understand why *Brown v. Board of Education* has not lived up to its promise, I propose a paradigm shift from racial liberalism to racial literacy.

※ ※ ※

Racial Liberalism and the Interest-Divergence Dilemma
Post–World War II racial liberalism rejected scientific racism and discredited its postulate of inherent black inferiority. At the same time, racial liberalism positioned the peculiarly American race "problem" as a psychological and interpersonal challenge rather than a structural problem rooted in our economic and political system. Reeling from the horrors of fascism abroad, fearing the specter of totalitarian domination, and facing continued pressure to fight racial inequities at home, proponents of greater tolerance suggested that racism was irrational and would surrender to logic and interpersonal contact. Equality before the law, through the persistent pursuit of civil rights, was the goal. That goal would be realized through racial integration. The defining elements of postwar racial liberalism were its pragmatic devotion to a single strategy, its individualized and static view of American racism, and its focus on top-down social reform.

Guided by the assumption that closer contact with whites would assure dignity and citizenship rights for blacks, racial liberals failed to connect their version of the psychology of blacks with an equally probing analysis of the psychology of whites. The bargain struck by northern elites — that desegregation would restore credibility to the United States during the Cold War and provide social stability as it eased the dissonance experienced by black veterans returning from World War II — disregarded the substantial investment poor whites had in their superior social status vis-à-vis blacks. Relying on the psychological evidence of the intangible damage segregation does to black personality development also enabled many white allies to maintain their social and economic advantages without giving up the moral high ground.

* * *

In the ideology of racial liberalism, the class and geographic interests of rural and poor southern whites — and of working-class northern whites — receded from view. That inattention had two consequences. First, many poor and working-class whites saw themselves as victims. Second, they saw desegregation as downward economic mobility. To poor whites, compulsory association with blacks brought no added value and endangered the sense of autonomy and community they did have. *Brown*'s racial liberalism did not offer poor whites even an elementary framework for understanding what they might gain as a result of integration. Neither the opinion nor the subsequent legal strategy to implement *Brown* made clear that segregation had offered elites an important means of exercising social control over poor and working-class whites as well as a means of dominating or disadvantaging blacks.[21]

* * *

In the South, for example, integration was successfully portrayed as downward mobility through compulsory association with blacks. The dramatic events accompanying the integration of Central High School in Little Rock, Arkansas, illustrate the dynamic. In 1957 there were three high schools serving Little Rock: the new all-white Hall High School, the all-black Horace Mann High School, and Central. Central had been the only white high school in Little Rock, but in summer 1957, Hall opened in the western and more affluent portion of the city. Middle- and upper-middle-class white students transferred to the new high school just before the school year began. This meant that once the senior class at Central graduated in 1958, Central would lose its "citywide character." The school board had approved a plan to integrate Central in 1955. It was

Teenage Boys Against Integration
A crowd of teenage boys protest against school integration and wave Confederate flags in Montgomery, Alabama, in 1963.

scheduled to take effect in fall 1957, at the very time when affluent whites were exiting to attend the new school. Horace Mann would remain all-black; Hall would be all-white. Only Central would experience integration, albeit with nine carefully chosen black students. Despite the academic credentials and middle-class appearance of the black trailblazers, those white students who remained at Central perceived a twisted symmetry: poor blacks and rich whites would remain in the isolated, racially homogeneous environments of Horace Mann and Hall high schools, while working-class whites became the guinea pigs in the integration experiment at Central. In their minds, the "symmetry" was not coincidental; school superintendent Virgil Blossom had "sold" his desegregation plan to the leadership in Little Rock by reassuring them that their children could attend the new Hall High School, "a high school segregated by both class and race." As Elizabeth Huckaby, who was then assistant principal of Central High School, recalled, "Except for a hundred of our seniors who had elected to stay at Central for their final year, we would have no more boys and girls from [the northwest] section of Little Rock where the finest houses were being built, where the families of the most successful businessmen were moving, where the country clubs are."[24]

The exodus of white elites from Central High School threatened working-class dreams of upward mobility and put working-class students' virtual membership in the "dominant class" at risk. The sociologist Beth Roy subsequently interviewed some white students who were then at Central. Even thirty years later, her interviewees criticized the disruption desegregation brought into their lives: "I became very disenchanted with the whole thing. I just kept thinking, This is my senior year, and this is not what I was looking forward to. This is just unfair." Another, searching for a way to explain her hatred for one of the black students who entered Central in 1957, exclaimed, "She walked the halls as if she belonged there." To working-class whites, integration, timed to coincide with the flight of the city's elite, was a stigmatizing force that interfered with their ability to pursue the American dream. Thus they resisted it.[25]

Goaded on by the racial demagoguery of local politicians, such whites viewed the potential economic consequences of desegregation in psychological terms. Politicians preyed on their sense of betrayal and unfair sacrifice, deliberately organizing the conversation about desegregation around a white racial consciousness. Although working-class whites initially saw this "experiment in interracial education" in class terms, a racially polarized contest was easily manufactured using antebellum conceptions of race and class that had crystallized under segregation. Lacking a vocabulary of either class or structure, Roy's working-class white informants were still fluent in the language of racial scapegoating some thirty years later. Disappointed with their own economic and social status, they blamed blacks. Cause and effect were reduced to race.[26]

❖ ❖ ❖

Interest Divergence: Stigmatizing Race

Brown helped change the quality of life for many blacks. It educated the country about the changing meaning of the United States Constitution and allowed blacks to claim the Constitution as theirs despite the tragic role race had played in its earliest formulation. It overruled *Plessy v. Ferguson*, the constitutional straitjacket in which the Court had put itself in 1896. It represented the triumph of racial liberalism over scientific racism and other theories of inherent black inferiority. It also served for most of the second half of the twentieth century as the "principal ideological inspiration" to those who sought racial justice through the courts, according to Jack Greenberg, Thurgood Marshall's successor as head of the NAACP LDEF and one of the lawyers who argued a companion case to *Brown*.[39]

Yet as Marshall's colleague Robert Carter concluded, *Brown* promised more than it could give. *Brown*'s analysis was limited by its singular focus on the harm segregation caused the personality development of black children. Predicated on experiments purportedly showcasing blacks' lack of self-esteem, the opinion reinforced the stigma long associated with blacks, even as it attributed the stigma to segregation rather than biology. Subsequent cases added insult to injury as the Court began to label the legal claim as arising from differential treatment rather than demeaning treatment within a racialized hierarchy.[40]

Significantly, the Court's analysis was framed as requiring racial desegregation to end damage to black psyches. The district court judge and later the Supreme Court adopted almost verbatim testimony by the psychologist Louisa Holt in the Kansas case that segregation, especially when sanctioned by law, had a detrimental effect on "the personality development of the Negro child." One of the lawyers in *Brown* found in her testimony, which he attributed to a "God-given eloquence," "the seeds of ultimate victory." Linking responsibility for educational disadvantage to black self-loathing and connecting that to a psychological abstraction did little, however, to disrupt the powerfully negative views of blacks in the popular imagination. As Charles R. Lawrence III has written, many whites do not believe that racial discrimination is the principal cause of black inequality. The explanation lies instead in some version of black inferiority. "Few will express this belief openly. It is no longer consistent with American ideology to speak in terms of inherent racial traits. But the myth of racial inferiority remains embedded in the fabric of our culture."[41]

Basing its opinion on the psychological research of the time, the Court misunderstood the source of self-esteem for many blacks and unwittingly contributed to the divergence of interests along class and geographic lines within and without the black community. These outcomes can be traced, in part, to the flawed studies on which plaintiffs relied to prove that physically equal but segregated facilities had a negative psychological impact on all black children. The most famous of the psychological studies cited by the Court was the doll experiment of Kenneth Clark and Mamie Clark. The Clark study aggregated findings of northern and southern black children, light-skinned and dark-skinned black children, and middle-class and poor black children to conclude that segregation caused feelings of inferiority among all blacks. Black children in the more integrated North had more frequently preferred the white dolls than black children in the South. Many northern black children also verbalized unease when prompted to consider their physical similarity to the brown dolls, yet Kenneth Clark concluded that northern black children were actually psychologically healthier. A historian has summarized Clark's argument: The reaction of the northern children showed their "discomfort with the complicated and harsh reality of racial mores rather than resignation," whereas racial segregation and isolation had caused southern black children to accept their inferior social status as normal. "Such an accept-ance," Clark reported, "is not symptomatic of a healthy personality." Clark argued that the racial identification of the southern children, almost 80 percent of whom identified themselves in some way with the brown dolls, was tainted because of the terms they used to verbalize their choices. The southern black children described the black dolls as "pretty," "nice," or "good," but accompanied their choices with statements such as, "This one. It's a nigger. I'm a nigger."[42]

Kenneth Clark
(1970)

Clark's message was that group self-hatred among blacks begins at an early age, involves the rejection of brown skin color by black children, and becomes embedded in the personality of blacks as a result of the "damage inherent in racial segregation." These conclusions may have had some merit, but none was entirely consistent with his research. According to Daryl Scott, Clark's conclusions (unlike his data) also contradicted other contemporary studies that suggested that black children with greater contact with whites experienced the most psychological distress. While many blacks hailed the Court decision, especially for its vast symbolic value, the opinion's emphasis on the psychological damage segregation does to blacks camouflaged the ways desegregation "hurt" some blacks, while segregation motivated others to excel, a possibility Holt had conceded. For some black children, segregated schools provided a sanctuary from psychological conflict. More recently, psychological literature has also suggested that those blacks who are the most invested in achieving academically within the larger society are often more vulnerable to what Claude Steele and others term stereotype threat, the situational threat of being negatively stereotyped. Unlike Clark's "self-fulfilling prophecy" that black students internalize and then fulfill negative stereotypes and low expectations for achievement, stereotype threat is context-dependent rather than intrinsic. Moreover, social psychologists have found that in some circumstances the ability to maintain a sense of self-worth in a hostile environment may actually enhance self-esteem. The key point is that data on self-esteem differences between black kids and white kids were not well developed then; even today "there's not much evidence of chronic psychological damage done to blacks' self-esteem as a result of segregation" per se.[43]

A desegregation solution based on concerns about psychological stigma did not necessarily have the desired effect of providing meaningful educational and economic opportunity even for those middle-class blacks whom compulsory segregation had denied a first-class education. For example, desegregation meant that some black teachers, the backbone of the black middle class at the time, lost their jobs. And the mentoring provided to high-achieving, middle-class black students at some all-black elite public high schools, such as Dunbar High School in Washington, D.C., was neither replaced nor reproduced in more integrated environments. Within integrated schools, the interaction with white students was often limited literally and figuratively by tracking, skepticism about blacks' intellectual ability by their teachers and white classmates, and the loss not only of black mentors but also of a sense of community in which the adults were invested in the students' achievement.[44]

In addition, the prejudice-centered approach set in motion forces that have cemented the connection between public education and damaged goods in a way that disadvantaged poor blacks in particular. Much of Derrick Bell's scholarship and that of others presents evidence that poor blacks were abandoned by middle-class blacks who now had the opportunity to choose educational situations consistent with their class interests. Similarly, Carter, an NAACP LDEF lawyer in *Brown*, later concluded that "to focus on integration alone is a luxury only the black middle-class can afford. They have the means to desert the public schools if dissatisfied." Poor blacks suffered as urban public schools became the primary locus of integration; the change fomented an unhealthy battleground of racial tensions. Race became synonymous with poor blacks, and public education itself became stigmatized as it became more and more closely associated with racialized poverty.[45]

The focus on educational quality soon abated, as administrators, teachers, and students became political figures or political pawns rather than learners; educational funds were diverted to conflict avoidance and resolution and education budgets manipulated to promote political goals about race policy. Although *Brown* heralded the crucial role that public education plays in a democracy and gave eloquent voice to the importance of an educated citizenry to society as a whole, its legal analysis forestalled political interest convergences to the detriment of poor people of all colors: black, brown, and white, urban and rural. The Court's analysis became the basis for a doctrinal distinction between race and class that lifted unequal resource distribution out of the constitutional canon.[46] What appeared to be "eloquence from God" in the testimony of a witness at the trial court in Kansas that compulsory segregation damages children's ability to learn soon became manifest in a different prophecy: that black children simply cannot or do not wish to learn. Legally compelled segregation became socially acceptable separation; separation became stigma; stigma became association with blacks who still occupied and defined separate, albeit public, education. Integration was reduced to diversity, a benefit to be enjoyed by a critical mass, but not by the masses.

Sadly, it was the appellees in *Brown* whose prognostications came closest to describing current realities. In his oral argument before the Supreme Court in the companion case of *Davis v. County School Board*, Attorney General Lindsay Almond of Virginia argued that integration would "destroy the public school system as we know it today" because the "people would not vote bond issues through their resentment to it." Colgate Darden, then president of the University of Virginia and a former governor of Virginia, testified that desegregation would "impair the opportunities for both races" because good will toward the public school system would be "badly impaired," which would lead to a "sizable falling off of the funds required for public education." Indeed, urban and rural public schools became stigmatized as the dumping ground for those with nowhere else to go.[47]

The ambiguity of *Brown*'s legacy is as much a consequence of interest divergence as of the temporary alliance between northern elites and civil rights advocates to promote social reform through biracial top-down cooperation grounded in the values of racial liberalism. The Court relied on incomplete data regarding the damage segregation did to the self-esteem of blacks while it underestimated the potentially negative impact of desegregation on the self-esteem of some blacks and perhaps inadvertently reinforced the identification of blackness with inferiority and stigma in the minds of whites. There was also a divergence of interests inside the black community between poor and middle-class blacks arising from the practical consequences of *Brown* (including the loss of community and the exodus of middle-class blacks from urban public schools). That the divergences were relegated to the background was partly a result of the prejudice-centered orthodoxy of racial liberalism. That the divergences remain mostly intact may also have been a function of the elevated and preeminent role of legal analysis in fashioning a social change strategy. The Court, acting alone, was not in a position to explore the triangulation of interests along race, class, and geographic lines.

Racial Literacy and the Interest-Divergence Dilemma

The apparent interest convergence between northern liberals and southern blacks ultimately perpetuated a more durable divergence of interests within and between the black and white communities. The ideals of racial liberalism produced a legal icon but did little to disrupt the historic pattern in which race was used to manufacture dissensus, complicating relationships within and outside communities of color. That dissensus was not produced by race, but by social and economic conflict that was simultaneously revealed and concealed by race. Post-*Brown*, the ability to use race to code and cloak diverging interests sustained racial hierarchies—a phenomenon that tainted our founding arrangements and remains at our ideological core.

Through the creation and maintenance of racialized hierarchies, the plight of poor blacks and poor whites was mostly ignored; similarly, under the shibboleth of equal opportunity, urban and rural communities were abandoned as the maldistribution of material resources persisted undisturbed. Just as significant, the psychological bribe that segregation offered working-class and poor whites was not examined or countered even as white racial solidarity assumed crucial importance in the decision's aftermath. Indeed, the focus on race as a source of one-way psychological stigma had deleterious consequences for the public school system. Public education became a battlefield rather than a constructive gravitational force within many communities. Race was used to pathologize blacks rather than to reveal how economic and social privilege hid behind racial fault lines. Ultimately, the class interests of those who could afford to invest personally in their children's education triumphed.

The first step in understanding these diverging interests is to make them legible. A racially literate analysis seeks to do just that by deciphering the dynamic interplay among race, class, and geography. In contrast to racial liberalism, racial literacy reads race as epiphenomenal. Those most advantaged by the status quo have historically manipulated race to order social, economic, and political relations to their benefit. Then and now, race is used to manufacture both convergences and divergences of interest that track class and geographic divisions. The racialized hierarchies that result reinforce divergences of interest among and between groups with varying social status and privilege, which the ideology of white supremacy converts into rationales for the status quo. Racism normalizes these racialized hierarchies; it diverts attention from the unequal distribution of resources and power they perpetuate. Using race as a decoy offers short-term psychological advantages to poor and working-class whites, but it also masks how much poor whites have in common with poor blacks and other people of color.[48]

Racial liberalism triumphed in *Brown* by presenting racism as a departure from the fundamentally sound liberal project of American individualism, equality of opportunity, and upward mobility. But racial liberalism's individualistic and prejudice-centered view of formal equality failed to anticipate multiple interest divergences, helped fuel a white backlash, and doomed both integration and the redistribution of resources. Racial literacy, in contrast, requires us to rethink race as an instrument of social, geographic, and economic control of both whites and blacks. Racial literacy offers a more dynamic framework for understanding American racism. There are many differences between what I call racial literacy and racial liberalism, but for the purposes of this essay three stand out. First, racial literacy is contextual rather than universal. It does not assume that either the problem or the solution is one-size-fits-all. Nor does it assume that the answer is made evident by thoughtful consideration or expert judgment alone. Racial literacy depends upon the engagement between action and thought, between experimentation and feedback, between bottom-up and top-down initiatives. It is about learning rather than knowing. Racial literacy is an interactive process in which race functions as a tool of diagnosis, feedback, and assessment.

Second, racial literacy emphasizes the relationship between race and power. Racial literacy reads race in its psychological, interpersonal, and structural dimensions. It acknowledges the importance of individual agency but refuses to lose sight of institutional and environmental forces that both shape and reflect that agency. It sees little to celebrate when formal equality is claimed within a racialized hierarchy. Although legally enforced separation was identified as a dignitary harm and the issue being litigated ridiculed as a matter of "racial prestige" by John W. Davis, attorney for South Carolina in the *Brown* case, it soon became distorted into an issue of mere separation rather than subjugation. Indeed, it is precisely as a legal abstraction that we are now being asked to honor equality. But things seldom are equal, as W. E. B. Du Bois pointed out in 1935 as he weighed the benefits of segregated and integrated education for blacks. He concluded that blacks needed education for their minds, not just integration of their bodies: "Other things being equal, the mixed school is the broader, more natural basis for the education of all youth. It gives wider contacts; it inspires greater self-confidence; and suppresses the inferiority complex. But other things seldom are equal, and in that case, Sympathy, Knowledge, and the Truth, outweigh all that the mixed school can offer."[49]

White Anti-Integration Protesters
In Chicago, jeers, cat-calls, and clowning groups greet cars bearing civil rights marchers as they gathered to continue their drive for open occupancy in an all-white neighborhood. (1966)

Third, while racial literacy never loses sight of race, it does not focus exclusively on race. It constantly interrogates the dynamic relationship among race, class, geography, gender, and other explanatory variables. It sees the danger of basing a strategy for monumental social change on assumptions about individual prejudice and individual victims. It considers the way psychological interests can mask political and economic interests for poor and working-class whites. It analyzes the psychological economy of white racial solidarity for poor and working-class whites and blacks, independent of manipulations by "the industrialists and the lawyers and politicians who served them." Racial literacy suggests that racialized hierarchies mirror the distribution of power and resources in the society more generally. In other words, problems that converge around blacks are often visible signs of broader societal dysfunction. Real interest convergences among poor and working-class blacks and whites are possible, but only when complex issues are analyzed and acted upon with their structural, not just their legal or their asymmetric psychological, underpinnings in mind. This means moving beyond a simple justice paradigm that is based on formal equality, while contemplating what it will take to create a moral consensus about the role of government and the place of the public itself.[50]

One of the original architects of the *Brown* strategy apparently understood the importance of further interrogating the interest divergences that promote a purely formal, legal equality within a system where social and economic inequalities persist. Charles Hamilton Houston, the former vice dean at Howard Law School, director-counsel of the NAACP LDEF and the consummate social engineer, declared six years before the case was decided:

> *There come times when it is possible to forecast the results of a contest, of a battle, of a lawsuit all before the final event has taken place. So far as our struggle for civil rights is concerned, the struggle for civil rights is won. What I am more concerned about is that the Negro shall not be content simply with demanding an equal share in the existing system. It seems to me that his historical challenge is to make sure that the system which shall survive in the United States of America shall be a system which guarantees justice and freedom for everyone.*[51]

Conclusion

Race is a powerful explanatory variable in the story of our country, which has been used to explain failure in part by associating failure with black people. Racial literacy suggests that legal equality granted through the courts will not extirpate the distinctive, racialized asymmetries from the DNA of the American dream. The courts can be and often have been a critically important ally, but neither the judiciary nor lawyers acting alone possess the surgical skill required to alter the genetic material of our organizing narrative. Nor is the attainment of civil rights by itself an adequate measure of success, in part because the problem is not just race but race as conjugated by class, geography, and the organizing narrative of upward mobility.

Through its invocation of the language of prejudice, the Court in *Brown* converted the structural phenomenon of racism into a problem of individual psychological dysfunction that whites and blacks are equally capable of exhibiting. In the 1950s prejudice was understood as an aberration in individuals who disregard relevant information, rely on stereotypes, and act thoughtlessly. Prejudice was a function of ignorance. Educated people, it was assumed, are not prejudiced. Yet many who acquiesce in racialized hierarchy derive tangible benefits from such a hierarchy. They are acting rationally, not irrationally, when they ignore the ways hierarchy systematically disadvantages groups of individuals and privileges others consistent with socially and culturally constructed definitions of race that predictably order and rank.

In legal terms, *Brown*'s rule of "equality by proclamation" linked segregation to prejudice and reinforced the individuating of both the cause of action and the remedy. By defining racism as prejudice and prejudice as creating individual psychological damage, the Court's opinion paved the way for others to reinterpret *Brown* as a case mandating formal equality and nothing more. Subsequent courts have tended to limit the equal protection clause of the Fourteenth Amendment by a symmetrical, perpetrator-oriented focus on color blindness. If the problem is that separate is inherently unequal, then equality is simply presumed when the separation is eliminated. Any remaining inequality is the fault of black people themselves.[52]

In the end, *Brown*'s racial liberalism had little to offer poor and working-class whites to counter the psychological benefits of white racial solidarity. Jim Crow was a caste system that oppressed all blacks, regardless of class and geographic lines, but the psychology of Jim Crow allowed white elites to limit the educational and economic opportunities of poor and working-class whites. Working-class whites were also complicit, as they perceived their own advancement as dependent on their ability to separate and distinguish themselves from blacks as a group. It is the conflation of psychological benefits with economic and political self-interest that crafts the popularly accepted fiction that failure is not only measured by race but also *explained* by it.

Brown's effect on public education, for example, showed why it is critical to link race and class without losing sight of race and in ways that invite the people most directly affected to speak for themselves. *Brown* relied on the lawyers' and the justices' understanding of the key role played by public education in a democracy. Yet it unwittingly nationalized the southern white racial consciousness, which downplayed the collective interest in a vigorous public in favor of the social interest of one class in private, individual choice. Nevertheless, it is important to remember that, although the trisection of interests along race, class, and regional lines haunted *Brown* from the beginning, the stark lines of divergence emerge more clearly in retrospect, viewed from the perspective of significant social progress that was inconceivable in 1954.

To be sure, the NAACP lawyers were audacious social engineers. Their ingenious litigation strategy bolstered insurgent efforts to dismantle *de jure* segregation. But for all their brilliance, the lawyers in *Brown* were unable to kindle a populist revolution in which the people, not just the lawyers, come to understand the crippling effects of race and racism on our entire social, economic, and political order. Race matters not just for blacks, in other words, but for every citizen of the United States. Because of its foundational role in the making of this country's history and myths, race, in conjunction with class and geography, invariably shapes educational, economic, and political opportunities for all of us.

My proposed paradigm shift to racial literacy is more a thought experiment than a judicial brief. We need to learn to use the courts as a tool rather than a panacea to overcome the structured dissension race has cemented in our popular consciousness as well as in our lived experience. If we can become more literate about the role racism continues to play in structuring and narrating economic and political opportunity, we may be better able to combine legal and legislative advocacy that enlists support among people of all colors, whites as well as blacks. It may be that the time has come for "a new policy compass," as Derrick Bell recently wrote, "to assert petitions for racial justice in forms that whites will realize serve their interests as well as those of blacks." But however petitions for racial justice are framed, they need to avoid confusing tactics with goals, forever freezing a formalistic theory of racial equality into the Constitution, which can then be used to undermine opportunities for progressive innovation in the future.[53]

If there is only one lesson to be learned from *Brown*, it is that all Americans need to go back to school. The courts acting alone cannot move us to overcome, and the federal government has not assumed leadership in this arena since the 1960s. At the beginning of the twenty-first century, a racially literate mobilization of people within and across lines of race, class, and geography might finally be what it takes to redeem the optimistic assessment of those early academic commentators. Of course, a racially literate analysis, meaning the ability to read race in conjunction with both contemporary institutional and democratic hierarchies and their historical antecedents, may not resolve the interest-divergence dilemma. Nor should it. But at least it may help us understand why *Brown* feels less satisfying fifty years later.

Lani Guinier is Bennett Boskey Professor of Law, Harvard Law School. The phrase "interest-divergence dilemma" in the title of this essay modifies and elaborates on the "interest-convergence dilemma" proposed by Professor Derrick A. Bell, Jr.

I thank Stephanie Camp, Kevin Gaines, Danielle Gray, Evelyn Brooks Higginbotham, Ken Mack, Joanne Meyerowitz, Frank Michelman, Martha Minow, Gerald Torres, and David Wilkins for enormously helpful comments on earlier drafts. Jay Cox, Jenee Desmond, Amos Jones, and Nathan Kitchens provided excellent research assistance. Susan Armeny, Lori Creed, Jenee Desmond, Amos Jones, and Samuel Spital provided very useful editorial and substantive feedback.

For a full version of the original essay, see 91, *Journal of American History*, 92 (June 2004).

[1] On the importance of the *Brown* decision, see Jack Greenberg, *Crusaders in the Courts: How a Dedicated Band of Lawyers Fought for the Civil Rights Revolution* (New York, 1994), 197; James T. Patterson, Brown v. Board of Education: *A Civil Rights Milestone and Its Troubled Legacy* (New York, 2001), xxvii–xxviii; Jordan Steiker, "American Icon: Does It Matter What the Court Said in *Brown?*," *Texas Law Review*, 81 (Nov. 2002), 305; Martin Guggenheim, "Symposium: Translating Insights into Policy: Maximizing Strategies for Pressuring Adults to Do Right by Children," *Arizona Law Review*, 45 (Fall 2000), 779; David A. Strauss, "Interdisciplinary Approach: Afterword: The Role of a Bill of Rights," *University of Chicago Law Review*, 59 (Winter 1992), 547; and Jack M. Balkin, ed., *What* Brown v. Board of Education *Should Have Said: The Nation's Top Legal Experts Rewrite America's Landmark Civil Rights Decision* (New York, 2001), 3. See also Ronald S. Sullivan, Jr., "Multiple Ironies: Brown at 50," *Howard Law Journal*, 47 (Fall 2003), 29.

[2] Nancy McArdle, "Beyond Poverty: Race and Concentrated-Poverty Neighborhoods in Metro Boston," Dec. 2003, *The Civil Rights Project, Harvard University* <http://www.civilrightsproject.harvard.edu/research/metro/ poverty_boston.php> (Jan. 22, 2004). For figures on declining levels of school-age children enrolled in Boston public schools by race and as total percentages of the population, see "Lessons for the Boston Schools," *Boston Globe*, March 14, 2004, p. A1. After ten years of court-ordered desegregation, barely 1% of black children in the eleven southern states attended school with whites, according to Gerald N. Rosenberg, *The Hollow Hope: Can Courts Bring About Social Change?* (Chicago, 1991), 52. See also Adam Fairclough, *Better Day Coming: Blacks and Equality, 1890–2000* (New York, 2001), 329; Patterson, *Brown v. Board of Education*, 202–4, 211–12, 229, 231; and Lani Guinier, "Admissions Rituals as Political Acts: Guardians at the Gates of Our Democratic Ideals," *Harvard Law Review*, 117 (Nov. 2003), 113, 118–19nn24–27. Mark Tushnet, "The Significance of *Brown v. Board of Education*," *Virginia Law Review*, 80 (Feb. 1994), 175.

[3] *Brown v. Board of Education*, 347 U.S. 483, 494 (1954). Decisions that rejected race-conscious governmental policies and/or required a showing of prior intentional discrimination to justify a limited racial classification as a remedy include *Regents of the University of California v. Bakke*, 438 U.S. 265 (1978); *City of Mobile v. Bolden*, 446 U.S. 55 (1980); *Wygant v. Jackson Board of Education*, 476 U.S. 267, 274 (1986) (plurality opinion); and *Richmond v. J. A. Croson Co.*, 488 U.S. 469, 496 (1989). The Court held that a school desegregation plan must be limited to districts with an actual history of racial discrimination in *Milliken v. Bradley*, 418 U.S. 717, 744–45 (1974).

[4] Derrick A. Bell, Jr., "*Brown v. Board of Education* and the Interest-Convergence Dilemma," *Harvard Law Review*, 93 (Jan. 1980), 518–33.

[5] Ibid., 523.

[6] For the interest-convergence principle framed broadly, see Derrick A. Bell, Jr., *Race, Racism, and American Law* (Boston, 1980). On desegregation and the Cold War, see Greenberg, *Crusaders in the Courts*, 164–65; Mary L. Dudziak, "Desegregation as a Cold War Imperative," *Stanford Law Review*, 41 (Nov. 1988), 61–120; and Mary L. Dudziak, *Cold War Civil Rights: Race and the Image of American Democracy* (Princeton, 2000). On the arousal of civil rights consciousness among blacks during World War II, see, for example, Earl Lewis, *In Their Own Interests: Race, Class, and Power in Twentieth-Century Norfolk, Virginia* (Berkeley, 1991), 173–76; Martin Sosna, *In Search of the Silent South: Southern Liberals and the Race Issue* (New York, 1977); and Michael J. Klarman, "*Brown*, Racial Change, and the Civil Rights Movement," *Virginia Law Review*, 80 (Feb. 1994), 17–18. On desegregation and southern industrialization, see ibid., 56. The brief on behalf of the United States is quoted in Yale Kamisar, "The School Desegregation Cases in Retrospect: Some Reflections on Causes and Effects," in *Argument: The Oral Argument before the Supreme Court in* Brown v. Board of Education of Topeka, 1952–55, ed. Leon Friedman (New York, 1969), xiv. On Special Assistant to the Attorney General Philip Elman, see Robert J. Cottrol, Raymond T. Diamond, and Leland B. Ware, "*Brown v. Board of Education*: Caste, Culture, and the Constitution" (Lawrence, 2003), 161–62. On the embarrassment to foreign visitors who were mistaken for American blacks, see Brief for the United States as Amicus Curiae at 4–5, *Brown v. Board of Education*, 347 U.S. 483 (1954) (No. 1).

[7] The Court itself refocused on segregation per se: "Here, unlike *Sweatt v. Painter*, there are findings below that the Negro and white schools involved have been equalized, or are being equalized, with respect to buildings, curricula, qualifications and salaries of teachers, and other 'tangible' factors. Our decision, therefore, cannot turn on merely a comparison of these tangible factors in the Negro and white schools involved in each of the cases. We must look instead to the effect of segregation itself on public education." *Brown v. Board of Education*, 347 U.S. at 492. On racial liberalism, see Daryl Michael Scott, *Contempt and Pity: Social Policy and the Image of the Damaged Black Psyche, 1880–1996* (Chapel Hill, 1997), xiii. On constituencies *Brown* ignored, see David S. Cecelski, *Along Freedom Road: Hyde County, North Carolina, and the Fate of Black Schools in the South* (Chapel Hill, 1994), 8, 12. According to the National Association for the Advancement of Colored People (NAACP) lawyer Constance Baker Motley, many black teachers became major foes of school

desegregation after *Brown*. See Adam Fairclough, *Teaching Equality: Black Schools in the Age of Jim Crow* (Athens, Ga., 2001), 62–65, esp. n. 46. See also Martha Biondi, *To Stand and Fight: The Struggle for Civil Rights in Postwar New York City* (Cambridge, Mass., 2003), 164–65, 170–71, 180–85.

[8] The social scientist survey on the psychological effects of segregation submitted to the Supreme Court as an appendix in *Brown* is cited in Kenneth B. Clark, *Prejudice and Your Child* (Boston, 1955), 39–41. Scott, Contempt and Pity, xii–xiv, 125–26, 138; W. E. B. Du Bois, *Black Reconstruction in America, 1860–1880* (New York, 1935), 700.

[9] For an example of the judiciary's perception of racism as a matter of prejudice, see Justice Anthony M. Kennedy's concurrence in *Board of Trustees of the University of Alabama v. Garrett*, 531 U.S. 356, 374–75 (2001). On the development of a specific intent theory of equal protection, see John Charles Boger, "Willful Colorblindness: The New Racial Piety and the Resegregation of Public Schools," *North Carolina Law Review*, 78 (Sept. 2000), 1794. *Washington v. Davis*, 426 U.S. 229 (1976); *Mobile v. Bolden*, 446 U.S. 55 (1980). On the cost of segregation to black schoolchildren and ultimately their communities, one source noted "the contrasts in support of white and Negro schools are appalling . . . the median expenditure per standard classroom unit in schools for white children is $1,160 as compared with $476 for Negro children." See Brief of the American Federation of Teachers as Amicus Curiae at 9, *Brown v. Board of Education*, 347 U.S. 483 (1954) (No. 1). Derrick A. Bell, Jr., "Bell, J., Dissenting," in *What* Brown v. Board of Education *Should Have Said*, ed. Balkin, 185–200. Stephen E. Gottlieb, "*Brown v. Board of Education* and the Application of American Tradition to Racial Division," *Suffolk University Law Review*, 34 (2001), 282–83. See also George Lipsitz, *The Possessive Investment in Whiteness: How White People Profit from Identity Politics* (Philadelphia, 1998), 34. But contrast Fairclough, *Teaching Equality,* 66. Cheryl I. Harris, "Whiteness as Property," *Harvard Law Review*, 106 (June 1993), 1714.

[10] On the Court's deference to southern whites, see Harris, "Whiteness as Property," 1753n9. For criticism of integration efforts, see Derrick A. Bell, Jr., "Serving Two Masters: Integration Ideals and Client Interests in School Desegregation Litigation," *Yale Law Journal*, 85 (March 1976), 470–516. For a critique of Bell's view that it was midde-class blacks who sought integration, see Tomiko Brown Nagin, "Race as Identity Caricature: A Local Legal History Lesson in the Salience of Intraracial Conflict," *University of Pennsylvania Law Review*, 151 (June 2003), 1913–76. On tokenism, consider that as recently as 2002, in a flagship state school that was the subject of a precedent on which *Brown* relied, nearly 90% of the undergraduate classes "with five to twenty-four students had no or only one African American to contribute their experiences or perspectives to a class discussion." Office of Admissions, University of Texas at Austin, "Diversity Levels of Undergraduate Classes at the University of Texas at Austin, 1996–2002," Nov. 20, 2003 <http://www.utexas.edu/student/admissions/research/ClassroomDiversity96-03 .pdf> (Feb. 3, 2004). Cf. *Sweatt v. Painter*, 339 U.S. 629 (1950).

[11] Michael J. Klarman, "How Brown Changed Race Relations: The Backlash Thesis," *Journal of American History*, 81 (June 1994), 81–118; Klarman, "*Brown*, Racial Change, and the Civil Rights Movement," 7–150. Some commentators have suggested Klarman may have exaggerated the possibilities of northern and southern biracial cooperation or treated the role of litigation without sufficient nuance. See, for example, David Garrow, "Hopelessly Hollow History: Revisionist Devaluing of *Brown v. Board of Education*," *Virginia Law Review*, 80 (Feb. 1994), 151. Robert Korstad and Nelson Lichtenstein, "Opportunities Found and Lost: Labor, Radicals, and the Early Civil Rights Movement," *Journal of American History*, 75 (Dec. 1988), 787. On the role of courts in implementing desegregation, see *U.S. v. Jefferson County Board of Education*, 372 F. 2d 836, 847 (1966); Rosenberg, Hollow Hope, 52.

[12] Cecelski, *Along Freedom Road*, 8, 10, 12, 15, 34, 36. Cf. Fairclough, *Better Day Coming*, 148, 219, 221–23; and Fairclough, *Teaching Equality*, 62–65. Patterson, *Brown v. Board of Education*, xxvi–xxix, 201–5. See also Bell, "Serving Two Masters," 470–516.

[13] For a definition of racism, see Lani Guinier and Gerald Torres, *The Miner's Canary: Enlisting Race, Resisting Power, Transforming Democracy* (Cambridge, Mass., 2002), 302. On the role of racial hierarchy in American history, see, for example, David Brion Davis, "Free at Last: The Enduring Legacy of the South's Civil War Victory," *New York Times*, Aug. 26, 2001, sec. 4, p. 1; Garry Wills, "The Negro President," *New York Review of Books*, Nov. 6, 2003, pp. 45, 48–49; Gordon S. Wood, "Slaves in the Family," *New York Times*, Dec. 14, 2003, sec. 7, p. 10; and Lipsitz, *Possessive Investment in Whiteness*, 18. Eric Foner, *The Story of American Freedom* (New York, 1998), 31–32; Henry Wiencek, "Yale and the Price of Slavery," *New York Times*, Aug. 18, 2001, p. A15; Davis, "Free at Last," 1.

[14] Biondi, *To Stand and Fight*, 183; Foner, *Story of American Freedom*, 21.

[15] On racism as the "dominant interpretative framework" for understanding and securing social stability in the United States, see Bell, "Bell, J., Dissenting," 185, 187–190. See also Lipsitz, *Possessive Investment in Whiteness*, 2, 19. On the difficult relationship between the legal rights in *Brown* and potential remedies, see Jack M. Balkin, "*Brown v. Board of Education*—A Critical Introduction," in *What Brown v. Board of Education Should Have Said*, ed. Balkin, 64–71. Robert Carter, "A Reassessment of *Brown v. Board*," in *Shades of Brown: New Perspectives on School Desegregation*, ed. Derrick A. Bell, Jr., (New York, 1980), 23. See also Kenneth B. Clark, "The Social Scientists, the *Brown* Decision, and Contemporary Confusion," in *Argument*, ed. Friedman, xl. Lewis, *In Their Own Interests*, 199–200.

***

[21] Beth Roy, *Bitters in the Honey: Tales of Hope and Disappointment across Divides of Race and Time* (Fayetteville, 1999), 318; Pete Daniel, *Lost Revolutions: The South in the 1950s* (Chapel Hill, 2000), 270. Many whites believed that if race relations changed, they could only lose social status and power. See Robert J. Norrell, *Reaping the Whirlwind: The Civil Rights Movement in Tuskegee* (New York, 1985), 107.

***

[24] Daniel, *Lost Revolutions*, 251; Elizabeth Huckaby, *Crisis at Central High: Little Rock, 1957–58* (Baton Rouge, 1980), 1–13. The Central High School integration plan had originally called for the desegregation of grades ten through twelve with 300 black students. Over time, the number was scaled back to 25. See Greenberg, *Crusaders in the Courts*, 228–29. On the twisted symmetry of the integration process, see Daniel, *Lost Revolutions*, 254–55; and David R. Goldfield, *Black, White, and Southern: Race Relations and Southern Culture, 1940 to the Present* (Baton Rouge, 1990), esp. 108. Huckaby, *Crisis at Central High*, 2. In 1960, the per capita income in the geographic region associated with Central High was $3,826; in the region associated with Hall High it was $8,012. See Donald Bogue, "Census Tract Data, 1960: Elizabeth Mullen Bogue File" (University of Chicago, Community and Family Study Center, 1975), computer file, Inter-University Consortium of Political and Social Research (ICPSR) version <http://www.icpsr.umich.edu:8080/ICPSR-STUDY/02932.xml> (Feb. 3, 2004).

[25] Daniel, *Lost Revolutions*, 257; Roy, *Bitters in the Honey*, 179, 206, 338, 343–44.

[26] On the role of Gov. Orval Faubus and others in manufacturing the conflagration and violence that attended the desegregation of Central High in Little Rock, see Greenberg, *Crusaders in the Courts*, 228–43. Goldfield, *Black, White, and Southern*, 108.

***

[39] *Plessy v. Ferguson*, 163 U.S. 537 (1896). Jack Greenberg made the statement in a 1974 speech delivered to the New York City Bar Association. See Gerald N. Rosenberg, "*Brown* Is Dead! Long Live *Brown*!: The Endless Attempt to Canonize a Case," *Virginia Law Review*, 80 (Feb. 1994), 171n32.

[40] Robert Carter quoted in Kamisar, "School Desegregation Cases in Retrospect," xxv. In recent cases challenging affirmative action, the Court's analysis often sees race merely as phenotypic difference, fails to recognize the asymmetrical ways in which race functions in American society, and allows whites to claim reverse discrimination. See Guinier and Torres, *Miner's Canary*, 32–66.

[41] Greenberg, *Crusaders in the Courts*, 130–32. Cf. Brief for the United States as Amicus Curiae at 3, *Brown v. Board of Education* (No. 1). Lawrence, "Id, the Ego, and Equal Protection," 322, 374–75, esp. 375. Scott, *Contempt and Pity*, 71–91; Charles R. Lawrence III, "If He Hollers Let Him Go: Regulating Racist Speech on Campus," *Duke Law Journal* (June 1990), 439–40, 466.

[42] Initially hailed for bringing a measure of reality into the legal proceedings, the evidence cited in *Brown's* famous footnote 11 was primarily (though not exclusively) from one social science—psychology. In the years after *Brown*, it was the doll studies that gained cultural salience. The Court also cited a sociologist and an economist: E. Franklin Frazier, *The Negro in the United States* (New York, 1949); Gunnar Myrdal, *An American Dilemma: The Negro Problem and Modern Democracy* (2 vols., New York, 1944). The other citations in footnote 11 of *Brown*, which described the psychological effects of segregation, included Max Deutscher and Isidor Chein, "The Psychological Effects of Enforced Segregation: A Survey of Social Science Opinion," *Journal of Psychology*, 26 (1948), 259–87; and Isidor Chein, "What Are the Psychological Effects of Segregation under Conditions of Equal Facilities?," *International Journal of Opinion and Attitude Research*, 3 (Summer 1949), 229–34. For the doll studies, see, for example, Midcentury White House Conference on Children

and Youth, "The Effects of Prejudice and Discrimination," in *Personality in the Making: The Fact-Finding Report of the Midcentury White House Conference on Children and Youth*, ed. Helen Lelan Witmer and Ruth Kotinsky (New York, 1952), 135–58, esp. 142; and Clark, *Prejudice and Your Child*, 19–20, 22–24. On the methodological problems of these studies, see Scott, *Contempt and Pity*, 93–136. On the children examined in the doll studies and Kenneth Clark's conclusions about them, see a historian's account: Ben Keppel, "Kenneth B. Clark in the Patterns of American Culture," *American Psychologist*, 57 (Jan. 2002), 29–37, esp. 32.

⁴³ Clark, *Prejudice and Your Child*, 50. Scott, *Contempt and Pity*, 124. On contemporary testing situations that trigger vulnerability to negative stereotypes, see Claude M. Steele, "Thin Ice: 'Stereotype Threat' and Black College Students," *Atlantic Monthly*, 284 (Aug. 1999) <http://www.theatlantic.com/issues/99aug/9908stereotype2.htm>, part 2, para. 2 (April 2, 2004). On how stigmatization may strengthen self-esteem, see Jennifer Crocker and Brenda Major, "Social Stigma and Self-Esteem: The Self-Protective Properties of Stigma," *Psychological Review*, 96 (Oct. 1989), 608–30. On the lack of evidence that segregation by itself damaged self-esteem, see Geoffrey Cohen to Lani Guinier, e-mail, Dec. 4, 2003 (in Lani Guinier's possession). See also David Glenn, "Minority Students with Complex Beliefs about Ethnic Identity Are Found to Do Better in School," *Chronicle of Higher Education*, [online version], June 2, 2003, now available at <http://sitemaker.umich.edu/daphna.oyserman/files/ chronicle_of_ higher_education.htm> (March 2, 2004); and D. Oyserman, M. Kemmelmeier, S. Fryberg, H. Brosh, and T. Hart-Johnson, "Racial-Ethnic Self-Schemas," *Social Psychology Quarterly*, 66 (Dec. 2003), 333–47.

⁴⁴ On black teachers losing their jobs due to integration, see Cecelski, *Along Freedom Road*, 8. On the loss of outstanding black high schools, see Derrick Bell, Jr., *Silent Covenants: Brown v. Board of Education and the Unfulfilled Hopes for Racial Reform* (New York, 2004), 124–25.

⁴⁵ Bell, "Serving Two Masters," 470–516; Brown-Nagin, "Race as Identity Caricature," 1913–76. See also Coleman, Kelly, and Moore, *Trends in School Segregation*, 53–80; Armor, *Forced Justice*, 174–93; Lewis, *In Their Own Interests*, 199–202; and Sugrue, *Origins of the Urban Crisis*, 268. On efforts by middle-class blacks to separate themselves from poorer blacks, see Grace Carroll, *Environmental Stress and African Americans: The Other Side of the Moon* (Westport, 1998), 9; Orfield and Thronson, "Dismantling Desegregation," 774; Lisa W. Foderaro, "A Suburb That's Segregated by Money More than Race," *New York Times*, Nov. 24, 2003, p. A22. Class differences within the black community also influenced who led in challenging segregation. See Goldfield, *Black, White, and Southern*, 90–91. But cf. Klarman, "*Brown*, Racial Change, and the Civil Rights Movement," 56–62. On "racial outsiders" who have sought the privileges of whiteness, see Lipsitz, *Possessive Investment in Whiteness*, 3. See also Patterson, *Brown v. Board of Education*, 42–44, 200–201; and Cecelski, *Along Freedom Road*, 34. Carter, "Reassessment of *Brown v. Board*," 28.

⁴⁶ The Court rejected the possibility that the Fourteenth Amendment implicated distributional considerations, striking down a judicial attempt to mandate equalization of resources, stating that "at least where wealth is involved, the equal protection clause of the Fourteenth Amendment does not require absolute equality or precisely equal advantages." See *San Antonio Independent School District v. Rodriguez*, 411 U.S. 1, 24 (1973). Dissenting, Justice Thurgood Marshall lamented the Court's refusal to consider how much governmental action itself had caused the wealth classifications. *Ibid.*, 123–24.

⁴⁷ *Davis v. County School Board*, 103 F. Supp. 337 (E.D. Va. 1952). For Lindsay Almond's statements, see "Oral Argument," in *Removing a Badge of Slavery: The Record of* Brown v. Board of Education, ed. Mark Whitman (Princeton, 1993), 157. For Colgate Darden's testimony, see "Colgate Darden," *ibid.*, 83, 84.

⁴⁸ I define racial literacy at greater length in Guinier, "Admissions Rituals as Political Acts," 201–12. See also Guinier and Torres, *Miner's Canary*, 29–31.

⁴⁹ John W. Davis quoted in "1953 Argument," in *Argument*, ed. Friedman, 216. W. E. B. Du Bois, "Does the Negro Need Separate Schools?," *Journal of Negro Education*, 4 (July 1935), 335.

⁵⁰ Norrell, *Reaping the Whirlwind*, esp. 57.

⁵¹ Charles Hamilton Houston (1949) quoted in *The Road to Brown*, dir. Mykola Kulish (California Newsreel, 1990).

⁵² Emphasis on formal equality gave birth to the (Warren E.) Burger and (William H.) Rehnquist Courts' legal doctrine interpreting the Constitution narrowly, limiting relief to proven acts of intentional discrimination. See, for example, *Washington v. Davis*, 426 U.S. 229 (1976); and *City of Mobile v. Bolden*, 446 U.S. 55 (1980). Even when the Court finds diversity to be a compelling governmental inter-

est, it diverts concern and resources away from the real barriers to educational opportunity, according to Derrick A. Bell, Jr., "Diversity's Distractions," *Columbia Law Review*, 103 (Oct. 2003), 1622–33.

[53] Derrick A. Bell, Jr., "Comments from the Contributors," in *What* Brown v. Board of Education *Should Have Said*, ed. Balkin, 206. Bell, *Silent Covenants*, 119–20; W. E. B. Du Bois, *Dusk of Dawn: An Essay toward an Autobiography of a Race Concept* (New York, 1940), 303.

Lani Guinier is a legal scholar and former civil rights lawyer who specializes in the areas of voting rights law, democratic theory and practice, educational pedagogy, and social justice with an emphasis on issues of race, gender, and class. In 1998, Guinier was appointed professor of law at Harvard Law School, becoming the school's first black woman tenured professor. She was a professor at the University of Pennsylvania for 10 years prior to joining the faculty at Harvard Law School. Her teaching interests range from law and the political process, professional responsibility, and public interest lawyering to issues of race, class, gender, and social change. She has written widely on topics related to voting rights, democratic theory, affirmative action, and legal education, and she coauthored a major study of women and law school. Guinier received an AB from Radcliffe College of Harvard University in 1971 and a JD in 1974 from Yale Law School.

African American Students Entering Desegregated School
Students watch as the first African American students, Floyd and Dwight Armstrong, enter Graymont School in Birmingham, Alabama, during desegregation.

What Has *Brown* Wrought?

Anthony Lewis

Fifty years on, what has *Brown* wrought? I found my answer to that question at the University of Arkansas—in the person of a second-year law student, Michele Stamps. Ms. Stamps is African American. She was born and brought up in what used to be the heartland of American racism, Jackson, Mississippi. But she shows not a trace of concern about the color of her skin. Faculty and students treat her as a leader. She helped to found and became president of a group called the Media, Entertainment and Sports Law Association, and she invited me to Fayetteville to talk about the failures of the American press in reporting what has happened to civil liberties in this country since the terrorist attacks of Sept. 11, 2001.

She first thought about becoming a lawyer as a child, she said, so she could fight discrimination —religious discrimination. She is a Seventh Day Adventist, and was concerned about denial of the right to worship, not work, on Saturdays. When she graduates, she is going to be a law clerk to a federal judge in Mississippi. Then she might become a prosecutor, to help fight the crime that infests her neighborhood at home, or a defense lawyer. She knows about the struggle against racial discrimination; she has studied the civil rights movement. But for her it is history.

Michele Stamps is something I could not have imagined fifty years ago: a black young woman from Mississippi unmarked by racial discrimination. There were great women in Mississippi in the segregated past. Fannie Lou Hamer said she was "sick and tired of being sick and tired," and she stood up to President Lyndon Johnson at the 1964 Democratic National Convention to fight the all-white Mississippi delegation. But Michele Stamps is something else. She is free.

She went to a public school that was nearly all black, so what she represents is not a triumph of school integration. What she demonstrates is that even though racial lines still mark much of American public education, the ideals proclaimed by *Brown v. Board of Education*—the ideals of freedom and equality—have had a profound effect on our society.

No one can pretend that the fears and prejudices of racism are gone from America fifty years after *Brown*. But it is a different country in its attitudes toward race.

In 1954, schools were segregated in the capital of the country. African Americans could not eat at drugstore lunch counters in Washington, D.C., and they had to sit separately in movie theaters. In seventeen southern and border states, with 40 percent of the country's public school enrollment, state law commanded segregation. Thurgood Marshall could not attend the University of Maryland law school.

In the Deep South the dominant theme of politics and culture was keeping the Negro in his place. African Americans were kept from registering and voting by fraud, force, even murder. They were relegated to separate and inferior public facilities of all kinds, from hospitals to cemeteries, cradle to grave.

Racism has deep roots in America. When Thomas Jefferson drafted the Declaration of Independence, he owned more than a hundred slaves. Slavery was, in fact, the mainstay of his existence. He had been a real estate lawyer, doing dull work, when he inherited one hundred slaves from his father-in-law and was able to become a gentleman farmer with an interest in architecture, politics, and the philosophy of freedom.

But, from the beginning, there was another strain of thought, of conscience: one that saw the servitude of an entire people because of their race as inconsistent with American ideals. And in the earliest days at least one court took seriously a state constitution's declaration of freedom and equality. That was the Supreme Judicial Court of Massachusetts, newly established when it heard the case of Quock Walker in 1783.

Quock Walker was a slave—Massachusetts had slaves then. He had been promised his freedom when he turned twenty-five. But when he did not get it from a new owner, he ran away. The owner, Nathaniel Jennison, found him, beat him, and brought him back. Jennison was prosecuted for assault and battery. His defense was that slavery was established in Massachusetts law, and he had every right to seize and punish a runaway.

Massachusetts had a new constitution, drafted by John Adams in 1780 while the Revolutionary War was still going on. (It is still in force, with amendments, in Massachusetts.) The Supreme

Judicial Court was composed of five judges from the court that it had replaced, all conservatives of their day. But they were well aware of the constitution, which, as Chief Justice William Cushing put it, "sets off declaring that all men are born free and equal and that every subject is entitled to liberty." Cushing said that, by the constitution's language, "slavery is in my judgment as effectively abolished as it can be. . . ." The chief justice spoke not only of Adams' language, but also of the belief in liberty that had been a rhetorical hallmark of the Revolution. With that, slavery was abolished in Massachusetts.

The federal Constitution did not follow the Massachusetts model on freedom. At the Constitutional Convention of 1787, the price of southern agreement to the formation of the union was the provision that slaves, who of course could not vote, should each be counted as three-fifths of a person in allotting seats to states, by population, in the House of Representatives. The effect was to give the South much greater weight, not only in the House, but also in the electoral college. Without those added electoral votes, Jefferson would probably not have won his narrow victory over Adams for the presidency in 1800.

Over the next sixty years, much of the American political struggle turned on southern efforts to maintain slavery and expand it into new territories. Then, in 1857, the pro-slavery forces won what they thought was a decisive victory in the Supreme Court, the *Dred Scott* decision. Chief Justice Roger B. Taney wrote for the majority that Negroes could not be citizens of the United States. At the time of the Revolution, Taney said, they were deemed "beings of an inferior order, and altogether unfit to associate with the white race, either in social or political relations; and so far inferior that they had no rights which the white man was bound to respect."

Dred Scott was described by Chief Justice Charles Evans Hughes as one of the Supreme Court's self-inflicted wounds. It helped to bring on the Civil War. It was overruled by the Fourteenth Amendment, which starts off by saying that all persons born or naturalized in the United States are citizens.

Chief Justice Roger B. Taney

For a brief period after the Civil War, the country and Congress were committed to the welfare of the former slaves. Congress passed three comprehensive Civil Rights Acts. The mood was reflected in the Supreme Court, which in 1880 held that a state law barring Negroes from serving on juries violated the Fourteenth Amendment. The case was *Strauder v. West Virginia*. The jury bar to Negroes, Justice William Strong wrote, "is practically a brand upon them, affixed by law, an assertion of their inferiority, and a stimulant to that race prejudice which is an impediment to securing to individuals of the race that equal justice which the law aims to secure to all others."

But soon northern politicians lost interest in the cause of Negroes, and so did the public, or much of it. The Republican Party, which dominated the presidency for decades, was chiefly interested in making the country safe for capitalism. And the Supreme Court's interpretation of the Fourteenth Amendment and its promise of justice for the former slaves changed as political attitudes did.

In *Strauder*, the Court said the amendment was "primarily designed" for the "protection" of black Americans. But sixteen years later the Court decided *Plessy v. Ferguson* and looked the other way. Homer Plessy, objecting to a Louisiana law requiring that Negroes ride in separate railroad cars, said the law labeled them as inferior—exactly as *Strauder* had held. But the Court now rejected the argument. Its "fallacy," Justice Henry B. Brown said, was the "assumption that the enforced separation of the two races stamps the colored race with a badge of inferiority. If this be so, it is not by reason of anything found in the act but solely because the colored race chooses to put that construction upon it."

How brutally cynical that sounds today. We live after the Nazis made Jews wear a yellow star, and we can have no doubt that the intention of Jim Crow laws was to make blacks wear a badge of inferiority. Justice Brown cited no authority for his proposition, no precedent or work of scholarship. It was, we could say, a sociological hypothesis. There is a certain irony in that, for southerners who objected when *Brown v. Board* overruled *Plessy* used "sociology" as a term of abuse.

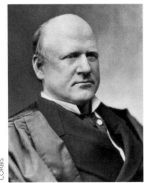

Justice John Marshall Harlan

Plessy v. Ferguson is famous for anointing the doctrine of "separate but equal" facilities for Negroes. But it hardly needs to be said that the doctrine was mocked by reality in the South. Black schools and everything else were grotesquely unequal. As late as 1931, six southeastern states spent three times as much on white schools as on black. When *Brown* was decided in 1954, despite years of heavy spending to equalize black schools in fear of having to desegregate, the disparity in spending was still one and one-half to one. And in other ways, life for Negroes was as burdensome and dangerous as the sole dissenter in *Plessy*, Justice John Marshall Harlan, had predicted. Legalizing "separate but equal" facilities, he said, would "stimulate aggressions, more or less brutal and irritating, upon the admitted rights of colored citizens."

During the period after the Civil War, blacks had played an active part in the politics of the South; now they were purged from the voting rolls. Jim Crow laws multiplied. And the Ku Klux Klan flourished. By the end of the nineteenth century more than one hundred black men were being lynched every year.

It is necessary to recall that grim history. America is a country with little historical memory, the land of forgetting. But if we are to understand the issue of race in our society, we have to remember. We have to face the reality, past and present, of racism.

Many years ago I was visiting South Africa, apartheid South Africa, when I found myself seated on a plane next to an Anglican bishop. We talked, and after a while he said to me that white South Africans suffered from "existential blindness." In order to exist, he explained—in order to live untroubled lives—they had to blind themselves to the cruelties imposed on South Africans of a different skin color. The bishop was right, and not only about South Africa. Jefferson well understood the nature of slavery. In his *Notes on the State of Virginia*, he wrote about its devastating effects, on slave and master; at the end of the passage he said, "I tremble for my country when I reflect that God is just." But he closed his mind to the realities that surrounded him every day in order to live as he wished.

In a sense, what has happened in the United States on the issue of race has been an exercise in ending existential blindness—in persuading Americans to look at the realities of racism. In that process I think there were two elements: law and conscience. The role of law is well known; but it is worth underlining how, step by step, the courts undermined the acceptance of discrimination.

In 1938, the Supreme Court held that Missouri could not satisfy the separate-but-equal test by paying the tuition of a Negro applicant to the Missouri law school at an out-of-state school. Chief Justice Hughes said the state had to provide equal facilities in Missouri. Justice James Clark McReynolds, dissenting alone, said Missouri could now abandon its law school or "break down the settled practice concerning separate schools and thereby, as indicated by experience, damnify both races." Professor Paul A. Freund of the Harvard Law School commented that Justice McReynolds, who favored segregation, "saw which way the winds of doctrine were blowing, and he did not like what he saw. What he saw was a steady, unmistakable progression on the part of the Court in applying the guarantee of equal protection of the laws. . . . The Court was recognizing the developing consciousness of the country that equal protection of the laws was to be given a full and not a qualified meaning."

Chief Justice Charles Hughes

There were more cases about admission to graduate schools. Then, in 1950, the Supreme Court held that a new law school created by Texas for Negroes flunked the test of equality. The University of Texas law school, for whites, Chief Justice Fred M. Vinson said, "possesses to a far greater degree those qualities which are incapable of measurement but which make for greatness in a law school"— such as position of the alumni, traditions, prestige. When such factors were put in the scale, it was hard to see how any separate law school could ever be equal.

But it was not inevitable—far from it—that the Supreme Court would find public school segregation unconstitutional. Indeed, Chief Justice Vinson was reportedly ready to reject the plaintiffs' case in *Brown*, until he died and was replaced by Earl Warren. Unlike higher education, attendance at school was compulsory, and involved millions of children. Association of children with those of another race was what southern segregationists feared.

The decision in *Brown v. Board of Education* set off attacks on the Supreme Court unmatched in scope and virulence. Southern governors swore they would use means up to and including closing the public schools to maintain segregation. The Virginia political machine of Senator Harry F. Byrd called for "massive resistance." In 1956 more than one hundred southern members of the House and Senate signed the Southern Manifesto, condemning the Supreme Court for "abuse of power." As late as 1960, not one black child attended a public school with whites in Alabama, Georgia, Mississippi, Louisiana, or South Carolina—and their state universities remained totally segregated. Only 4 percent of black citizens of voting age were registered in Mississippi, 14 percent in Alabama.

The walls of law and intimidation eventually came tumbling down. That they did resulted in good part from the second of the two elements mentioned above, conscience.

Gunnar Myrdal wrote about the importance of conscience in *An American Dilemma*, the first great study of the country's race problem, published in 1944. "When we say there is a Negro *problem* in America," he wrote, "what we mean is that the Americans are worried about it. It is on their minds and on their consciences." At the time, it was hard to see much evidence of the American conscience being touched. Blacks were fighting in World War II in segregated Army units. They were second-class citizens in Washington, D.C. But I think Myrdal was not so much wrong as premature.

What awoke the American conscience in a powerful way was, ironically, southern resistance to school desegregation. Its brutal, violent tactics made many in the North who had not paid much attention to racial discrimination see what it meant. On their television sets in 1957 they saw white youths outside Central High School in Little Rock, Arkansas, shouting at a handful of black children: "Niggers, keep away from our school, go back to the jungle." They saw riots there and in New Orleans. Professor Alexander M. Bickel of the Yale Law School wrote: "Compulsory segregation, like states' rights and like 'The Southern Way of Life,' is an abstraction and, to a good many people, a neutral or sympathetic one. These riots, which were brought instantly, dramatically and literally home to the American people, showed what it means concretely. Here were grown men and women furiously confronting their enemy: two, three, a half-dozen scrubbed, starched, scared and incredibly brave colored children. The moral bankruptcy, the shame of the thing, was evident."

Black Students Integrate Little Rock's Central High School Elizabeth Eckford, one of the nine black students whose admission to Little Rock's Central High School was ordered by a federal court following legal action by NAACP Legal Defense Fund attorneys. (1957)

Lawsuits over many decades were a way of reaching out to the American conscience. They were a means of expression for a people without political power. One of the extraordinary things about the black fight for justice was its faith in American institutions, in judges and the Constitution, and its faith in the ultimate good will of Americans. Despite long years of disregard and even contempt from the white majority, and years of judicial betrayals like *Plessy v. Ferguson*, most blacks continued to believe in this country and its people.

Law was not the only way of seeking to awaken the American conscience. On December 1, 1955, the year after *Brown v. Board of Education*, Rosa Parks refused to move to the back of a bus in Montgomery, Alabama. The strategy that came to be called direct action was born. The black people of Montgomery carried out a bus boycott with amazing determination, yielding neither to threats nor to exhaustion.

Dr. Martin Luther King, Jr., arose from the bus boycott as a new kind of leader. He spoke of following Mohandas Gandhi's nonviolent protests as a strategy. For both Gandhi and Dr. King, protests were a way to reach the conscience of the oppressor. It should be added that the oppressor has to have a conscience for the strategy to work; Adolf Hitler would not have been moved by protest. Law helps, too. In the end it was a Supreme Court decision that ended the Montgomery bus boycott in victory, desegregating the buses.

Woolworth's Lunch Counter Sit-In Four African American college students sit in protest at a whites-only lunch counter at a Woolworth's in Greensboro, North Carolina. (1960)

Dr. King did not touch the hearts of southern sheriffs who kept blacks from voting and set police dogs on peaceful demonstrators. What he did, with spectacular success, was to make northerners who had been indifferent become aware of the viciousness of racism. And it was not just Dr. King. The spirit of equality spread. In early 1960, four college students in Greensboro, North Carolina, sat down at a Woolworth's lunch counter. When they were not served, they just sat there. They, and then many others around the South, sat in quiet determination to get equal service, persisting despite taunts from onlookers and liquids poured over them. Six months later, the lunch counter at Woolworth's in Greensboro started serving Negroes.

The strategy of awakening the national conscience worked in good part because southern segregationists overplayed their hand so crudely. National journalists horrified readers and viewers by simply recording what happened. Claude Sitton, the great southern regional correspondent of the *New York Times*, wrote from Sasser, Georgia, on July 26, 1962. Thirty-eight Negroes and two whites were holding a voter registration rally in the Mount Olive Baptist Church. Sheriff Z.T. Mathews told Sitton, "I tell you, cap'n, we're a little fed up with this registration business." As his deputy walked around the church holding a revolver, the sheriff asked the crowd, "Can you vote if you are qualified?" The crowd said, "No." "Do you need people to come down and tell you what to do?" "Yes." "Haven't you been getting along well for a hundred years?" "No."

At length, some segregationists understood why Dr. King was so effective on a national scale. He depended on national journalists to show the American public racism and its violent enforcers. The press showed the reality, when what the segregationists wanted was an undisturbed picture of magnolias and southern charm. So they tried to frighten the national press out of covering the Civil Rights movement.

In 1960, the *New York Times* published an advertisement by supporters of Dr. King and the movement that described the violence and trickery used by what the ad called southern violators of the Constitution. It named no names. But a city commissioner of Montgomery, Alabama, L.B. Sullivan, sued the *Times*, claiming that people would connect him with some of the events described in the ad and would think worse of him. (When the case came to the Supreme Court, Justice Hugo L. Black, who came from Alabama, said that if any white citizens of Alabama had seen the ad and thought it referred to Sullivan, his social and financial prestige was probably enhanced.) Commissioner Sullivan was awarded $500,000 by an all-white jury in an Alabama court. Others sued over the ad, and the *Times* was set to lose $2.5 million—enough to put it out of business in those days. And libel actions were filed over news stories in the *Times*, CBS television, and *Time* magazine. The *Montgomery Advertiser*, whose editor had urged Sullivan to sue, ran a story about the case with the headline, "State Finds Formidable Legal Club to Swing at Out-of-State Press."

But Sullivan lost his damage award, and segregationists their legal club, in the Supreme Court. In *New York Times v. Sullivan*, Justice William J. Brennan, Jr., wrote for the Court that the right to criticize officials is "the central meaning of the First Amendment." Officials cannot recover libel damages, the Court held, unless they show that a false and damaging statement about them was published with knowledge of its falsity or with reckless disregard for the truth. The decision put constitutional limits on libel suits for the first time, and lifted a menacing threat to the Civil Rights movement. Once again, overreaching by southern racists had provoked a powerful reaction.

In the story of the civil rights struggle we can see that *Brown v. Board of Education* was more than a decision about school segregation—more, indeed, than a landmark in the law. It was the beginning of a social and political revolution in this country. Without *Brown*, I think Rosa Parks would have moved to the back of the bus—at least until later, probably years later. It was the message of hope in the *Brown* decision that inspired Dr. King and the students in Greensboro and the would-be voters in the Mount Olive Baptist Church in Sasser, Georgia.

The revolution worked by showing racism for what it was. When they saw it bare, Americans did not like it. They pressed Congress to act, and Congress did. In the civil rights legislation of 1964 and 1965 it enlisted the federal government definitively on the side of equal rights. And, effectively at last, after failed past attempts, it guaranteed black Americans in the South the right to register and vote. They voted, and they changed the political landscape. The result was not to create a liberal paradise. Most whites shifted to the Republican Party and expressed their

Blacks Registering to Vote in Alabama
Long lines of African Americans wait to register to vote in a makeshift office in Alabama after passage of the Voting Rights Act. (1966)

conservative views there. But southern blacks were now treated with political respect. They ran for office, and they were elected.

Ralph McGill was the great editor of the *Atlanta Constitution*, an opponent of racial discrimination when that was a lonely and sometimes dangerous position. Some years after the civil rights legislation of the 1960s, a friend stopped by McGill's office and said he wanted to show McGill something. They went to a hall where black southern elected officials were meeting. It was a large hall, full of people. McGill stood in the back of the room, and tears ran down his face.

One of the lawyers who took the *Brown* case to the Supreme Court, Jack Greenberg, has said that, "in retrospect, it wasn't a school case; it was a case that transformed the politics of America." I think it transformed more than politics. It changed our attitudes toward each other, our expectations of each other. It changed our culture.

When *Brown v. Board of Education* was decided, fifty years ago, hate mail inundated the sponsor of a television program when the star, comedian Eddie Cantor, put his arm around Sammy Davis, Jr., African Americans were portrayed in movies as shiftless, happy-go-lucky beings. No black man or woman headed a major corporation or university. In Mississippi and large parts of other states in the Deep South, the culture of fear dominated; business leaders joined the White Citizens' Council.

All of that has been transformed. African Americans can live normal lives in Mississippi. They can aspire to leadership in law or politics without looking in the rear-view mirror with anxiety when they drive down a lonely road at night. *Brown v. Board of Education* made possible what has been a revolution. It made possible Michele Stamps.

Anthony Lewis was a columnist for the *New York Times* from 1969 to December 2001. He has twice won the Pulitzer Prize. In 2001 he was awarded the Presidential Citizens Medal. He is the author of three books: *Gideon's Trumpet*, about a landmark Supreme Court case; *Portrait of a Decade*, about the great changes in American race relations; and *Make No Law: The Sullivan Case and the First Amendment*. Mr. Lewis was for fifteen years a lecturer on law at the Harvard Law School, teaching a course on the Constitution and the press. He has taught at a number of other universities as a visitor, among them the Universities of California, Illinois, Oregon, and Arizona. Since 1983 he has held the James Madison Visiting Professorship at Columbia University.

Segregationists Protesting
African American students march past two demonstrators protesting desegregation at Southern High School, Baltimore, scene of a near riot. Escorting the students to class is the Reverend James L. Johnson (rear). Some 2,000 white teenagers, shouting anti-black slogans, paraded through the streets and staged noisy demonstrations outside of several high schools. In nearby Washington, D.C., more demonstrations occurred at two high schools. (1954)

Did *Brown* Matter?

Cass R. Sunstein

On the fiftieth anniversary of the fabled desegregation case, not everyone is celebrating.
Originally published in *The New Yorker*

On May 17, 1954, the Supreme Court announced its decision in the case of *Brown v. Board of Education*. "Separate educational facilities are inherently unequal," the Court ruled unanimously, declaring that they violated the equal protection clause of the Fourteenth Amendment. It thus overturned the doctrine of "separate but equal," which had been the law of the land since 1896, when *Plessy v. Ferguson* was decided. The *Brown* ruling—the culmination of a decades-long effort by the NAACP—has today acquired an aura of inevitability. But it didn't seem inevitable at the time. And the fact that it was unanimous was little short of miraculous.

When the school-segregation cases first came before the Court, in 1952, the justices, all Roosevelt and Truman appointees, were split over the constitutional questions. Only four of them (William O. Douglas, Hugo L. Black, Harold H. Burton, and Sherman Minton) were solidly in favor of overturning *Plessy*. Though there is no official record of the Court's internal deliberations, scholars of the decision—notably Michael J. Klarman, a professor of law and history at the University of Virginia—have been able to reconstruct what went on through the justices' conference notes and draft opinions. Chief Justice Fred M. Vinson, a Truman appointee from Kentucky, argued that *Plessy* should be permitted to stand. "Congress has not declared there should be no segregation," Vinson observed, and surely, he went on, the Court must be responsive to "the long-continued interpretation of Congress ever since the Amendments." Justice Stanley F. Reed, also a Kentuckian, was even more skeptical of overturning segregation. "Negroes have not thoroughly assimilated," he said; segregation was "for the benefit of both"

Franklin Delano Roosevelt
(1936)

blacks and whites, and "states should be left to work out the problem for themselves." The notes for Justice Tom C. Clark, a Texan, indicate greater uncertainty, but he was clearly willing to entertain the position that "we had led the states on to think segregation is OK and we should let them work it out."

Justices Felix Frankfurter and Robert H. Jackson, though staunchly opposed to segregation, were troubled by the legal propriety of overturning a well-established precedent. "However passionately any of us may hold egalitarian views," Frankfurter, an apostle of judicial restraint, wrote in a memorandum, "he travels outside his judicious authority if for this private reason alone he declares unconstitutional the policy of segregation." During the justices' deliberations, Frankfurter pronounced that, considered solely on the basis of history and precedent, "*Plessy* is right." Jackson, for his part, composed a draft opinion reflecting his ambivalence. He acknowledged that the Court's decision "would be simple if our personal opinion that school segregation is morally, economically and politically indefensible made it legally so." But, he asked, "how is it that the Constitution this morning forbids what for three-quarters of a century it has tolerated or approved?" Both Frankfurter and Jackson had been deeply affected by the New Deal era, during which a right-wing Supreme Court had struck down progressive legislation approved by their beloved Franklin Delano Roosevelt, including regulations establishing minimum wages. Frankfurter and Jackson believed in democracy and abhorred judicial activism. They also worried that the judiciary would be unable to enforce a ban on segregation, and that an unenforceable decree would undermine the legitimacy of the federal courts. And so the justices were at odds. In an unusual step, the Court postponed its decision, and asked both sides to reargue the case.

In September of 1953, just before *Brown* was to be reargued, Vinson died of a heart attack, and everything changed. "This is the first indication that I have ever had that there is a God," Frankfurter told a former law clerk. President Eisenhower replaced Vinson with Earl Warren, then the governor of California, who had extraordinary political skills and personal warmth, along with a deep commitment to social justice. Through a combination of determination, compromise, charm, and intense work with the other justices (including visits to the hospital bed of an ailing Robert Jackson), Warren engineered something that might have seemed impossible the year before: a unanimous opinion overruling *Plessy*. Thurgood Marshall, a principal architect of the litigation strategy that led to *Brown*, recalled, "I was so happy I was numb." He predicted that school segregation would be entirely stamped out within five years.

That's how *Brown* looked fifty years ago. Not everyone thinks that it has aged well. Many progressives now argue that its importance has been greatly overstated—that social forces and political pressures, far more than federal judges, were responsible for the demise of segregation. Certainly, *Brown* has disappointed those who hoped that it would give black Americans equal educational opportunities. Some scholars on the left even question whether *Brown* was rightly decided. The experience of the past half century suggests that the Court cannot produce social reform on its own, and that judges are unlikely to challenge an established social consensus. But experience has also underlined *Brown*'s enduring importance. To understand all this, we need to step back a bit.

A quiz: In 1960, on the sixth anniversary of the *Brown* decision, how many of the 1.4 million African American children in the Deep South states of Alabama, Georgia, Louisiana, Mississippi, and South Carolina attended racially mixed schools? Answer: Zero. Even in 1964, a decade after *Brown*, more than 98 percent of African American children in the South attended segregated schools. As Klarman shows in his magnificent *From Jim Crow to Civil Rights: The Supreme Court and the Struggle for Racial Equality*, the Court, on its own, brought about little desegregation, above all because it lacked the power to overcome local resistance.

Not that it made any unambiguous effort to do so. In the 1954 decision, the Court declined to specify the appropriate remedy for school segregation, asking instead for further arguments about it. The following year, in an opinion known as *Brown v. Board of Education II*, the Court declared that the transition to integration must occur "with all deliberate speed." Perhaps fearing that an order for immediate desegregation would result in school closings and violence, the justices held that lower-court judges could certainly consider administrative problems; delays would be acceptable. As Marshall later told the legal historian Dennis Hutchinson, "In 1954, I was delirious. What a victory! I thought I was the smartest lawyer in the entire world. In 1955, I was shattered. They gave us nothing and then told us to work for it. I thought I was the dumbest Negro in the United States." As a Supreme Court justice, Marshall—for whom I clerked in 1980—liked to say, "I've finally figured out what 'all deliberate speed' means. It means 'slow.' "

Real desegregation began only when the democratic process demanded it—through the 1964 Civil Rights Act and aggressive enforcement by the Department of Justice, which threatened to deny federal funds to segregated school systems. But Klarman doesn't claim that *Brown* was irrel-

Orval E. Faubus
Arkansas Governor Orval E. Faubus bitterly attacked the action of the federal government in sending troops to "occupy" Little Rock. (1957)

evant to the desegregation struggle. In his view, the decision catalyzed the passage of civil rights legislation by, in effect, heightening the contradictions: inspiring southern blacks to challenge segregation—and southern whites to defend it—more aggressively than they otherwise would have. Before *Brown*, he shows, southern politics was dominated by moderate Democrats, who generally downplayed racial conflicts. The *Brown* ruling radicalized southern politics practically overnight, and in a way that has had lasting consequences for American politics.

A case in point is Orval E. Faubus, who became a national figure in 1957, when, as the governor of Arkansas, he used the state's National Guard to defy the courts and stop African American children from attending high school in Little Rock. But Klarman reminds us that, three years earlier, he had been elected on a liberal, race-neutral platform of spending more money on education and old-age pensions. (His father, a socialist organizer, gave him the middle name Eugene, in honor of Debs.) In the early days of his term, he appointed blacks to the Democratic Central Committee for the first time, and desegregated public transportation. Only after public indignation over *Brown* swept through his state, and his chief political opponent accused him of being insufficiently zealous in resisting the decision, did he reposition himself as a racial hard-liner.

Or consider "Big Jim" Folsom, once a popular governor of Alabama. Folsom was a racial moderate who refused to join other southern governors in a statement condemning *Brown*, and went so far as to invite Adam Clayton Powell to the governor's mansion. Folsom was defeated in the 1958 election by an extreme segregationist. During the *Brown* deliberations, Justice Black reportedly predicted that overturning *Plessy* would mean the end of mid-century southern liberalism, and his prediction was largely borne out.

Klarman's story doesn't stop there, however. Because "the post-*Brown* racial fanaticism of southern politics produced a situation that was ripe for violence," he writes, northerners soon found themselves outraged by televised scenes of police brutality against peaceful black demonstrators. The civil rights legislation of the sixties, including the very laws that led to the enforcement of *Brown*, arose from a sort of backlash to the backlash. Given these complicated causal chains, how important to our civil rights history, in the end, was Chief Justice Vinson's fatal heart attack? Not very, in Klarman's accounting: "Deep background forces"—notably, the experience of the Second World War and the encounter with Nazi racial ideology—"ensured that the United States would experience a racial reform movement regardless of what the Supreme Court did or did not do."

Klarman is far from alone in demoting the Court's historic role in the civil rights movement. In *All Deliberate Speed: Reflections on the First Half-Century of* Brown v. Board of Education, Charles J. Ogletree, Jr., a law professor at Harvard, contends that *Brown* did nothing "to address the social inequality that predominantly harms African Americans." Ogletree still regards Thurgood Marshall as a genuine hero. But he believes that, under the spell of both Marshall and the *Brown* ruling, civil rights advocates may have placed too much emphasis on the courts, which are often unresponsive or ineffective. If you want to improve educational opportunities for poor blacks, he suggests, you might do better to put your energies into, say, charter schools and after-school programs. (He tells us about some promising examples.) In Ogletree's view, *Brown*'s unfulfilled promise reflects not so much the Court's limited authority as the nation's limited commitment to racial justice. He points to a series of Supreme Court decisions, starting in the late 1970s, that sharply confined the scope of affirmative action programs and that amounted to a "process of undoing *Brown*."

This argument can be pressed even further, as Derrick Bell shows in *Silent Covenants:* Brown v. Board of Education *and the Unfulfilled Hopes for Racial Reform*. In his view, *Brown* has been not merely a disappointment but a grotesque failure. Bell connects that failure to a more general claim about "interest convergence." America makes progress toward racial equality, he thinks, only when such progress is in the interest of whites. For him, *Brown* is a clear illustration: the Court knew that invalidating segregation would help the nation in its competition with Communist nations and undermine subversive elements at home.

The argument (which Mary L. Dudziak's 2000 book *Cold War Civil Rights* explored at length) isn't as implausible as it might at first seem. The Department of Justice, in its brief before the Court, quoted Secretary of State Dean Acheson, who maintained that racial discrimination gave unfriendly governments "the most effective kind of ammunition for their propaganda warfare," and remained "a source of constant embarrassment to this government in the day-to-day conduct of its foreign relations." (More recent support for Bell's claim about "interest convergence": when, just a year ago, the Supreme Court stopped short of invalidating all affirmative action plans, it referred to briefs it had received from businesses and former military leaders arguing that affirmative action was necessary for both corporate success and national defense.) "Interest convergence" motivated only the abolition of *de jure* segregation; the nation, in Bell's view, had no larger appetite for racial justice.

Like Ogletree, Bell points out that, even without compulsory segregation, millions of African American children continue to attend all-black schools, and often receive a second-rate education, or worse. In the nation's urban centers, millions of African Americans are jobless, badly educated, and without marketable skills, and are thus propelled into crime, domestic violence, and, ultimately, despair. And he suggests that *Brown* shares some of the blame: "The statement that separate facilities were inherently unequal served to legitimate current arrangements. Thereafter, those blacks who remained poor and disempowered were viewed as having failed to take advantage of their definitionally equal status." *Brown*, then, may have been something worse than useless: an alibi for inaction.

If *Brown* was destined to fail, as Bell believes, what would he have had the Supreme Court do in 1954? Surprisingly, he argues that the Court should have reaffirmed *Plessy* and permitted segregation to continue—but should have insisted that separate must be genuinely equal. Recognizing that "predictable outraged resistance could undermine and eventually negate even the most committed judicial enforcement efforts," the Court should have required full enforcement of *Plessy* with a decree that would have equalized educational opportunity immediately, with federal district judges monitoring the process to insure compliance.

It's a bold and sobering counterproposal. But it would have done nothing about the injury produced by segregation, and it would have put federal courts in an impossible position. How could judges decide, in particular cases, whether segregated schools really were equal? To produce genuine equality, would they have had to ask local school boards to raise taxes, or to take funds from white schools for the benefit of black schools? The challenge of monitoring "separate but equal" would have been at least as formidable as the challenge of desegregation.

Brown has attracted scrutiny from another set of legal scholars, who are concerned with the proper role of judicial authority. What is at issue, for them, isn't the wisdom of the decision itself but what the decision later helped to establish and fortify—the widespread belief that the Supreme Court has been a major and indispensable force for expanding our liberties. In the 1975 foreword to the classic history of *Brown*, *Simple Justice*, Richard Kluger declares, "The nine Justices, as has often been said, constitute the least democratic branch of the national government. Yet this, most likely, was one reason why the Court felt free to act: it is not compelled to nourish the collective biases of the electorate; it may act to curb those unsavory attitudes by the direct expedient of declaring them to be intolerable among a civilized people." For liberal critics of federal judicial power, such talk represents a perilous delusion. They argue that the meaning of the Constitution should not be in the hands of unelected judges; if people have been persuaded otherwise, it's in part because the cult of *Brown v. Board of Education* has conferred excessive prestige on an institution whose tendencies are better symbolized by *Bush v. Gore*.

Fifty years later, *Brown* does seem increasingly anomalous. Before the Warren Court, the justices were almost never a force for social reform, and they have rarely assumed that role in the past two decades. Most of the time, the judiciary has been an obstacle to racial equality. Before the Civil War, the Supreme Court, in the *Dred Scott* case, interpreted the Constitution so as to entrench slavery. After the Civil War, the Court sharply limited Congress's power to protect the newly freed slaves. During the first half of the twentieth century, the Court did little to promote racial justice (and for much of that time, as Frankfurter and Jackson were painfully aware, it was hostile to legislative attempts to reduce economic inequality); in the last quarter of the century, the Court's most important racial-discrimination decisions struck down affirmative action programs.

But if the Supreme Court justices aren't the ultimate authority on what the Constitution means, who is? In *The People Themselves*, Larry D. Kramer, a New York University law professor, makes a subtle and striking argument for popular control over constitutional meaning. Central to his account is a distinction between "popular constitutionalism" and "judicial supremacy": He thinks that the framers of the Constitution favored the former, but that, in recent decades, we have lost sight of their design, ceding constitutional supremacy to the judiciary. Roosevelt's contention that the Constitution should be seen as "a layman's instrument of government" and not "a lawyer's contract" perfectly captured the founders' spirit, Kramer believes. "The Supreme Court is not the highest authority in the land on constitutional law," he writes. "We are."

In a system of popular constitutionalism, the president, Congress, and the Supreme Court are bound by the founding document; they swear an oath to uphold it, and they must obey it as they understand it. For this reason, courts have the authority to strike down legislation that they deem to be unconstitutional. But judicial decisions on constitutional meaning are not to be treated as uniquely authoritative. If the Supreme Court rules that school segregation is unlawful or that affirmative action programs are unacceptable, the public and its elected representatives are entitled to insist that the Constitution has been misread and to seek change. To the extent that *Brown*'s harshest critics operated within the law, they were within their rights to object that the

Court mangled the Constitution, and to use political channels to attempt to limit or even to over-rule *Brown*. They need not have treated *Brown* as if it had been carved in stone.

Historically, there has rarely been a chasm between popular will and judicial rulings. A century ago, Finley Peter Dunne's fictional wiseacre Mr. Dooley remarked that "no matter whether th' constitution follows th' flag or not, th' supreme court follows th' iliction returns." The Court doesn't really do that, but its members live in society, and they are inevitably affected by the beliefs of society and its elected representatives. When, recently, the Court invalidated Texas's ban on same-sex sodomy, it relied on the fact that this ban was inconsistent with prevailing national values; most Americans just do not support criminal prosecutions for consensual sexual relations among adults. *Brown* can be understood in similar terms: By 1954, segregated schools were perceived as an outrage by at least half of the nation's citizens. In fact, American Presidents — Roosevelt, Truman, and, to some extent, even Eisenhower — supported a strong judicial role in the protection of civil rights. Courts do not rule in a vacuum, and when they appear most aggressive they are likely to be responding to evolving social values.

In *Reconsidering Roosevelt on Race: How the Presidency Paved the Road to* Brown, the political scientist Kevin J. McMahon elaborates this point. He thinks that we have exaggerated the roles of Thurgood Marshall and Earl Warren and undervalued the role of Franklin Delano Roosevelt. In McMahon's account, interpretation of the Constitution fundamentally depends on presidential decisions. Presidents have a more or less explicit "constitutional vision," and *Brown*, he believes, was a direct product of Roosevelt's. Constrained by the need to maintain southern support for the New Deal, Roosevelt did proceed cautiously on issues of racial equality. But, in reshaping the federal bench, he destroyed the long-standing alliance between the Supreme Court and the South. Starting in the late thirties, his Justice Department took many steps to protect African Americans, initiating litigation against police brutality, lynching, the poll tax, and the "white primary." And Roosevelt's judges, McMahon demonstrates, were quite willing to use the Court's authority to protect the rights of the disadvantaged.

The "presidency-focussed approach," as McMahon calls it, has its limits. (Consider Earl Warren, whose appointment to the court Eisenhower called "the biggest damn fool mistake I ever made.") But it certainly accords with the radical shift from the liberal Warren Court to the conservative Rehnquist Court — a shift engineered, above all, by Presidents Ronald Reagan and George H. W. Bush, who appointed five of the nine justices currently serving. In this light, what Ogletree and Bell deplore as the failed promise of *Brown* would seem to be a result of presidential decisions. Because the rulings of the Supreme Court are influenced by the occupants of the White House, and in that sense by popular will, popular constitutionalism is alive and well—and is largely responsible for *Brown*'s limited effects.

And yet to declare, with Bell and Ogletree, that *Brown* has been "undone" presupposes a particular account of what *Brown* is taken to "do." Perhaps *Brown* means that governments must be color-blind—that they may never take race into account in their decisions. If so, Supreme Court decisions that strike down affirmative action programs are continuing in *Brown*'s path. Both Bell and Ogletree argue forcefully that *Brown* should be understood to require not color blindness but an end to white supremacy and the subordination of African Americans. Thurgood Marshall himself emphasized the problem of subordination, or lower-caste status, in his arguments in *Brown*. I agree that this is the preferable interpretation of the equal protection clause, and, if it's right, affirmative action programs are fully consistent with *Brown*. But how should we choose between the color-blindness principle and

President Eisenhower Hosting Supreme Court Members First row (l. to r.), Justices William Douglas and Stanley Reed, Chief Justice Fred Vinson, President Eisenhower, and Justices Hugo Black and Felix Frankfurter. Back row (l. to r.) Sherman Adams (assistant to the president), Attorney General Herbert Brownell, and Justices Sherman Minton, Tom Clark, Robert Jackson, and Harold Burton. (1953)

the anti-subordination principle? The Rehnquist Court has mostly opted for color blindness, and *Brown* itself does not expressly prohibit that choice.

Was *Brown*, then, a failure? Suppose that this is the real meaning of the Court's decision: states may not, by law, separate citizens from one another by race, simply because forcible separation imposes a kind of stigma, or second-class citizenship, that offends the most minimal understanding of human equality. It is one thing to attend all-black schools. It is quite another to live under a legal system that announces, on a daily basis, that some children are not fit to be educated with others. *Brown* ruled that, under the Constitution, states may not humiliate a class of people in that way. It may have taken a while, but this ruling, at least, has stuck. And on the occasion of its fiftieth anniversary it justifies a celebration.

But it does not justify triumphalism. *Brown v. Board*, despite the unanimity of the decision, was the product of a divided Supreme Court and a divided nation. Its current meaning is up to us, not to previous generations or even to the Court that decided it.

Cass R. Sunstein is Karl N. Llewellyn Distinguished Service Professor at the University of Chicago Law School. A former law clerk for Justice Thurgood Marshall of the U.S. Supreme Court, he worked as an attorney-advisor in the Office of the Legal Counsel of the U.S. Department of Justice. Mr. Sunstein has been involved in constitution-making and law reform activities in a number of nations, including Ukraine, Poland, China, South Africa, and Russia. Mr. Sunstein has been Samuel Rubin Visiting Professor of Law at Columbia and visiting professor of law at Harvard. Mr. Sunstein is the author of many articles and a number of books, including *The Second Bill of Rights: FDR's Constitutional Vision and Why We Need It More Than Ever (2004)*.

Bettmann/CORBIS

Bused Students with Heavy Police Escort
Black students are bused back to the Roxbury section from South Boston under a heavy police guard September 16, the third day of court-ordered busing in Boston as a means of public school integration. (1974)

Implementing, Transforming, and Abandoning *Brown*

Mark Tushnet

I n 1954 and 1955, the Supreme Court's decisions invalidating segregated education were ambiguous about what the Constitution actually required. As one prominent southern judge put it after *Brown*, one possibility was that the Court was demanding only desegregation, not integration. By that he meant that *Brown* simply invalidated government policies that assigned students to schools on the basis of their race. All other ways of designating the schools a child should attend were open, such as neighborhood schools or placement according to performance on tests, for example. The alternative was that *Brown* required integration, meaning that the racial composition of each school should roughly match the racial composition of the school district as a whole.

Brown was ambiguous because accomplishing desegregation was legally simple but politically problematic. Setting up neighborhood school assignment systems would have taken no time at all. Yet, the Court contemplated some delay in implementing its rulings, through the famous statement that school systems should comply with "all deliberate speed." Pretty clearly the Court was worried about the possibility—soon to be a reality—that many southern school systems would resist complying with the Constitution. At the same time, though, the Court could not, and did not, acknowledge the possibility of resistance. Indeed, it said explicitly that disagreement with the Court's decisions provided no justification for delay in compliance.

Resistance occurred, of course. Some forms of defiance were more subtle than others. Southern legislators got a lot of attention for their dramatic campaign of "massive resistance" to desegregation, which included the prospect of closing the public schools when final desegregation orders were entered. That possibility was realized in Prince Edward County, Virginia, until the courts ordered the schools reopened and white parents realized that they were inflicting real damage on their own children's education. James Jackson Kilpatrick, then the editor of a major Virginia newspaper, revived John C. Calhoun's old theory that the Constitution allowed the states to "interpose" their authority between the national government and their citizens when, in the states' view, the national government was itself violating the Constitution—a theory that, one would have thought, the Civil War's result, if nothing else, had reduced to ashes.

The Supreme Court basically stayed out of the desegregation business for more than a decade. Lower courts generally took *Brown* to require only desegregation. They upheld plans that would desegregate schools one grade at a time, sometimes working from first grade to high school, sometimes working down from high school to first grade. At least in concept, desegregation of that sort could also produce integration.

Other plans that the lower courts approved pretty clearly endorsed desegregation over integration. The courts upheld neighborhood school plans and freedom-of-choice plans that allowed students to choose their schools. They also upheld "pupil placement plans," in which school boards adopted a list of complicated criteria—student interest, space availability, program suitability, and more—that they purported to apply to each student in the district.

The problems with these plans emerged as they were implemented, although the difficulties could have been anticipated. School boards redrew the boundaries of neighborhood schools, so that neighborhood schools were tied closely to areas of residential racial segregation. Freedom-of-choice plans produced little change in patterns of enrollment, because the violence that accompanied desegregation led parents to "choose" to enroll their children in the same, previously segregated schools they had been attending. And pupil placement plans were pretty clearly manipulated to ensure that only a handful of African Americans were placed in predominantly white schools, and that no white children were placed in predominantly African American schools.

Eventually the courts got fed up. Once judges understood what was going on, they readily concluded that the manipulations of school boundary lines and pupil placement plans were unconstitutional under *Brown*; these methods actually involved the assignment of students to schools based on their race, despite their seeming use of criteria that didn't include race. The experience with these evasions of *Brown*'s core mandate also led courts to understand that it might be difficult for them to ferret out race-based decision making. Courts began to focus on the *results* of desegregation plans, drawing the natural inference from continued patterns of racial segregation that somewhere behind the scenes someone was continuing to base assignments on race even if the courts couldn't quite identify who was doing that, or how it was being done.

The Supreme Court endorsed the results-oriented approach in 1968. The case involved the adoption of a freedom-of-choice plan in a rural county of Virginia. The county was not residentially segregated, so a neighborhood school plan would have desegregated the county's high schools *and* integrated them. Under the freedom-of-choice plan, however, nearly every white student chose to attend

Women Arguing and Holding Placards
Women exchange words at Sayre Elementary School as Chicago's school busing plan goes into effect. Sayre was one of eight all-white schools receiving black students from two overcrowded schools. (1968)

the school that had been reserved for whites under segregation, and nearly every African American chose to attend the school to which African Americans had been previously assigned by law. Justice William J. Brennan, writing for the Court in *Green v. County School Board of New Kent County*, insisted that the time for deliberate speed had passed, and that school boards had to come up with plans that "promise[d] realistically to work, and promise[d] realistically to work now." The idea that desegregation plans had to work came close to explicitly eliminating the ambiguity in *Brown* by making integration, not desegregation, the goal.

Close, but not entirely. The Court's refusal to take the final step was rooted in experience with resistance to *Brown*, and the implications of what judges had learned. They had learned that students could be assigned to schools on the basis of their race by intentional decisions of school boards in the absence of laws explicitly requiring segregation. That knowledge meant that *Brown* could no longer be confined to the South. Northern school boards could engage in practices that amounted to deliberate segregation—deliberate assignment of children to schools because of their race—even in the absence of state laws requiring segregation, and even in the presence of state laws prohibiting it. The result was that *Brown* moved northwards.

Yet, in the North, the argument that separation of races in the schools resulted from choices by parents about where to live, coupled with residential segregation that wasn't the responsibility of school boards, carried more weight than it had in the South. These northern districts, were, after all, not burdened with the legacy of explicit segregation statutes. In addition, northern school boards rarely made deliberate decisions designed to guarantee that *all* African Americans would attend one set of schools, all whites another. At most, the school boards tinkered with assignment policies to reinforce school enrollment patterns that arose primarily from residential racial segregation.

As *Brown* moved northwards, the courts grappled with the decision's implications. The courts could not, and did not, immunize northern school boards from the consequences of their deliberate decisions to separate some children from others because of their race. Neither did they take *Brown* to require integration—directly. The courts continued to insist on a strong distinction in law between *de jure* segregation, the product of statutory law or administrative decisions to assign children to schools based on their race, and *de facto* segregation, the (mere) fact that observers could describe schools as "white" or "black," or, in the terminology that the courts came to endorse, as racially identifiable.

Saying that *de facto* segregation was unconstitutional would have been to say that *Brown* required integration. The courts refused to do so. They believed that the social costs of integrating the schools, particularly in the nation's larger cities (North and South), would have been too great—or, perhaps, they believed that the courts lacked the power to accomplish integration of the nation's school systems. Judges became increasingly concerned that seeking integration would be futile, as white parents uncomfortable with integrated schools withdrew their children from the public schools that were subject to judicial order—by sending their children to private schools or by moving to suburbs not affected by the court orders.

Instead of finding *de facto* segregation unconstitutional, courts focused on deliberate decisions to separate children by race. In the first important northern *desegregation* case, decided in 1973, the Supreme Court found that the Denver school board had indeed made deliberate decisions that kept some of the city's schools racially identifiable. That finding, the Court said, authorized the lower courts to insist on desegregation remedies that encompassed the entire city, even though the deliberate decisions it identified affected only a part of the city. The Court did so because of the natural inference that decisions affecting a significant part of the district probably had ripple effects throughout the city, and perhaps because of its experience with southern desegregation. That experience taught that judges might find it quite difficult to identify particular decisions that enhanced segregation even though they were quite confident that someone had made such decisions.

Almost simultaneously with the Supreme Court's adoption of the results-oriented approach, Republican politicians came to understand that the push to integration could be used as a weapon in their attempt to recapture national political power. Barry Goldwater and then Richard Nixon adopted the so-called "southern strategy," which was designed to build the Republican Party in the South. The objective was to recruit whites disaffected with the Supreme Court and the Democratic administrations that, after 1964, were enforcing *Brown* vigorously. As *Brown* moved northward, so did the southern strategy: Republicans found similar disaffection with Democrats among whites in the North affected by *Brown*'s application.

That disaffection was multiplied by what the courts did to remedy intentional segregation. The only effective means of monitoring school-district decision making was to see whether each school's enrollment roughly matched the racial composition of the district as a whole. That is, the remedy designed to implement the requirement of *desegregation* became nearly identical to what integration would have required. The courts used a number of more specific remedies, but the most prominent was transportation of children to schools that the courts monitored to ensure that race played no role at all in determining assignments.

Transportation remedies — busing — became a central feature in political challenges to the federal courts. Senator Jesse Helms and other congressional colleagues sponsored legislation that purported to restrict the power of federal courts to order busing, but it was so badly drafted that it was ineffective except for political purposes. The opposition to the courts' decisions in northern segregation cases, coupled with the adverse economic and social consequences of policies associated with the Democratic Party (including those concerning Vietnam), gave Republicans a chance to regain the presidency. That change in leadership also affected appointments to the federal courts.

Advocates of desegregation — or integration — had a sense that they faced a different judicial environment after the early 1970s. Strikingly, they continued to win in the Supreme Court, although the victories were clearly hard-won and their advocates believed that they were snatching victories from the jaws of defeat. The Warren Court's desegregation decisions had all been unanimous, because the justices agreed that showing a united front was important if the lower courts were to overcome resistance to desegregation decrees. The Burger Court broke the tradition of unanimity, at first in a relatively unimportant case, but then in more important ones. While unanimously upholding the power of federal courts to order busing as a remedy for segregation, the majority also ruled — this time over dissent — that northern school districts were subject to precisely the same requirements as southern districts.

Given the racial realities of urban America in the 1970s, these decisions meant that lower courts had the power to compel any urban school district to adopt extensive busing programs. And many judges did. The Burger Court was plainly uncomfortable with how aggressive lower courts had become, and began to rein them in. The most important decision involved Detroit and its suburbs. Stephen Roth, a conservative federal judge, was persuaded by the evidence that the Detroit school board had purposefully segregated the city's black children in separate schools for generations. Over time, the city had more and more blacks, fewer and fewer whites. Judge Roth realized that a desegregation order limited to the city's borders would do little to help. Most of the city's schools would still be racially identifiable, and white parents might well accelerate their departure to the suburbs, converting a difficult job of desegregation into an impossible one. Judge Roth responded by ordering an "interdistrict remedy"; that is, he ordered that Detroit and its suburbs cooperate in desegregating the schools. The plan that he adopted ingeniously created districts shaped like pie pieces, so children would not have to ride buses for much longer than would have been necessary in a plan involving only the city.

The Supreme Court balked. Writing for a sharply divided Court, Chief Justice Burger said that Judge Roth's interdistrict remedy punished the suburbs for Detroit's sins. A few years later

Busing in Berkeley Schools
White students ride from the school they voluntarily chose in an African American neighborhood of Berkeley, California. (1971)

Burger tried to repair the damage in an opinion holding that federal judges could order *educational* "remedies" to alleviate the inadequacies of segregated schools, but the initial Detroit decision meant that the Supreme Court had basically withdrawn from the project of achieving integrated schools in urban areas.

A later desegregation case from Kansas City, Missouri, gave the Rehnquist Court the chance to cut back further on the use of educational measures in such cases. Barred from pulling the city's suburbs into a desegregation plan, federal district judge Russell Clark ordered the city and the state to increase their investments in the city's schools by reducing the average class sizes, creating specialized programs in science and the arts, renovating run-down facilities, and installing computers. One further requirement gave critics an obvious target—swimming pools.

Judge Clark had two theories for what he did. The first was that improving urban schools would encourage whites to move back into the city, making it easier to achieve integration without busing to the suburbs.

However, to Rehnquist and the Court's majority, Judge Clark was improperly trying to achieve effects outside Kansas City. Magnet schools were one thing, a "magnet district" another. Judge Clark's decree seemed like the equivalent of the interdistrict remedy the Court had disapproved for Detroit.

Judge Clark's second theory was that African American children in Kansas City's schools couldn't get an education equal to that available in integrated districts, and so deserved something else as compensation. The majority didn't take up this theory, but Justice Clarence Thomas did. He challenged Judge Clark's implicit assumption that "anything that is predominantly black must be inferior." Judge Clark, according to Thomas, was "experiment[ing] with the education of [Kansas City's] black youth," trying out untested theories about what improved educational quality without any basis for thinking that the students weren't able to get a good education under the ordinary, predominantly black conditions in the city's schools.

The Rehnquist Court's retreat went further. It encouraged lower courts to get out of the business of trying to integrate the schools altogether. In a case from Oklahoma City, the Court said that federal judges should stop supervising school districts when they found that the districts were no longer violating the Constitution and weren't likely to start up again. And, in a case from Atlanta, the Court told judges to withdraw from supervision step by step: As soon as a school district showed that it was complying with the Constitution in one regard—no longer discriminating in assigning teachers to particular schools, for example—the judge should stop monitoring that part of the desegregation order even if the district still was violating the Constitution in some other way, for example in drawing neighborhood school district lines to keep the races apart.

After 1995, the Rehnquist Court didn't hear a single case involving desegregation. A benign view of the Court's actions is that it adopted the strategy that Senator George Aiken suggested for getting out of the hopeless Vietnam War: Integrating the nation's urban schools appeared impossible, so the Rehnquist Court declared victory and went home.

Consistent with the modesty of the Aiken strategy, the Rehnquist Court's decisions in desegregation cases neither identified broad principles nor defended a vision of multicultural relations that the Constitution required or even encouraged. The majority opinions were technical, focusing on the scope of the federal judicial power to order remedies for identified constitutional violations and expressing concern for judicial micro-management of state and local government policy.

By contrast, Justice Thomas took the lead in articulating a constitutional vision, which somewhat awkwardly combined an ideal of color blindness with a sort of black nationalism that may have been the residue of Thomas's enthusiasm for that ideology during his college years. For Justice Thomas, racial "imbalance" was not in itself of constitutional concern. Imbalances resulting from deliberate state policies designed to separate the races were impermissible, but imbalances resulting from maintaining institutions with distinctive traditions were acceptable. The contributions of historically black institutions provided educational justifications—such as instilling pride in African Americans' accomplishments—for racial disparities at those institutions.

Justice Thomas showed his disdain for constitutional rules predicated on the mere existence of racial imbalance in what is probably his most widely quoted statement on education for African Americans. In the Kansas City case he stated, "It never ceases to amaze me that the courts are so willing to assume that anything that is predominantly black must be inferior.... If separation itself is a harm, and if integration therefore is the only way that blacks can receive a proper education, then there must be something inferior about blacks. Under this theory, segregation injures blacks because blacks, when left on their own, cannot achieve." Rejecting this assumption, Justice Thomas suggested that black middle and high schools "can function as the center and symbol of black communities, and provide examples of independent black leadership, success, and achievement." He concluded, "We must forever put aside the notion that simply because a school district today is black, it must be educationally inferior."

Justice Thomas remains committed to the elimination of racial hierarchy. But he insists that black institutions can demonstrate that African Americans can accomplish just as much as whites—although perhaps in different domains, and with accomplishment measured along many dimensions. How, though, can the nation move from here to there?

The currently preferred social policy for doing so is affirmative action, which Justice Thomas thinks is unconstitutional. He has also suggested that affirmative action programs—at least those in elite law schools—may be inadequate for this purpose and constitute a cheap response to a problem with deeper roots. There are too few minority lawyers, and significant progress will demand attention to policies other than affirmative action. Even those who think affirmative action should be a tool available to policymakers must acknowledge that affirmative action in law school admissions comes too late to remedy the small pool of qualified minority applicants. Scholars of career paths agree that interventions to broaden the "pipeline" to the profession have to occur much earlier than law school policymakers often assume. Law-oriented enrichment programs in colleges help a bit, but what really matters are interventions in secondary and even elementary schools. Fourth and fifth graders are interested in *everything*, and the trick is to figure out ways of sustaining their interest in professional education through their high school and college educations. Designing appropriate interventions will call on the talents of educators far more than lawyers and judges. Legal academics, however, could assist the process through strategies such as expanding social-justice service learning opportunities in elementary and secondary schools.

Justice Thomas's vision is one of a color-blind Constitution, in the sense that policies to improve the educational (and social) achievements of African Americans cannot, in his view, take race into account. Justice Antonin Scalia has a similar view. As he once memorably put it in an affirmative action case, "We are just one race here. It is American." The insistence on the irrelevance of race in government decision making amounts to an unequivocal interpretation of *Brown* as a case involving desegregation, not integration.

Black Children and Parents on Bus
Garfield Heights, Ohio, students and their parents are set to ride the bus from the east-side Cranwood School to their new assignments at schools across town, under the desegregation plan of the Cleveland School Board. Turnout was low for the second day of a three-day open house at the schools. (1979)

Notably, however, Justices Thomas and Scalia have not carried the day in the Rehnquist Court. Instead, an ambivalent commitment to the integrationist interpretation of *Brown* seems to have prevailed. The very technicality of the Rehnquist Court's majority opinions suggests how difficult it is for today's justices openly to reject the integrationist vision even as they limit its implementation.

More important, perhaps, are the Court's affirmative action cases culminating in the 2003 decision in *Grutter v. Bollinger* holding that "diversity" provided a compelling justification for race-based affirmative action programs in colleges and universities. Even on the surface, *Grutter* rejects a "desegregation" interpretation of *Brown*, because the majority expressly allows public policy makers to take race into account. *Grutter* seems to accept the integrationist vision on a deeper level as well. In finding diversity acceptable as a justification for affirmative action, the Court seems to contemplate classrooms filled with students of multiple races and ethnicities—if not necessarily in proportion to their presence in the population as a whole, still something closer to the integrationist ideal than not.

And yet, just as Justice Thomas's endorsement of constitutional color blindness sits uneasily with his insistence on the value of historically black institutions, so too does the integrationist vision sit somewhat uncomfortably with the *reasons* the Court gave for finding diversity a compelling justification for affirmative action programs. Justice Sandra Day O'Connor's opinion for the Court in *Grutter* insisted that the Fourteenth Amendment "protect[s] *persons*, not *groups*." Even a diversity-based justification for affirmative action relies to some extent on the fact that students from minority groups are indeed members of *groups*, and Justice O'Connor was unable to dissipate the tension between her individualistic focus and affirmative action itself. The law school insisted that its program did not rest on the view that minority students "always (or even consistently) express some characteristic minority viewpoint on any issue." Still, Justice O'Connor's opinion also seemed to impute *something* distinctive to all minority students: "Just as growing up in a particular region or having particular professional experiences is likely to affect an individual's views, so too is one's own, unique experience of being a racial minority in a society, like our own, in which race unfortunately still matters." The way in which one experiences race may differ from one minority member to another, but there is something that distinguishes all those unique experiences from the different ways nonminority students experience the society.

Here too, the tensions within *Brown* and its legacy are apparent. Race does not matter, constitutionally, because the Constitution deals with individuals, not groups; but race does matter, constitutionally, because the experiences of the nation's racial groups differ. We want integrated classrooms *both* because everyone is the same in constitutional terms, but also because the actual differences among us will help us educate each other about what our nation means.

Comparing *Grutter* and the Court's retreat from desegregation of the public schools demonstrates that the tensions within *Brown* have not disappeared. As Americans, we seem to think both that eliminating race as a basis for government decision making is an important national goal, and that because race does matter in shaping our experiences, governments should be allowed and sometimes encouraged to take race into account in making policy. *Brown*'s legacy has been to show that grappling with the tensions in our views about race and social policy will be a continuing challenge in the next fifty years as well as the last.

Rhoda Baer

Mark Tushnet is Carmack Waterhouse Professor of Constitutional Law at the Georgetown University Law Center. He is the co-author of four casebooks, including the most widely used casebook on constitutional law, has written twelve books, including a two-volume work on the life of Justice Thurgood Marshall, and has edited four others. He was president of the Association of American Law Schools in 2003. In 2002 he was elected a fellow of the American Academy of Arts and Sciences. His book, *A Court Divided: The Rehnquist Court and the Future of Constitutional Law,* will be published in January 2005 by W. W. Norton Co.

PART III
THE FUTURE

Najah Feanny/CORBIS SABA

Demonstration in Support of Affirmative Action
Students from the University of Michigan demonstrate in support of affirmative action. The demonstration is part of a National Day of Action to Defend Affirmative Action. (1998)

Turning *Brown's* Hope into Reality

Stephen G. Breyer

Fifty years ago, the Supreme Court decided the case of *Brown v. Board of Education of Topeka*.[1] Here is the question the case presented: "Does segregation of children in public schools solely on the basis of race, even though the physical facilities and other 'tangible' factors may be equal, deprive the children of the minority group of equal educational opportunities?" The Court answered this question unanimously: "We believe that it does."

The announcement of the decision marked a great moment in the history of the Supreme Court. Before that day, the Court read the Fourteenth Amendment's words, "equal protection of the laws," as if they protected only the members of the majority race. After that day, it read those words as the framers who wrote them immediately after the Civil War intended them to be read, as offering the same protection to citizens of every race.

Thurgood Marshall, who later became a member of the Court, represented the schoolchildren in the case. He argued that separating children by race violated the Constitution's promise of equal protection. The Court adopted Marshall's argument and told the nation that segregation based on race is wrong and that the law cannot tolerate that wrong. *Brown* helped the nation to understand that our Constitution was meant to create a democracy that worked not just on paper but in practice—one that can work only if every citizen understands that the Constitution belongs not to the majority, or to the lawyers, or to the judges, but to us all.

The Court's decision in *Brown* helped us to understand that the Constitution is "ours," whoever we may be. In so doing, it embraced the Constitution's insistence that the law equally respect

Students Escorted into School
African American students are escorted by soldiers into Little Rock's Central High School on the first full day of integration. (1957)

members of each race, majority and minority alike. The Court asked whether the practice of segregated education was consistent with this constitutional promise. The Court answered that segregation was not consistent with that promise, and the Court then began the lengthy task of translating the words of its opinion into a legal reality.

Chief Justice Earl Warren also emphasized that "education is perhaps the most important function of state and local governments," serving as "a principal instrument in awakening the child to [our Nation's] cultural values."[2] Justice O'Connor, quoting Justice Powell, recently elaborated on this theme, stating that "nothing less than the 'nation's future depends upon leaders trained through wide exposure to the ideas and mores of students as diverse as this Nation of many peoples.' "[3]

The *Brown* decision had two important legacies—one fulfilled, one unfulfilled. The first is its strong statement committing the Court and the nation to the rule of law over prejudice. This legacy was fulfilled in the struggle to enforce *Brown* in the years following the Court's decision. The task of translating the Constitution's words into practical reality by dismantling the legal structure that supported segregation was not easy. Doing so required the nation to ask itself whether it believed in a rule of law—a rule of law that the nation's history had too often denied, a rule of law that President Eisenhower enforced in 1957, when he sent federal paratroopers to Arkansas to take those black schoolchildren by the hand and walk them safely through that white schoolhouse door. We now accept that rule of law as part of our heritage, thanks to *Brown* and to its aftermath, although too often we take that rule of law for granted, without recalling the conditions of fifty years ago and without adequate appreciation for those whose struggles made it possible.

Brown's second, unfulfilled legacy lies in its assumption that the nation would achieve equal, high-quality education for all children, regardless of race. Our Court continues to debate the constitutional leeway available to those who search for the best way to attain this goal. Last Term, for example, the Court, in *Grutter v. Bollinger*, considered the Michigan Law School's admissions program, a program that used minority race as a factor favoring admission.[4] And it held, by a narrow majority, that the Fourteenth Amendment permitted affirmative use of race—in the context of individualized consideration of applications—in order to help " 'achieve that diversity which has the potential to enrich everyone's education.' "

Some members of the Court based their conclusion in part upon the need to use race, carefully but affirmatively, to overcome the effects of past discrimination, thereby bringing about equality of treatment. As Justice Ginsburg wrote (dissenting in a different case) "[W]e are not far distant from an overtly discriminatory past, and the effects of centuries of law-sanctioned inequality remain painfully evident in our communities and schools."[5] The majority based its conclusion in part upon the breadth of decision-making authority that the Constitution provides to universities, a breadth of authority related to the First Amendment's protection of liberty of expression.

The majority's conclusion also rested upon its understanding that the contrary interpretation of the Equal Protection Clause—an interpretation that forbids any use of affirmative action—would risk closing the doors of too many institutions to too many members of a minority race who might successfully participate. Too many Americans of minority race might then come to believe that this nation and its government are "theirs," not "ours." If they did, the democratic form of government that the Constitution creates could not work. The Court agreed with the Government's argument in the *Grutter* case that participation by all groups "in the civic life of our Nation is essential if the dream of one Nation, indivisible, is to be realized." I would add that participation is essential if the democracy that the Constitution creates is to arise from the written page and work in practice.

The Court's opinion in *Grutter* provides constitutional breathing room for other institutional efforts to improve our children's education. And such efforts are necessary. From an educational perspective, *Brown* rings hollow. Data for the years 2000–2001, for example, show that 71.6 percent of African American children, 76.3 percent of Hispanic children, and 49.7 percent of Native American children attended a school in which minorities made up a majority of the student body.[6] The data indicate that nearly two in five African American and Latino children attended an "intensely segregated" school, with a student body that was at least 90 percent minority.[7] And studies show a trend toward resegregation in schools in the South and other regions, after those schools reached a peak of integration in the mid-1980s.[8]

The data show that segregation makes a seriously negative difference: Only 15 percent of highly segregated white schools (less than 10 percent black or Latino students) were schools of concentrated poverty (where more than half of the students are on free or reduced price lunch). By contrast, 88 percent of schools with less than 10 percent white students had that kind of concentrated poverty.[9] The research shows that very poor schools turn out students who have received a worse education and achieve less.[10] Schools that are predominantly minority lag behind others in the educational resources they receive and the quality of the education they provide.[11]

Given these grim facts, suggesting a form of resegregation, what is perhaps remarkable about the Michigan Law School statistics is not that the number of minority applicants meeting Michigan's basic admissions standard was so few, but rather that it was so many. The number of minority applicants qualifying for admissions to top law schools like Michigan's, without reference to affirmative action, remains steady or on the rise over the past 15 years, both absolutely and relative to the total number of top applicants. In 1985, for example, there were 101 minority applicants with a grade point average above 3.5 and an LSAT score above 38 (the rough equivalent in percentile terms of 160 in the current LSAT scoring system[12]), representing almost 2 percent of all applicants in that tier.[13] By 2000, there were 297 minority applicants in this tier, representing almost 4 percent of all applicants in the tier.[14] This rising achievement has taken place despite the presence of increasingly segregated schools, and despite the inadequate and unequal educational opportunities provided to many minority students.

At the same time, the public's desire for improved public education systems is strong.[15] Given these positive trends in the face of continued adversity, it is reasonable, not only to hope, but to expect, that progress toward nondiscrimination and genuine equal opportunity and participation will continue.

The Court expressed this hope in its *Grutter* majority opinion. It "expects" that, a generation from now, the kind of affirmative action program found at the Michigan Law School will no longer prove necessary. But for that to occur, other institutions must begin to formulate, not constitutional law, but educational policy. A world with no need for affirmative action in graduate school admissions twenty-five years from now foresees children entering educationally adequate pre-schools, kindergartens, primary schools, and high schools beginning eight to ten years from now. Building those schools requires legislation, policies, and programs in place perhaps five years from now. And that means that the will to improve our schools—translatable into policy—must exist now. Judges can see the need, but it is decisions by policymakers, not case law, that will make the difference.

Brown and *Grutter* express the same educational hope, a hope that concerns "the opportunity of an education." *Brown* says that it is a "right which must be made available to all on equal terms." *Grutter* adds that educators must have "affirmative action" leeway so that they, together with others, may turn *Brown*'s hope into reality.

[1] 347 U.S. 483 (1954).

[2] Id. at 493.

[3] *Grutter v. Bollinger*, 539 U.S. 306, 324 (2003) (quoting *Regents of Univ. of Cal. v. Bakke*, 438 U. S. 265, 313 (1978)).

[4] 539 U.S. 306 (2003).

[5] *Gratz v. Bollinger*, 539 U.S. 244, 298 (Ginsburg, J., dissenting).

[6] See E. Frankenberg, C. Lee, & G. Orfield, "A Multiracial Society with Segregated Schools: Are we Losing the Dream?" p. 28, Fig. 4 (Jan. 2003), http://www.civilrightsproject.harvard.edu/research/reseg03/AreWeLosingtheDream.pdf.

[7] Ibid.

[8] See G. Orfield and C. Lee, "*Brown* at 50: King's Dream or Plessy's Nightmare?" p. 19 Table 7 (Jan. 2004), http://www.civilrightsproject.harvard.edu/research/reseg04/brown50.pdf.

[9] Id., at 21.

[10] Id., at 21–22.

[11] See Frankenberg, supra, at 11.

[12] The Law School Admission Council, The Law School Admission Test: Sources, Contents, Uses 13–14 (Sept. 1991).

[13] See Law School Admission Council, National Statistical Report, 1985–86 through 1989–90, at 3, 57, 75, 119, 139, 179 (1991).

[14] See Law School Admission Council, National Statistical Report, 1996–97 through 2000–01, at A-5, D-13, E-13, G-13, H-13, J-13 (2002).

[15] See Public Opinion Research Conducted by Peter D. Hart and Robert M. Teeter for the Educational Testing Service, A National Priority: Americans Speak on Teacher Quality, 2, 11 (2002); The No Child Left Behind Act of 2001, Pub. L. No. 107–110, 115 Stat. 1425 (2002) (codified at 20 U. S. C. §7231).

Collection of Supreme Court of United States

Stephen G. Breyer received an A.B. from Stanford University, a B.A. from Magdalen College, Oxford, and an LL.B. from Harvard Law School. He served as a law clerk to Justice Arthur Goldberg of the Supreme Court of the United States during the 1964 Term, as a special assistant to the Assistant U.S. Attorney General for Antitrust, 1965–1967, as an assistant special prosecutor of the Watergate Special Prosecution Force, 1973, as special counsel of the U.S. Senate Judiciary Committee, 1974–1975, and as chief counsel of the committee, 1979–1980. He has taught at Harvard Law School, the Harvard University Kennedy School of Government, the College of Law, Sydney, Australia, and the University of Rome. From 1980–1990, he served as a judge of the United States Court of Appeals for the First Circuit, and as its chief judge, 1990–1994. President Clinton nominated him as an associate justice of the Supreme Court, and he took his seat August 3, 1994.

Bettmann/CORBIS

James Meredith with Constance Motley
James Meredith (L) and his attorney Constance Motley (R) were followed by pickets when they left the Federal Courts Building September 28 during the noon recess of the U.S. Fifth Circuit Appeals Court in New Orleans. Medgar Evers is half-obscured behind James Meredith. (1962)

Excerpts from

Crusaders in the Courts, Anniversary Edition: Legal Battles of the Civil Rights Movement

Jack Greenberg

Reprinted by permission from *Crusaders in the Courts: Legal Battles of the Civil Rights Movement, Anniversary Edition*, Copyright © 2004 by Twelve Tables Press, 462 Broome St., #4W, New York, NY 10013, www.twelvetables-press.com, 917-658-2294.

James Meredith Goes to Ole Miss

United States District Judge Constance Baker Motley, with me and other lawyers of the NAACP Legal Defense and Educational Fund, represented Meredith. On February 2, 2004, as part of a colloquium of lawyers who were counsel for plaintiffs in *Brown v. Board of Education*, she told of recently having been on the campus of the University of Mississippi. She thought it now might be the best integrated university in the country. A far cry from when Meredith entered Ole Miss.

In 1961 James Meredith, who was attending black Jackson State College, sent a transfer application, letters of recommendation from five blacks, and his picture to the University of Mississippi. Ole Miss replied that it was overcrowded although the following semester it admitted more than three hundred more students than before.

Mississippi then limited transfers to students from accredited institutions. Jackson State wasn't accredited. With R. Jess Brown, Connie filed our complaint in United States District Court on May 31, 1961, asking for a preliminary injunction so Meredith could attend the June 8 summer session.

Judge Sidney C. Mize set the hearing for June 12, after school was scheduled to open. In mid-hearing he suspended and reset the proceedings for July 10, after the end of the first summer session, when he reset it for August 10, past the start of the second summer session. He held hearings August 10, 15, and 16. Fall registration ended September 28, but Mize didn't deny a preliminary injunction until December 12. He found that Meredith had not been rejected because he was black.

James Meredith Studying in His Dorm
James Meredith, the first black student to enroll at the University of Mississippi, studies in his dorm room. The night before his admittance triggered riots by white students across the campus. (1962)

By this time, Thurgood Marshall had left LDF to take his seat on the court of appeals, and I was in charge.

Connie sped to the Fifth Circuit. A month later Judge John Minor Wisdom's opinion rejected Mississippi's incredible claim that it did not segregate, ridiculed Ole Miss's argument that we had to prove that its students all were white, and concluded, "We take judicial notice that the state of Mississippi maintains a policy of segregation in its schools and colleges." The court ordered a fresh district court hearing and that it decide promptly, in view of the fact that a new school term was scheduled for February 6, 1962.

On February 3 Mize concluded, "The proof shows and I find as a fact, that the University is not a racially segregated institution." Connie went once more to the court of appeals.

While the appeal was pending, on June 6, Mississippi arrested Meredith, because he had registered to vote in Jackson, where he attended Jackson State, although his residence was in Kosciusko. We got an injunction from the court of appeals restraining the prosecution. On June 25, the court of appeals reversed Judge Mize. Wisdom called the defense "a carefully calculated campaign of delay, harassment, and masterly inactivity. It was a defense designed to discourage and to defeat by evasive tactics which would have been a credit to Quintus Fabius Maximus." Maximus was a Roman army commander known as a master of attrition and described as famed for "conducting harassing operations while avoiding decisive conflicts." Meredith had seen a psychiatrist while in the air force (one of Ole Miss's arguments for rejecting him), from which Wisdom concluded that his "record shows just about the type of Negro who might be expected to try to crack the racial barrier at the University of Mississippi: a man with a mission and with a nervous stomach."

Three weeks later, on July 17, the court's order went down to Judge Mize. Four times Judge Ben F. Cameron, a member of the court of appeals and a Mississippian, but who had not sat on the case, ordered a stay of the order. The court of appeals vacated his orders the day he entered them. Ole Miss trustees rejected Meredith's application.

Ole Miss also petitioned the Supreme Court to hear the Meredith case. On September 10, Justice Black announced that he had consulted all other members of the Court and that "there is very little likelihood that this Court will grant certiorari to review the judgment of the Court of Appeals…." He enjoined Ole Miss from "taking any steps to prevent enforcement of the Court of Appeals judgment and mandate."

Connie went back to Mize for an injunction. Sitting alongside Mize was Harold Cox, a new Kennedy appointee, and possibly the most racist judge ever to sit on the federal bench. Mize, who had senior status, would soon give up the Meredith case to Cox, and was acquainting him with the case. Cox began indicating that he would deny Connie's motion. But Mize placed his hand on Cox's arm and said, "It's all over, Judge Cox." On September 13, Mize ordered Ole Miss to admit Meredith.

Governor Ross Barnett, on September 13, went on statewide television and invoked the right of "interposition" under the Tenth Amendment, claiming it gave Mississippi the right to defy federal court orders. He issued a proclamation, full of "whereases" and "therefores" and "in witness whereofs," to which he "caused the great Seal of the State of Mississippi to be affixed, on this the 13th day of September in the Year of Our Lord, One Thousand Nine Hundred and Sixty-Two." Musical comedy material, but many of Mississippi's racists took it seriously.

On September 20, violating a June 13 federal court order, which prohibited prosecuting Meredith for false registration, Mississippi charged and convicted him of that offense. It also passed a law, Senate Bill 1501, prohibiting any person who has a "criminal charge of moral turpitude pending against him or her" from entering any state institution. The law excepted "any charge or conviction of traffic law violations, violation of the state conservation laws and state game and fish laws, or manslaughter as a result of driving while intoxicated." These exceptions covered thousands of Mississippians.

The court of appeals gave us an order enjoining enforcement of S.B. 1501 and prohibiting "any steps to effectuate the conviction and sentence … of James Meredith for false registration."

The university's board of trustees, on September 20, "invest(ed) Honorable Ross R. Barnett … with the full power … to act upon all matters pertaining to or concerned with the registration or non-registration, admission or non-admission and/or attendance or non-attendance of James H. Meredith." The orotund style suggested that they thought the words had a magical quality.

In the meantime, from the Justice Department, Bobby Kennedy, Burke Marshall, and John Doar called the governor, attorney general, and lawyer friends in the state in an effort to get

Meredith into Ole Miss peacefully. But from the outset, Connie and I thought that the only way to get Meredith into Ole Miss was with so overwhelming a show of force that violence would be seen as futile.

On September 20, the Justice Department took Meredith from Millington Air Force Base in Memphis, on the Mississippi border, to the university campus in Oxford in a border patrol car. In the auditorium of the university's Continuation Center, the registrar told Meredith that only the governor could register him. The governor then denied Meredith's application.

Meredith then returned to Memphis. Connie and I drove to Meridian to Judge Mize's court and, with the Justice Department at our side, petitioned for an order holding the registrar and other university officials in contempt. But on the following day, September 21, Mize ruled that they were not guilty—the trustees had turned the matter over to Barnett and were powerless to admit Meredith.

The Fifth Circuit Court of Appeals was in New Orleans. We set up LDF headquarters at the Dillard University guest house—a two-story cottage, with a half-dozen bedrooms and a kitchen, an ample lawn and lovely trees—courtesy of its president, Albert Dent, father of Tom Dent, then our public information director.

After a while the place began to resemble a fraternity house. One night, Meredith ventured out to a dance on the Dillard campus. He later wrote that when the students learned who he was "they literally swamped me for at least forty-five minutes to an hour…. I could not guess how many women must have offered themselves to me or asked me to go home with them."

Many of our meals consisted of takeout food from Levata's, a ramshackle seafood joint near the Dillard campus. Big bags containing boiled crabs, oyster rolls (fried oysters on a roll), lemon meringue pie, and Coca-Cola were brought in daily. This diet gave me a bad case of acne by the time the case ended.

On September 24, Barnett issued another proclamation directing the summary arrest and jailing of any representative of the federal government who arrested or attempted to arrest, or who fined or attempted to fine, any state official in the performance of his official duties.

The same day, Connie and I and the Justice Department lawyers were back at the court of appeals. The court took the extraordinary step of gathering eight judges, all the eligible judges, plus the highly respected, retired Joseph C. Hutcheson of Texas, a conservative law-and-order type, who had the right to sit but was not required to. Cameron alone didn't show up. Hutcheson ascended the bench with great difficulty. He was outraged and wanted to be there.

In a hearing that went from 11:30 A.M. to 6:32 P.M. the court heard testimony and received evidence, almost unheard of in appellate courts. Hutcheson, in referring to the trustees' order giving the governor control of Ole Miss, asked the attorney general of Mississippi, "Did you advise them that this monkey business of coming around pretending to take over the school was legal?" Finally, the president of the Board of Trustees announced that the board was willing to obey the court's orders. The registrar agreed to register and admit Meredith.

Mississippi Lieutenant Governor Blocking Integration
Mississippi Lieutenant Governor Paul Johnson blocks James Meredith, U.S. Marshal J. P. McShane, and Justice Department attorney John Doar from entering the University of Mississippi campus. Meredith became the first black student to enroll. (1962)

Robert Kennedy and Ross Barnett conferred by phone. Kennedy told Barnett that the federal courts had ruled, and Barnett replied that the Mississippi courts had ruled to the contrary. Barnett would not agree to permit Meredith to register nor would he guarantee Meredith's safety.

At 8:30 A.M. on the morning of September 25, the court of appeals entered a temporary restraining order prohibiting Barnett, State Attorney General Patterson, and a raft of other officials from interfering with Meredith's registration.

During some of this time Meredith stayed in Memphis and at other times he stayed with us in New Orleans. He traveled by government plane to Mississippi to attempt to register. We drove from the Dillard guest house to the airport, where two identical aircraft, one carrying Meredith, the other a decoy, took off for the trip, a tactic designed to confuse any Mississippian who might try shooting down Meredith's plane. I thought that if they'd shoot down one plane they'd shoot down two. As it turned out, our greatest peril occurred when the car taking us to the airport, traveling fast, hit a campus speed bump, and we banged our heads against the roof.

At the state office building, Meredith, accompanied by John Doar and other Justice Department representatives, once more tried to register. Barnett, once more denied admission. The court of appeals slapped back an order that evening requiring the governor to appear in court in New Orleans at 10:00 A.M., September 28, "to show cause, if any he has, why he should not be held in civil contempt…." Bobby Kennedy and Burke Marshall continued their telephone negotiations.

I objected that there was no way the Justice Department would ever persuade Mississippi other than by a show of more than sufficient force, such as Eisenhower had used in Little Rock.

Nevertheless, Justice officers took Meredith from Dillard to Oxford once more on Wednesday, September 26, to try again. This time Lieutenant Governor Paul Johnson turned him away. The *New York Times* reported that the Little Rock confrontation "seemed tonight to be just a shadow of the crisis developing in Mississippi . . . Officials are in open defiance of Federal Law."

In the meantime Kennedy and Mississippi representatives were trying to work out a registration charade. Mississippi proposed that federal marshals should draw their guns, at which point Mississippi officials with a show of yielding to federal threats, would permit Meredith to enter the university. Kennedy countered that he preferred that only one marshal draw a gun. Kennedy upped his offer: One marshal would draw a gun; the others would put their hands on their holsters. That still wasn't enough for Barnett, and so Kennedy gave in and agreed that all the marshals would draw their guns.

Kennedy and Mississippi officials having come to an agreement, Meredith's once again tried to register. But when a federal convoy carrying Meredith got within fifty miles of Oxford on Thursday, September 27, the mobs had grown so threatening that the convoy headed back. I issued a statement announcing that enough was enough:

> *We had advised Mr. Meredith that we do not believe he should return to the University of Mississippi campus unless he is accompanied by sufficient force to assure his enrollment and continued attendance. He agrees with us. We have so informed the Department of Justice.*

We filed motions, along with the Justice Department, in the court of appeals asking that Barnett be held in civil contempt. At each stage we made sure to file our own motions and be in court ourselves, refusing to allow Justice to conduct alone the case that they had treated with a mix of dither, politics, and principle.

On Friday, September 28, in the court of appeals in New Orleans, Mississippi's lawyer was John C. Satterfield of Yazoo City, the crown jewel of the Mississippi bar and the 1961–62 president of the American Bar Association. Satterfield appeared for the state as a friend of the court. No one in the courtroom represented Ross Barnett. Barnett was ducking service; Satterfield was claiming he was a friend of the court, not Barnett's counsel, in order to take the position that the court couldn't find Barnett in contempt because he hadn't been served and was not represented.

Looking like a praying mantis, Satterfield tiptoed around the courtroom as he addressed the court in elaborate, deferential tones and filed a motion to dismiss the complaint against Barnett. But the judges immediately caught on. Judge Tuttle replied: "All the Court has given the State of

Mississippi the right to do, Mr. Satterfield, is to present the views of the State of Mississippi. The Court has thus far not authorized the State of Mississippi to file any pleadings on behalf of the Defendant … Barnett."

Tuttle conferred with the court and announced that Satterfield would not be allowed to proceed until the court determined whether Barnett had been served. Satterfield asked whether he might make objections to evidence. Tuttle, visibly irritated, answered, "You can assume Counsel for Amicus Curiae has no right to object to any of the evidence." Satterfield replied, "To which we except." Tuttle riposted, "You also have no right to except I might add." Satterfield, in drippingly deferential tones, responded, "Certainly. That is correct, sir. I am sorry." Tuttle added, "And you needn't do it anyway," pointing out Satterfield's ignorance of the Federal Rules, which had abolished oral exceptions.

The government then proved that Barnett had been served, in person, by mail, and by Western Union night letter, with the court order requiring him to admit Meredith. A deputy marshal testified that he went twice to Barnett's office to serve the contempt citation and found it closed, with a piece of paper reading "office closed" affixed to the door. Attempting to serve the citation for a third time, the marshal found a group of state police at the door. They refused to state their names, refused to accept service, and warned against leaving the papers on the floor. The marshal left. On a further attempt, the attorney general of Mississippi refused to receive service for the governor. In another effort the marshal was turned away from the governor's home.

Satterfield once more arose to say, "May I respectfully suggest to the Court, it might be of benefit to the Court to have the credentials he exhibited introduced." Tuttle shut him up: "Mr. Satterfield, I do not think you are in a position to make any suggestions." Satterfield, ever obsequious: "Thank you, sir." Judge Rives, exasperated, went after Satterfield, and asked whether he represented the governor. Satterfield said he did not.

Rives then asked, "What communication have you had with the Governor of Mississippi?"

Satterfield evaded, "Within what period of time?"

Rives said, "Since last Tuesday night."

Satterfield once more evaded, "I think it would take several hours to go into that fully."

Rives, becoming furious, continued the attack:

RIVES: Have you seen the Governor in person?

SATTERFIELD: Yes, of course.

RIVES: . . . Did you discuss this Order with the Governor?

SATTERFIELD: Do you care to have me sworn as a witness, may it please the Court?

RIVES: No, I am asking you as attorney.

SATTERFIELD: I thought I was not privileged to participate in the proceeding until later. I am sorry.

RIVES: You are an attorney and officer of the Court?

SATTERFIELD: Correct.

RIVES: And I ask you as an attorney and officer of the Court.

SATTERFIELD: May I respectfully object to being questioned by the Court unless I have the status of participating attorney, which I do not have.

RIVES: Yes, you may object, but I still want an answer.

Rives and Judge Brown then wrung from Satterfield that two days earlier he had discussed with the governor the order to show cause and the time for which it was scheduled to be heard, which Barnett had learned by reading the newspapers, and that Barnett had obtained copies of the recently prepared court papers.

Nevertheless, later Satterfield presented a motion to dismiss the contempt proceedings against Barnett. Tuttle called a brief recess to confer with the court. Satterfield asked for "the privilege of presenting authorities." Tuttle responded: "You don't know what I am talking about to the Court." When the Court finished conferring Tuttle announced, "The Court has unanimously voted to revoke its order permitting the State of Mississippi to appear as Amicus Curiae or in any other matter in the case. The Court will hear no further arguments on that. That is a final decision. I want to make it perfectly clear that the Court now revokes its order previously entered orally, permitting the State of Mississippi to appear in the case."

Satterfield tried to come back with another motion "with complete deference and respect." But Tuttle responded curtly, "The motion is denied."

Later that day the court entered its order holding Barnett in civil contempt, committing him to "the custody of the Attorney General of the United States and . . . [to] pay a fine to the United States of $10,000 per day unless on or before Tuesday, October 2nd, 1962 at 11 A.M.," he ceases resisting the orders of the courts. The order also required the governor to maintain law and order at Ole Miss "to the end that James H. Meredith be permitted to register and remain as a student."

On Saturday, September 29, the president, over the telephone, made a deal with Barnett by which Meredith would register in Jackson, while Barnett and John Doar would pretend to be in Oxford for the purpose of registering him, thereby diverting mobs from the scene. But then Barnett changed his mind.

In the meantime, at the Saturday night Ole Miss football game, fans displayed what must have been the largest Confederate flag in the world. Governor Barnett spoke, affirming his allegiance to the customs of Mississippi. Retired General Edwin A. Walker, who had commanded federal troops in Little Rock, and later became a John Bircher, called for volunteers to come to Mississippi to resist federal encroachment.

Finally, on September 30, President Kennedy issued a proclamation that directed all persons to cease and desist obstruction of justice against court orders that required Meredith's admission. Later that day, Kennedy directed the secretary of defense to take all appropriate steps to enforce orders of the courts in the Meredith case. The administration amassed a few hundred army troops and about five hundred marshals at the Millington Naval Air Station on the Mississippi border.

Late that afternoon, Meredith, with John Doar and United States marshal, James J. McShane, flew from Millington to Oxford. They drove to Baxter Hall, a campus dormitory. The Mississippi Highway Patrol, federal marshals, and troops were already on campus. Meredith went to a second-floor counselor's apartment, and began reading a school assignment. Most of the students apparently had gone to Jackson for the football game; they were beginning to return and, by 7:00 P.M., formed a mob that was becoming large and nasty, taunting and threatening marshals. One member of the mob sprayed a fire extinguisher in the face of an army truck driver. Rioters began throwing stones. Governor Barnett, or another official, ordered the highway patrol to leave the campus. Only strenuous efforts by Justice, including phone calls between Bobby Kennedy and the governor, got that decision reversed.

The mob attacked a TV cameraman, reporters, and photographers, and beat a faculty member who attempted to protect a camera. The crowd threw rocks, bottles, bricks, lead pipes, Coke bottles filled with flaming gasoline, and acid. Finally, the marshals fired tear gas at the mob and at the Highway Patrol.

President Kennedy went on radio and television. He called for adherence to law and urged Mississippians to consider that they had "a new opportunity to show

President Kennedy Confers with Brother Robert F. Kennedy
President Kennedy and his brother, Attorney General Robert F. Kennedy, conferred together most of the night on the Mississippi situation. (1962)

Bettmann/CORBIS

that you are men of patriotism and integrity." Around that time an unknown person shot and killed an Agence France-Presse photographer. More marshals came to the campus. More racists began arriving on campus from rural Mississippi. Gunfire against marshals erupted—by 10:00 P.M., four marshals had been hit. A bystander was killed and others badly wounded. State police pulled back.

The riot had been going on for three hours and Justice officials still had not called in troops. Finally, the White House permitted the National Guard to act. By then the mob was attacking the marshals and the guard with a bulldozer, a fire engine, and automobiles. They burned cars in the parking lot. The president, around midnight, called for troops at Millington to hurry to Oxford. Sometime after 2:00 A.M., they arrived on campus to restore order. By dawn the campus was under control and, before 8:00 A.M., Meredith was driven to the registrar's office in a battered border patrol car and registered.

In 1990, John Doar said that Justice had handled the Meredith case badly: "Would the Justice Department of the United States government ever have done it that way again? No, they wouldn't have. . . ."

Meredith began attending classes. Other students harassed him and armed guards lived in his suite, but he had an oddly relaxed attitude toward his studies. At the end of his first semester he announced that he would withdraw from the university and only just before classes resumed did he decide to return. When Connie and I told him that he hadn't done as well as we thought he could have, he responded that a black man had as much right to fail as a white man. We arranged

James Meredith Studying in Dormitory
James Meredith, the first African American student at the University of Mississippi, studies in his dormitory room with an FBI agent on the telephone nearby. (1962)

tutoring for him in Memphis on weekends. I flew there for the sessions but he spent his time with friends or at the bowling alley—anywhere but studying. Connie got him up to Yale for Christmas vacation, where she arranged for faculty to work with him. But he suddenly went to Chicago and then back to Mississippi. It was like trying to get one of your kids to study when he or she didn't want to.

Some years later, Meredith wrote, "The decisions that I had to make were concerned primarily with the question of my Divine Responsibility. . . . My mission was clear. I had to devote my life to the cause of directing civilization toward a destiny of humaneness." He was graduated from Ole Miss and then applied to Columbia Law School. Bill Warren, dean at the time, asked whether I thought the school should admit Meredith. I replied that I didn't know enough about his academic record to make a judgment. Meredith was admitted and graduated in 1968. Some faculty members have told me that he made useful and insightful contributions to classroom discussion. Later he became an assistant to Senator Jesse Helms of North Carolina, and in 1991, announced his candidacy for the office of president of the United States. At one time he worked with David Duke.

Southern segregationists were flummoxed by Connie Motley, who beat them, not only in *Meredith*, but almost every time. Once, Attorney General Joe Patterson of Mississippi, possibly feeling that I would confide in him because I was white, asked me whether she really was black. I said I was sure that she was but that I would check with her; I relayed his question to Connie. She replied, "Tell him I'm an Indian."

School Integration
Brown + 50

While, nationally, residential segregation has declined about 5 percent over the past 10 years, major urban areas remain about as densely segregated as before. Fair housing laws have not been enforced effectively, but even if they were, the 24 percent of blacks (and their higher proportion of children) who live in poverty cannot afford better housing. They could not move to integrated neighborhoods (ordinarily suburbs) without subsidies. The country is not in a mood to redistribute wealth to poor people. As a result, over 70 percent of blacks attend schools in which they are in the majority, so called majority-minority schools, segregated by race and wealth. Small town and rural southern schools, which have been the most integrated, are also becoming increasingly segregated. Most of this segregation does not violate any law. It results from ordinary school assignment policies. But there are legal techniques by which children may be integrated, which are not in use because they are politically controversial, or because of expense or inconvenience.

The Decline of Court Ordered Integration
On Martin Luther King, Jr.'s birthday in 2004, the Harvard Civil Rights Project described a decided decrease in integration:

- In many districts where court-ordered desegregation ended in the past decade, there has been a major increase in segregation. The courts assumed that the forces that produced segregation and inequality had been cured. They have not been.

- Among the four districts included in the original Brown decision…three of the four cases show considerable long-term success in realizing desegregated education.
- Rural and small town school districts are, on average, the nation's most integrated for both African Americans and Latinos. Central cities of large metropolitan areas are the epicenter of segregation; segregation is also severe in smaller central cities and in the suburban rings of large metros.
- There has been a substantial slippage toward segregation in most of the states that were highly desegregated in 1991.
- The vast majority of intensely segregated minority schools face conditions of concentrated poverty, powerfully related to unequal educational opportunity.

Despite the capacity of integration to deliver equal education, court ordered integration, which was once widespread, has become virtually impossible to sustain. Judges have been dissolving integration orders as systems have become "unitary" and no "vestiges" of segregation remain. With perhaps the rare exception of two judges in Alabama, they accept agreement between lawyers, who apparently just want the cases to be over, with little or no examination of whether race continues to play a part in school policies, such as tracking, resource allocation, drop-out prevention, graduation rates, and so forth.

While some integration is possible in an urban district not entirely bereft of whites, it becomes harder to accomplish because more whites have been moving to the suburbs. Court-ordered integration across district lines has become virtually impossible as a result of the doctrine that there will be no interdistrict remedy without an interdistrict violation, that is some collusion between city and suburb to segregate. The integration possibilities, therefore, reduce to: (1) integration within a metropolitan area with the small number of whites who remain; (2) integration within a suburban district, the extent depending on the size and location of black and white populations; (3) integration between districts (suburb and city, suburb and suburb) where population size, location and distances make it feasible.

The Advantages of Integrated Learning
Blacks in segregated schools, with few exceptions, have always received inferior, tangible, measurable educational facilities. That was the case before the Margold Report that launched the

campaign that led to *Brown v. Board of Education*. We know also that remedies that do not integrate may never provide equal buildings, libraries, teachers, and other components of instruction. Integrating equalizes by placing all children in the same schools. The ancient dictum, "green follows white," i.e., the funding goes towards white students, holds sway. That, of course, is apart from the deleterious effects of segregation, *per se*.

Segregation itself deprives low-income African American students of social networks that afford personal contact with universities, businesses, law firms, or art museums, for example, and others who can open their eyes to possibilities after high school. Schoolmates and teachers inform about career paths, scholarship programs, internships, help get summer jobs, and opportunities they never would have heard of. Integrated schools offer more challenging curricula and teach how to get along in a majority white world. After graduation from integrated schools, black children commonly enjoy higher salaries and better lifestyle than students who attended segregated schools, are less likely to hold negative views about whites, more likely to live in integrated neighborhoods, and interact with whites where they live, socially, politically, and economically. Interracial contact dispels stereotypes that whites have of blacks.

Moreover, by commonly accepted measures, black students who attend integrated schools do better. The largest upward leap in black standardized test scores occurred after 1970 following the Supreme Court decision in *Alexander v. Holmes County Board of Education*, which overruled the 1955 "all deliberate speed decision." The 1966 Coleman Report concluded that the most important factors that influence academic performance are family background and the school's social composition. Recent surveys of three separate cohorts of 200,000 Texas school children concluded: "*ceteris paribus* [all things being equal] schools with higher concentrations of minority students lead to lower achievement for Black students but minimal effects on whites or Hispanics."

James Liebman's synthesis of school integration reports that black students in desegregated schools are more likely to have higher IQs than their segregated counterparts, less likely to drop out, more likely to complete four-year colleges, and to receive high marks. Susan Eaton's *The Other Boston Busing Story* relates the superior academic performance and achievement of Boston black inner city schoolchildren who attended suburban schools through the Boston METCO program. METCO is a voluntary program in which 3,500 Boston black children attend suburban schools. It has a waiting list of 13,000 applicants. Amy Stuart Wells writes of black St. Louis school children in a city-to-suburb program:

[N]early twice as many of the transfer students are graduating from their suburban high schools in four years as compared to students who graduate from a City high school....

[F]or every 100 ninth graders in the St. Louis Public Schools, about 74 fail to graduate four years later, and of the 26 students who do graduate, only about 13 go on to post secondary education.... [A]pproximately eight of these 100 freshmen will find themselves in a four-year university five years after they enter high school.

.... on average, out of every group of 100 ninth grade students in the City schools, only six black students will graduate in four years and go on to attend a four-year college.

In contrast, the college-going rate for graduates of the 16 predominantly white suburban districts was about 75 percent on average.... [I]n the more affluent of these suburban districts ... the college-going rates were more than 90 percent.... Meanwhile, 68 percent of the African American transfer students who graduate from suburban schools are college bound. Forty-four percent ... attend four-year colleges...nearly three times the national average for black high school graduates. Thus, for every 100 African American transfer students who enroll in suburban schools by the ninth grade, about 60 graduate from the suburbs and 40 of these graduates go on to college.

Equal or Adequate Funding for City Schools

Unable to persuade or require schools to integrate and because majority-minority schools are generally inferior, equal rights advocates have sued to equalize school financing, or at least bring it to a level of adequacy. About a score of state supreme courts have required increasing the funding. Early suits sought equality. Now the aim is adequacy. In a celebrated decision, *Sheff v. O'Neill*, a case that is eight years old, the Supreme Court of Connecticut ordered that racial isolation of Hartford students be remedied. The legislature then passed laws which included a state takeover of the city schools and increased funding for interdistrict magnets and an expansion of a METCO-like Project Choice to other cities in the state. The interdistrict magnets have been successful, with waiting lists among suburban and urban parents. The Project Choice program also has a waiting list, even though there is little advertising or recruitment. Thirty years ago, the New Jersey Supreme Court ordered equalizing school funding between rich and poor districts, now moderated to a requirement that the poor districts receive adequate funding. In 2003 the New York Court of Appeals ruled that the state is under a duty to provide a sound basic education to all children. At this writing there has not yet been a legislative response.

Equal funding sometimes substitutes for integration. But funding alone cannot provide equality, although a school's potential could not be achieved without adequate funds, either. Kansas City spent $2 billion dollars and Detroit spent hundreds of millions that courts awarded to compensate for degradation of their school systems during years of segregation. The schools could have been integrated only across district lines, which was not possible under Supreme Court doctrine. The funds were spent in segregated schools on all sorts of things other than superior teaching and administration. There was no change in student performance.

Moreover, courts rarely order appropriations as large as those in Detroit and Kansas City. When they decide whether and what to appropriate, race apparently plays a part. As James E. Ryan has written:

> *minority districts do not win school finance cases nearly as often as white districts do, and in the few states where minority districts have successfully challenged school finance schemes, they have encountered legislative recalcitrance that exceeds, in both intensity and duration, the legislative resistance that successful white districts have faced. As this and additional evidence suggests, there are strong reasons to believe that the racial composition of the school district plays an influential role in determining its success or failure in school finance litigation and legislative reform.*

When legislatures have in fact appropriated funds in response to judicial orders, white schools usually have benefited most, or, to repeat the saying, "green follows white."

Proposals for Integrating Without Court Orders

Proposals abound for improving education. Some, while not primarily integration vehicles, could provide means for integrating: charters; vouchers; magnets; No Child Left Behind; voluntary cross-district transfers, exemplified by METCO; assignment by socio-economic class (more or less coinciding with race); assignment from across a range of test scores (coinciding pretty much with race); controlled choice, i.e., limited parental school selection, controlled to prevent racial concentrations. None can solve the school segregation problem alone. Within a metropolitan or suburban area, it might be that a number of the proposals in combination could improve black youngsters' educational opportunities.

Vouchers carry the controversial baggage of church-state issues and a battle over whether they threaten impairment or destruction of public education. They are not likely to become universal. Vouchers have been rejected in recent votes in Maryland, Michigan, Colorado, California, Washington, Michigan, and California by votes between 55 percent and 71 percent. Because of heavy opposition there may not be enough experience to conclude whether they will affect integration. But, enough is known so that the NAACP Legal Defense Fund, which surely would support them if it believed they would promote integration, is firmly opposed and filed a friend of the court brief taking that position in the Supreme Court's most recent voucher case.

Magnets have in some places been useful in integrating. They ordinarily do not draw students across the city-suburb boundary. They are no more likely to be integrated or segregated than the general run of schools. But when they are used to desegregate they may leave seats unfilled, saving them for white children, whose presence would be needed to integrate. Or, they may reject white children to make room for blacks. Both situations can create legal problems that could be mitigated by *Grutter*.

A charter school may be organized and its classes taught in different ways, so long as it meets certain requirements. But charters are more segregated than ordinary public schools and there is no reason to believe that they offer a path to integration. If the aim were to promote integration the state might give priority to charters located near district lines that would recruit students from urban and suburban districts. Charter schools do not offer an assurance of quality education, although, some charters are first rate. Recently, New York state closed one of its first three charter schools, partially closed another, and placed the third on probation. Catchy names and fresh forms of organization cannot solve problems of urban education.

Within cities or suburbs, controlled choice is ordinarily the most effective technique for integrating. Ordinarily, however, most districts don't have enough of a racial mix for it to serve as a widely used means to promote integration. In a controlled choice system parents select from a small number of, usually, magnet-like schools. Schools are all of the same quality. Travel distances are convenient. The final assignment is made by lottery but administrators may make adjustments to maintain some sort of racial balance. My granddaughters attend school in a choice district, Montclair, New Jersey, where the schools are excellent and well integrated. I have heard of no dissatisfaction with the program. There may be objection to magnets in a controlled choice system, which set aside some number of seats for minorities if choice does not produce a racially balanced class. Such issues have come up occasionally, and usually have been resolved against racial balance, but not always. The Supreme Court has not spoken on the question.

No single technique can work everywhere. In some, perhaps many places, segregated living is so extensive that integration, assuming a will to achieve it, will be difficult or unattainable. Because urban areas are almost all black, the main problem is how to integrate from city to suburb. Unless that is doable, integration will be very limited. James E. Ryan and Michael Heise have persuasively come to a sobering conclusion: The key to integrating schools is the willingness of the suburbs to relinquish their power to keep out racial minorities:

> *Our central claim is that unless the politics surrounding school choice are altered, school choice plans will continue to be structured in ways that protect the physical and financial independence of suburban public schools. As a result, school choice plans will be geographically constrained and will generally tend to be intradistrict. Voucher programs, in particular, are likely to be limited to urban areas, where parents feel little attachment to neighborhood public schools and are desperate for relief.*

Jack Greenberg was one of the attorneys who argued *Brown v. Board of Education* before the United States Supreme Court as co-counsel for the plaintiffs with Thurgood Marshall. A professor of law at Columbia Law School, he teaches courses and seminars in constitutional law, civil rights and human rights law, and civil procedure. His relationship with the NAACP Legal Defense and Educational Fund spanned nearly four decades; first as assistant counsel, beginning in 1949, and then, from 1961 to 1984, succeeding Thurgood Marshall as director counsel. As director counsel he briefed and argued forty cases in the Supreme Court of the United States, and hundreds in lower federal courts. Professor Greenberg continues to serve the NAACP as a member of the executive committee of the board. He has written numerous books and articles on civil rights, and in 2001 he was one of 28 distinguished Americans honored by President Bill Clinton with Presidential Citizens Medals at a White House ceremony.

David Butow/CORBIS SABA

Child with Pro-Affirmative Action Sign
A young boy demonstrating for affirmative action at the University of California at Berkeley. Students and families were protesting to keep affirmative action during a demonstration outside a Board of Regents meeting. (1995)

The Integration Ideal: Sobering Reflections

Charles J. Ogletree, Jr.

An excerpt from *All Deliberate Speed: Reflections on the First Half-Century of* Brown v. Board of Education
(W.W. Norton & Company, 2004)

Now that fifty years have passed since the *Brown* decision, we must examine some thorny questions about race matters in America. The years since 1954 have been difficult ones, particularly in addressing matters of race. The false promise of integration—and particularly of the "all deliberate speed" kind embodied in *Bakke*'s diversity rationale—is to perceive integration as an end in itself, rather than a means to an end. Viewing integration as simply an end, some commentators in the wake of *Brown* asserted that it had little impact on desegregation or on the civil rights movement. Gerald Rosenberg, in his book *The Hollow Hope*, was one of the first to do so. He points out, "For ten years, 1954–64, virtually nothing happened."[1] Looking at *Brown*'s effect on public opinion, other branches of government, and the press, Rosenberg doubts that *Brown* had even an indirect impact on any of the three: "[T]he claim that a major contribution of the courts in civil rights was to give the issue salience, press political elites to act, prick the consciences of whites, legitimate the grievances of blacks, and fire blacks up to act is not substantiated. The evidence suggests that *Brown*'s major positive impact was limited to reinforcing the belief in a legal strategy for change of those already committed to it."[2]

Other commentators, such as Michael Klarman, take Rosenberg's argument even further by documenting *Brown*'s "crystallizing effect on southern white resistance to racial change."[3] Yet Klarman's conclusion that *Brown* was to blame for much of the violence against civil rights demonstrators, which in turn was the catalyst for change, seems actually to illustrate *Brown*'s significance. The literature responding to Rosenberg and Klarman is voluminous, and the whole debate is now somewhat dated. The respondents insist that the "cultural significance" of the decision is under-stated in Rosenberg's analysis, which ignores *Brown*'s importance as a "moral resource" for the civil rights movement.[4] Perhaps the most effective response to Rosenberg details how, merely by becoming law, *Brown* not only "raised new obstacles to segregation" in legal and social contexts but also "challenged the assumption that there was no option but loyalty to the status quo."[5] This view challenges the thesis of the "hollow hope" argument by emphasizing that "[j]udicial decisions can change assumptions not only by opening new options for opposition, but also through their power to grant legitimacy to certain claims and to redefine norms of institutional action."[6]

Moreover, the "hollow hope" view fails to see integration and diversity as instrumental goods—a means of achieving a goal, not the goal itself. The challenge of *Brown* was not only to achieve integration but also to recognize that once integrated, all of us are diverse: we have all given up something to gain something more. Integration does not simply place people side by side in vari-ous institutional settings; rather, it remakes America, creating a new community founded on a new form of respect and tolerance. Implicit in that challenge was the recognition that white society had to change to acknowledge in substantive ways the achievements of African-American society. It was not enough simply to admit African-Americans to the table, or even to let them dine, but to partake of the food they brought with them.

The enslaved and segregated African-American community did no less than create the American voice and produce the New World culture that could speak distinctively in contrast to the Old. When Ken Burns creates his documents of American culture, he turns to jazz, to the Civil War, and to modern baseball's flowering out of two leagues, one white, one black. When Mark Twain captured the American voice, it was Huck Finn and Jim, each sounding like the other, black voice mingling with white. By the time F. Scott Fitzgerald captured the spirit of America's emergence as a world power, he called it the Jazz Age; George Gershwin's distinctively American sound was its classical musical expression. In the midst of the worst squalor and deprivation, a people were, if not thriving, then surviving, growing, creating, even celebrating, and what they achieved spoke to and defined much that was America. Some southern segregationists, from *Plessy* forward, even used this evidence of cultural strength to argue that "separate but equal" was good for African-Americans.

By the 1920s, African-American culture was certainly thriving, as around the country middle-class African-Americans engaged in the type of self-reliant enterprise endorsed by Booker T. Washington in his Atlanta Exposition speech of 1895. Many of those communities, however, were formed not from a compromise with southern whites but by an escape north or west to the emerging industrial towns. In New York in the 1920s, Harlem styled itself the black capital of the world. The Harlem Renaissance produced a concentration of talent rarely seen in American letters. But outside the Northeast, other African-American communities were thriving. Of particular note was the Greenwood District of Tulsa, Oklahoma, one of the most successful African-American communities in America.[7] As a result of Jim Crow segregation, Greenwood formed a self-sustaining economy having little contact with the white parts of town.[8]

Greenwood District Race Riot
June 1, 1921

Tulsa Historical Society

Often forgotten in the rush toward integration are the community leaders and middle-class entrepreneurs who made these communities flourish. Generations of teachers, newspapermen, shop owners, makers of beauty products, and providers of myriad services for the black community grew in the shadow of segregation. The real challenge of integration was not how to bring black children to white schools, or how to make space at formerly all-white firms for the new black professional class that emerged from the integrated educational spaces. The real challenge was to see how Americans would use the space created by the talents that already existed, by the already skilled—for those spaces existed in the African-American community.

Too often, integration is presented as an unalloyed benefit for African-Americans, as if we all had been clamoring to leave our communities. For many in the African-American community, however, integration was viewed with suspicion or something worse. Many communities at the center of the battle for integration, represented by the crusading lawyers of the NAACP, would have welcomed something less than the full integration demanded by the civil rights lawyers. Instead, these teachers, school principals, and janitors would rather have kept their schools, their jobs, and their positions of power and influence than see their charges bused to white schools run by white principals where white educators often made the children all too grimly aware of their distaste for the new state of affairs.

In fact, integration had a similar effect on large sections of the community. Now not only whites but middle-class blacks as well could live in the suburbs. Although the phenomenon of white flight made clear how ephemeral such an existence could be, many African-Americans chose to leave the inner cities, not so much to integrate with whites—although that was the goal of many—

W.E.B. Du Bois

as to create new communities in better areas. Leaving the black community, however, undermined one of the major goals Du Bois had created for his Talented Tenth: to maintain a connection with the poor and underrepresented in the black community to provide a means of self-betterment for the downtrodden. Disengaging the Talented Tenth from the community created a vacuum that was never properly filled; it led to a spiral of poverty in urban America that has yet to be adequately addressed. For many middle-class African-Americans, moreover, it has created a sense of loss of connection to the community. The current civil rights generation has spent so much time fighting those who would deny equal rights to African-Americans that the question what should be done with integration once it was achieved was put aside.

Does this mean that integration has failed and that African-Americans can thrive only culturally on the margins of American society in the newly resegregated towns and cities? Yes and no. Integration as a one-way street, imagining diversity as all that is not white, has failed. The challenge is for America to see *all* Americans in their diversity—to be not only plural but equal in our plurality. In the meantime, African-Americans, as those closest to their communities, as those most likely to look out for other African-Americans, may be in the best position—if not under the greatest obligation—to make integration work. Most recently, the failure of the Great Society marked the last time America promised to address the social inequality that predominantly harms African-Americans. For too many Americans, the concept of freedom for African-Americans admits of no degree but is simply based upon the absence of slavery or segregation.

Is there any solution to the problem of discrimination and inequality? There have certainly been moments, for example, after the Civil War and during the civil rights revolution, when America as a whole appears to have manifested a desire to change, to reform, to make whole. My mentor Professor Derrick Bell has provided an account of these moments in terms of "interest convergence,"[9] the claim that only when the interests of the majority converge with those of the minority will the minority achieve its goals. "When whites perceive that it will be profitable or at least cost-free to serve, hire, admit, or otherwise deal with blacks on a nondiscriminatory basis, they do so. When they fear—accurately or not—that there may be a loss, inconvenience, or upset to themselves or other whites, discriminatory conduct usually follows."[10] Bell finds that interest convergence accounts for the successful *Brown* litigation; it also provides a convincing account of the failure of integration in the wake of *Brown*.

There is indeed a cost to be paid for failing to heed the plea of the lawyers in the *Brown* case, half a century ago. In the meantime, we have lost the voice of passion with Dr. King's death and the voice of reason with Justice Marshall's. Many black people have run out of patience waiting for America to address the legacy of slavery. This country's failure to achieve even the modest goals of *Brown*, by providing all children with equal educational opportunities, has resulted in the creation of a movement that we all hoped to avoid: the demand for reparations by blacks. Whereas Justice Brennan's greatest quality was his ability to translate liberal readings of the Constitution into legal doctrine, Marshall's greatest quality was perhaps the empathy he brought to the cases, along with the passion of one seasoned by years of campaigning on behalf of the dispossessed.

The failure of pedagogical diversity at so many of our educational establishments may be an argument for preserving predominantly African-American or female colleges as an educational alternative. That was certainly the position Justice Thomas endorsed in *United States v. Fordice*,[11] an opinion upholding the right of historically black colleges and universities (HBCUs) to equal funding from the state.

Thomas's answer to the problem of resegregation and unequal funding is deeply radical, pessimistic, and perhaps anticipated by Orlando Patterson, a colleague of mine at Harvard University—that it is the "black person's burden" (to paraphrase Kipling) to reform American society through striving separately for equality. On the one hand, Patterson endorses a view espoused by Justice Ginsburg, that "the purpose of affirmative action is to redress past wrongs." He suggests, however, that an undue reliance on the diversity rationale has transformed this purpose, and that "many of its supporters see affirmative action as an entitlement, requiring little or no effort on the part of minorities." The consequence is that African-Americans must do more of what Patterson terms "the cultural work necessary to create what Martin Luther King, Jr., called the 'beloved community' of an integrated nation."[12] Now, I am as much a fan as anyone of the beloved community. But Patterson seems to have misread the last fifty years of American history as well as the current state of the affirmative action debate if he believes that any but the most extreme supporters of the program view

Martin Luther King, Jr., Addressing Crowd (1966)

Anti-Busing Demonstrators Marching
Anti-busing demonstrators, some dressed in colonial cos-
tume, march down Bunker Hill Street in Boston's
Charlestown section. As school desegregation got underway, thousands of white children boycotted classes. (1974)

it as an entitlement. It is more accurate to say that we view it as one of the last holdouts in the rollback of the civil rights agenda of the 1960s. Affirmative action is not a substitute for social change and cultural reconstruction. But it is generally regarded as easily the most important means of ensuring the integration Patterson unhesitatingly embraces as the goal of the American community.

The real problem, as I have argued elsewhere[13] and in this book, is not that African-Americans have failed to embrace the beloved community but that the history of integration since *Brown*, and the history of race relations preceding that decision, has been marked by a "go slow" attitude embodied in the phrase "all deliberate speed." For Patterson to suggest that integration has failed so far because of African-American unwillingness or complacency is a myopic indictment of the efforts of the civil rights movement and the actions of those people during the various, often violent, efforts to desegregate school systems throughout the 1970s. Boston, I have made clear, offers one example of the violence of resistance to integration, but there are many others. The failure of the American community to live up to Dr. King's ideals is not so much due to the collective failure of African-Americans or some amorphous sense of black entitlement. Rather, it is due to the concrete and often brutally painful failure of many whites to live up to the promises of Reconstruction or the Great Society.

The Boston busing case, along with *Brown* itself, raises an interesting question: Why did the courts (and later the executive branches of the various state and federal governments) ignore the "massive resistance" to these programs and go along with something as socially disruptive as integration? Derrick Bell's discussion of interest convergence provides one answer. Interest convergence explains how African-Americans are able to achieve political gains despite the essentially racist nature of American society. The white majority retains political and social power—in fact, a white minority that has power and wishes to conserve it retains true power, and the rest of white society is empowered only relative to African-Americans. Thus, while not only African-Americans but many whites are without effective political, social, or economic power, the relative position of African-Americans to the rest of society serves to mask the reality of disenfranchisement for the majority of whites.[14] Interest convergence suggests that, against this consolidation of power in an elite, redistributive gains are possible only when the interests of the elite and the rest coincide.

Bell suggests that racism is not some accidental by-product of American society or culture that can be undone by a sustained effort to eradicate it. Rather, racism is endemic in America, a definitive, structural feature of liberal democracy in America.[15] Far from being some problematic, but essentially transient, social or psychological condition, racism is a permanent feature of American society, necessary for its stability and for the well-being of the majority of its citizens.[16] Thus, according to Bell, "black people will never gain full equality in this country. Even those Herculean efforts we hail as successful will produce no more than temporary 'peaks of progress,' short-lived victories that slide into irrelevance as racial patterns adapt in ways that maintain white dominance."[17]

Accordingly, interest convergence works as a safety valve, to permit short-term gains for African-Americans when doing so furthers the short- or long-term goals of the white elite. As a side effect, it has the important consequence of convincing the minority population (or others that lack power) that social change is possible rather than ephemeral and that participation in the social and political system will provide redistributive benefits. This is an important check on widespread disaffection that may end in rioting or even revolution.

In particular, with regard to *Brown*, Bell suggests that the Cold War provided the impetus for a change in the courts' and federal government's attitude to segregation. The American propaganda of equality and democracy was effectively countered in the resource-rich countries of Africa by the communist propaganda surrounding the continued existence of segregation. This foreign policy interest appears in the government brief in *Brown* and is often cited as one of the major influences on the Court's thinking.

In the University of Michigan cases, interest convergence is plainly evident. Ginsburg's and Thomas's opinions in *Gratz* and *Grutter* make clear the symbiosis between elite school status and impoverished and resegregating public education. Affirmative action, whatever its merits, permits the system to exist while abandoning the majority of African-American and Latino students to a second-rate education. Tinkering with affirmative action by introducing income-based qualifications risks further obscuring the real problem: the discriminatory and race-based underfunding of our primary and secondary education systems. On the other hand, failing to address the underlying problem perpetuates it. Unwilling to risk the malign consequences of system failure and unwilling to change the system, majority and minority interests converge around affirmative action.

There is certainly a majority interest in continued participation by minorities in the workplace. The most widely hailed aspect of O'Connor's opinion in *Grutter* has been its acceptance of the business and military community's endorsement of affirmative action.[18] The support of these two vital groups is heartening, suggesting that even if some parts of the population don't "get" the importance of affirmative action, others in power do—and for similar reasons as in *Brown*. Affirmative action is important because the "aesthetic" values derided by Thomas are precisely those that appeal to business and the military: the consumers of their services (a global public; the disproportionately minority noncommissioned ranks) demand it. They want evidence that they can get on in their society regardless of race or that they can do business on equal terms (and thus wish to see such equality manifested in their business partners or superior officers). As Justice O'Connor put it,

> *The benefits [of affirmative action] are not theoretical but real, as major American businesses have made clear that the skills needed in today's increasingly global marketplace can only be developed through exposure to widely diverse people, cultures, ideas, and viewpoints. What is more, high-ranking retired officers and civilian leaders of the United States military assert that, "based on [their] decades of experience," a "highly qualified, racially diverse officer corps ... is essential to the military's ability to fulfill its princip[al] mission to provide national security."[19]*

The causes of educational failure are multiple, but one important factor is the attitude of teachers at public schools toward the minority youngsters in their charge. Many schools are becoming more and more internally segregated, as minority children are assigned to remedial learning classes at a rate that is disproportionately higher than that of white children, and without any justification for the high rate of assignment. Minority children are also more likely to be disciplined, and for longer, than white children for comparable offenses. Finally, because busing was essentially a one-way experience, with whites refusing to travel to African-American schools, the burden of integrated schooling is disproportionately borne by poor African-American children.[20]

So, finally, the wheel has turned full circle. Kenneth Clark's social science evidence, cited by Chief Justice Warren in the now infamous footnote 11 of *Brown v. Board of Education*, to demonstrate that "[s]egregation of white and colored children in public schools has a detrimental effect upon the colored children,"[21] has been trumped, in dissent at least, by Justice Thomas. Roy Brooks, of the University of California at San Diego, also contends that integration has been a failure that may be overcome by a strategy of limited separation. Both theories are pessimistic to the extent that they maintain that integration has failed many African-Americans and that there is lacking in the white community a generalized will to overcome race-based social and economic disparities.[22]

Certainly, there must be some form of social change on the education front. Whether this occurs through separation or in an integrated environment is a matter of great consequence for American society. Our experiment with integration started with a pronouncement, half a century ago in *Brown*, that integration was an important value with positive social consequences that should be embraced by all Americans. Twenty years later, real action to integrate our schools had only just started. We are but one generation into an integrated society, and the signs are that the majority of the population is tired with the process. Those at the top want to stay there, and those in the middle would rather hold on to what they have than give a little to get a lot. We have to decide whether this is a country that is comfortable with discrimination. Are we satisfied with the fact that many whites find minorities so repellent that they will move and change their children's schooling to avoid us? For, make no mistake, that is what underpins the supposedly "rational" decisions based on racial stereotyping: an inability on the part of the majority of Americans to acknowledge that minority citizens are "just like us."

Demonstration in Support of Affirmative Action
Students from the University of Michigan demonstrate in support of affirmative action. The demonstration was part of a National Day of Action to Defend Affirmative Action. (1998)

There is little surprise in acknowledging that there was substantial resistance by the white community to integration and later to affirmative action. But the theory of interest convergence suggests that most Americans cannot be bothered to engage that problem unless it directly affects them. They would rather turn away, uninterested, and perpetuate racial disadvantage than acknowledge it, let alone confront it. We have witnessed the *Brown* decision, followed by *Bakke* and, more recently, *Grutter v. Bollinger*. We have witnessed Dr. King's historic "I Have a Dream" speech and his subsequent assassination. We have heard the powerful words of President Johnson in his commitment to affirmative action, and President Bush's criticism of the Michigan plan as a program promoting racial preferences.[23] We have seen diversity plans approved by the Supreme Court and, in the same year, some HBCUs lose their accreditation and close. We continue to make progress, and suffer setbacks, in grappling with the persistent problem of race in America. But we must remain vigilant in our commitment to confront racial inequalities, even when we face persistent, even increasing resistance.

As I look back on the fifty years of my life that coincided with the *Brown* decision, the picture is not encouraging. Indeed, I see great disappointment in the effort to achieve a society of equality under the law, blindness to the harm that racial prejudice inflicts on African-Americans, and refusal to address the problem with candor or conviction. If *Brown I* signaled the end of equalization as a permissible educational strategy, *Brown II* indicated that, so far as the legislature was concerned, integration was to be pursued with hesitation. President Eisenhower accepted the *Brown* decision but emphasized that integration should happen slowly, and it did.

When I turned three years old and the ink on the *Brown* decision was barely dry, there were telling signs that *Brown* was already on unsteady ground, when it was tested in *Briggs v. Elliott* (1955). By the time I uttered my first coherent words as a child and prepared to enter kindergarten, the phrase "massive resistance" had already been coined and the "Southern Manifesto" been signed. Around the time I entered school, and rode on my first yellow school bus to get there, southern cities learned that in preventing desegregation they had a powerful weapon in actually closing schools.

As I moved from one underresourced and largely segregated elementary school in Merced to another, a number of southern states passed pupil placement laws designed to block transfers between white and black schools. The resistance to integration was not limited to the South. The pattern across America—from California to Massachusetts to Michigan—was being replicated along these lines. In fact, school integration was not achieved until the advent of busing, and then only at great social cost. When I graduated from Stanford in 1975, I recognized that the education I received, largely as a result of the *Brown* mandate, allowed me passage through formerly closed doors in society. I was on my way to the mecca of higher education, Harvard Law School. What could have been better? Well, in the shadow of Harvard, across the river from Cambridge, black, brown, and white children were facing a different reality. As late as 1975, and despite coming under the ambit of the U.S. Constitution and the Massachusetts Racial Imbalance Act, both of which mandated an end to racially discriminatory schooling, Boston resisted the mandate to integrate the local school system fully.

The Boston experience, which was repeated in other parts of the nation, indicates that the country resisted integrating the public school system for decades after the *Brown* decision, and large sections of the nation never entirely embraced integration. During the last thirty years, many Americans, perhaps even a majority, have acted to subvert the ideal of integration announced in *Brown I*. Within thirty years of achieving integration, it has failed de facto and may no longer be required de jure. A major cause of the end of the *Brown* ideal has been a Supreme Court that, once Warren retired, wasted little time in undoing the few gains that were so painstakingly and "deliberately" achieved.

With fifty years of hindsight, I believe that the tragic lesson of the two decisions in *Brown v. Board of Education* is that one described an aspirational view of American democratic liberalism (*Brown I*) and the other (*Brown II*) actually defined the reality of grudging educational reform, and the power of racism as a barrier to true racial progress in twentieth-century and, for that matter, twenty-first-century America. Whereas *Brown I* made possible the institutional equality first promised in 1776 with the Declaration of Independence ("All men are created equal") and again in 1865 with the ratification of the Thirteenth and Fourteenth Amendments, *Brown II* created the method and manner in which America would resist the mandate of the equality ideal. If *Brown I* made integration a legal imperative, *Brown II*, with its decision to proceed "with all deliberate speed," ensured that the legal imperative was not implemented as a social imperative. Almost immediately, "massive resistance" materialized at virtually every level of society, and it began from the day the decision was issued, through the efforts of national leaders, such as Governor Faubus's appearance on the steps of Little Rock's Central High School in 1957, to the Boston busing crisis of 1975, to the reverse-discrimination arguments that gained popular appeal in the years following *Brown*, and, most telling, to the resegregation of our schools and our communities in the twenty-first century. As an expression of moral rectitude, *Brown I* was the least the Court could have done, but the timidity expressed in *Brown II* nullified its import. To obtain the requisite unanimity, the Court in *Brown I* went too far to accommodate southern whites' opposition to the morality of segregation. To avoid offending the white segregationists, the Court famously eschewed identifying segregation as immoral or evil—although it was, and everyone knew it to be. Instead, Warren demanded that the opinion be "non-rhetorical, unemotional and, above all, nonaccusatory."[24] To identify segregation with evil, Warren and the rest of the Court feared, would provoke a massive rift between South and North and risk the legitimacy of the Court. Given the Court's own reluctance to mandate the forthright enforcement of integration, the legislative and executive branches had all of the reason they needed to ignore or resist urgent and comprehensive remedies.

Forgotten — or, at least, discounted — in all of this were the families and children who petitioned the *Brown* court to end the racial caste system. *Brown I* barely addressed the almost 100 years of Jim Crow suffering and the preceding 250 years of slavery that African-Americans, uniquely as a group in America, had already endured. As a gesture recognizing the pervasive impact of the racial disparity that plagued America then, and the effect of that suffering in the African-American community, *Brown I* included a footnote on the psychological damage inflicted by segregation.[25] If the Court's attitude is one of solicitude toward whites in *Brown I*, in *Brown II*, one can justifiably say, "there is no hint of solicitude for the feelings of Afro-Americans. The Court made no attempt to assuage the inevitable anger and anxiety that the decision would generate within the black community. The rhetoric of the opinion displays . . . complacency [toward the feelings of African-Americans]."[26]

In its solicitude toward the feelings of southern (and many northern) whites in refusing to describe segregation as an evil, the *Brown* decision ignores the restorative function of our legal system. Individuals come to the courts not only to obtain monetary or injunctive remedies but also to seek justice and relief from the suffering they have endured. As Warren surely recognized, *Brown I* offered the opportunity for America to start anew without dividing the nation on the question of race. But forgiveness need not include forgetfulness, and in accounting for *Brown*, we should not ignore that it enacted a collective amnesia that haunts the nation to this day.

It is instructive to compare the racial reconciliation enacted through *Brown I* and *II* with that enacted by President Lincoln, faced with similar stakes, during his second inaugural address. Unlike Warren, Lincoln saw slavery as a *national* sin for which the whole country was to be held responsible (and had been held responsible by God). The responsibility for atonement was therefore to be borne by the whole nation, even though the cost would be to account for "all the wealth piled by the bondsman's two hundred and fifty years of unrequited toil."[27]

The restraint shown by Warren in *Brown I* in identifying the magnitude of the evil of segregation led to the predictably modest remedy proposed by *Brown II*. African-Americans would, in theory, have the burden of segregation in public education removed from their shoulders, but the relief would come slowly, deliberately, and at the pace determined by those who resisted the change. *Brown*'s failure to achieve its admirable goals was compounded by the subsequent elimination of the formerly viable, though segregated, black communities and numerous black jobs in education that was a by-product of integration. When schools were integrated, whites did not attend black schools staffed by black teachers and black principals. Instead, blacks went to the better funded white schools. In this way, integration ended one vital aspect of the "equalization" strategy pursued by the NAACP in the cases leading up to *Brown I*, while at the same time perpetuating the segregation of public education.

The practical effect of judicial, legislative, and personal resistance to *Brown* is manifest today. For example, before *Brown*, the city of Topeka maintained segregated elementary schools. In 1951, there were eighteen elementary schools for whites and four for minorities.[28] After *Brown*, the Topeka board adopted a neighborhood school policy as a result of which three of the elementary schools remained all-black and two others became over 20 percent black. In 1954, less than 10 percent of the elementary students in the district were black.[29] The Kansas district court reopened the original *Brown* case in 1979, when the lead plaintiff, Linda Brown, along with other parents of school-age children, challenged the continued segregation in Topeka schools. In 1992, the Tenth Circuit concluded—having been asked by the Supreme Court to reconsider its earlier opinion in light of recent desegregation cases—that the Topeka school system had not yet achieved adequate integration of its public schools, and it continued to require court supervision.[30]

While public schools in many parts of the nation are experiencing resegregation in the twenty-first century, some opponents of affirmative action assert that racial diversity can be accomplished through 10 percent and 20 percent plans, as now practiced in California, Texas, and Florida, for example. They present them as diversity-sensitive, but not race conscious, alternatives to affirmative action, while ignoring the obvious fact that these plans, in order to guarantee admission to state colleges to the top 10 percent of students at every high school, actually depend upon segregated school systems to ensure minority participation at the tertiary level. The predominantly black schools in these states will provide admission to their students, as will the predominantly white schools. Race is the proxy that determines admission to the state university.

Even legally acceptable affirmative action efforts, as sanctioned in the Supreme Court's decision in *Grutter*, will not guarantee a "critical mass" of minorities in elite institutions. The Court, with a 5-to-4 majority vote, approved the admissions policy of the University of Michigan's law school, while at the same time rejecting a policy that ensures minority students access to its undergraduate division, the obvious pipeline to the law school, and ultimately failed to address the type of quality secondary education that is necessary if the affirmative action program is eventually to end. The irony could hardly be more graphic.

There has been no clearer example of the failure to ensure equal educational facilities than the treatment of historically black colleges and universities (HBCUs). Of the 103 currently existing HBCUs, it was reported in 2003, "fifteen percent are on warning or probation status with accreditation agencies. Many can barely meet their payrolls. Two—Morris Brown College in Atlanta and Mary Holmes College in West Point, Mississippi—have lost their accreditation. Grambling State University in New Orleans is on probation after auditors couldn't make sense of its accounting records."[31] The focus on integrated schooling has so undermined the status of the HBCUs that only Howard, Morehouse, and Spelman are thriving. Ironically, at a time when affirmative action was under attack by the Bush administration, in the *Grutter* and *Gratz* cases, those colleges that exist to support a predominantly African-American student body were under siege. Many HBCUs have faced discrimination from the states in which they are located, which fund HBCUs at a lower level than other state colleges. In *United States v. Fordice*, the Court found that Mississippi continued to discriminate against its HBCUs in such areas as admission standards and that such discrimination was traceable to the *de jure* segregation of the Jim Crow era.[32] The state's proposed solution, to close the HBCUs, was held unconstitutional.

The centrality of the HBCUs to black education can scarcely be overstated. They "helped educate much of the nation's black middle class. Thirty percent of blacks who hold doctorates earned them from black colleges, as did 35% of African-American lawyers, 50% of black engineers and 65% of black physicians."[33] As the Bush administration supports the demise of affirmative action at the college and graduate school levels, such institutions stand to become especially important at a time when many face budgetary crises unlikely to be undone by a proposed 5 percent increase in funding by the federal government.

The decision in *Brown I*, ending segregation in our public schools—and by implication *de jure* segregation everywhere—is justly celebrated as one of the great events in our legal and political history. Precedent did not compel the result, nor was the composition of the Court indicative of a favorable outcome. There is no doubt that the circumstances of many African-Americans are better now than they were before the *Brown* decision. But the speed with which we have embraced the society made possible by *Brown I* has indeed been all too deliberate. It has been deliberate meaning "slow," "cautious," "wary," as if Americans remained to be convinced of the integration ideal. It has been deliberate in the sense of "ponderous" or "awkward," as if each step had been taken painfully and at great cost. Yet the speed with which we have embraced integration has not been deliberate in the sense of "thoughtful" or "reflective"—on the contrary, our response has been emotional and instinctive, perhaps on both sides of the debate. These reactions, anticipated and epitomized in *Brown II*, I suggest, are the real legacy of *Brown I*.

It would be foolhardy to deny that progress has been made, or to dismiss the reality that *Brown I* is a momentous decision both for what it says and for what it has achieved. But there is more yet to do. *Brown I* should be celebrated for ending *de jure* segregation in this country—a blight that lasted almost 400 years and harmed millions of Americans of all races. Far too many African-Americans, however, have been left behind, while only a relative few have truly prospered. For some, the promise of integration has proved ephemeral. For others, short-term gains have been replaced by setbacks engendered by new forms of racism. School districts, briefly integrated, have become resegregated. Some distinctively African-American institutions have been permanently destroyed and others crippled. As we stand near the end or the transformation of affirmative action, things look set to get worse, not better.

For all their clear vision of the need to end segregation, *Brown I* and *II* stand as decisions that see integration as a solution that is embraced only grudgingly. Subsequent courts do not even seem to recognize integration as an imperative. And that, perhaps, is the worst indictment of the *Brown* decisions: their faith in progress and their failure to see how quickly people of a different mind could not only resist but, once the tide had turned, even reverse the halting progress toward a fully integrated society. This failure compels me to look to the past, and the future, and to suggest both modest and radical solutions to address *Brown*'s failure.

We must not let ourselves be deterred from achieving what so many of our forefathers achieved, in the face of even more formidable challenges. If Africans could survive the innumerable horrors of slavery, and if freed slaves could survive the cruelty and repugnance of the Jim Crow system, we as a nation can, must, and will survive the current manifestations of *Brown*'s failures. It is a challenge that we must face with unrelenting dedication and commitment, and when we do so, we will not fail.

[1] Gerald Rosenberg, *The Hollow Hope: Can Courts Bring About Social Change?* (Chicago: Univ. of Chicago Press, 1991), 52.

[2] Ibid., 156.

[3] Michael J. Klarman, "*Brown*, Racial Change, and the Civil Rights Movement," *Virginia Law Review* 80 (1994): 7, 10, 13.

[4] Mark Tushnet, "The Significance of *Brown v. Board of Education*," *Virginia Law Review* 80 (1994): 173, 176–77.

[5] David Schultz and Steven E. Gottlieb, "Legal Functionalism and Social Change: A Reassessment of Rosenberg's *The Hollow Hope: Can Courts Bring About Social Change?*" *Journal of Law and Politics* 12 (1996): 63.

[6] Ibid.

[7] Scott Ellsworth, *Death in a Promised Land: The Tulsa Race Riot of 1921* (Baton Rouge: Louisiana State Univ. Press, 1982): 22

[8] See, generally, Alfred L. Brophy, *Reconstructing the Dreamland*.

[9] See Derrick A. Bell, Jr., "*Brown v. Board of Education* and the Interest Convergence Dilemma," in *Critical Race Theory: The Key Writings That Formed the Movement*, ed. Kimberlé Crenshaw et al. (New York: Basic Books, 1992), 22.

[10] Derrick A. Bell, Jr., *Faces at the Bottom of the Well: The Permanence of Racism* (New York: Basic Books, 1992), 7.

[11] *Fordice*, 505 U.S. 717, 748–49 (1992) (Thomas, J., concurring).

[12] Orlando Patterson, "Affirmative Action: The Sequel," *New York Times*, June 22, 2003, sec. 4, at 11.

[13] See Charles Ogletree, "Repairing the Past: New Efforts in the Reparations Debate in America," *Harvard Civil Rights–Civil Liberties Law Review* 22 (1987): 282–84.

[14] See Bell, *Faces at the Bottom of the Well*, 7.

[15] Bell considers the relationship between racism and liberal democracy to be "symbio[tic]" such that "liberal democracy and racism in the United States are historically, even inherently, reinforcing; American society as we know it exists only because of its foundation in racially based slavery, and it thrives only because racial discrimination continues." Ibid., 10.

[16] As evidence of the permanence of racism, Bell points to the "unstated understanding by the mass of whites that they will accept large disparities in economic opportunity in respect to other whites as long as they have a priority over blacks and other people of color for access to the few opportunities available." Ibid., 9.

[17] Ibid., 12.

[18] See *Grutter*, 123 S.Ct. 2325, 2334–43 (2003).

[19] Ibid., 2340.

[20] Ibid., 2330–31.

[21] *Brown*, 347 U.S. 483, 494 n. 11 (1954).

[22] See Roy L. Brooks, *Integration or Separation?: A Strategy for Racial Equality* (Cambridge: Harvard Univ. Press, 1996), 185–213. Brooks's analysis is similar to Derek Bell's work on interest convergence.

[23] As an alternative to Michigan's diversity plan, President Bush recommended the race-neutral percentage plans. In my view, the arguments for these plans to achieve diversity are unsophisticated and unpersuasive; when closely examined, the plans, advanced by opponents of diversity, perpetuate a more sinister brand of racism. Moreover, percentage plans are inapplicable to the Michigan Law School. Most Michigan Law School students leave the state, any attempt to provide education benefits or access to leadership paths is addressed as a national problem, and under *Adarand* states cannot adopt race-conscious solutions to address generalized national race problems. Finally, recent empirical evidence suggests that these plans are not as effective as race-conscious plans in achieving diversity. See Catherine L. Horn and Stella M. Flores, *Percentage Plans in College Admissions: A Comparative Analysis of Three States' Experiences* (Cambridge: The Civil Rights Project at Harvard University, 2003).

[24] Randall L. Kennedy, "*McCleskey v. Kemp*: Race, Capital Punishment, and the Supreme Court," *Harvard Law Review* 101 (1988): 1388, 1418.

[25] *Brown I*, 347 U.S. at 494, n. 11.

[26] Kennedy, "*McClesky v. Kemp*," 1418.

[27] Abraham Lincoln, *Great Speeches* (New York: Dover 1991): 107

[28] *Brown v. Board of Education*, 98 F. Supp. 797, 797 (D. Kan. 1952).

[29] *Brown*, 892 F.2d 851, 856 (10th Cir. 1989).
[30] *Brown v. Board of Education*, 978 F. 2d 585, 587 (10th Cir. 1992).
[31] Ruby Bailey, "Colleges in Budget Squeeze; Crisis Hits Historically Black Schools as Lawsuits Threaten Affirmative Action," *Milwaukee Journal Sentinel*, March 9, 2003, news sec., at 7A.
[32] *Fordice*, 505 U.S. 717, 733–35 (1992).
[33] Ruby Bailey, "Colleges in Budget Squeeze; Crisis Hits Hstorically Black Schools as Lawsuits Threaten Affirmative Action," *Milwaukee Journal Sentinel*, March 9, 2003, news sec., at 7A.

Lou Jones

Charles J. Ogletree, Jr., the Harvard Law School Jesse Climenko Professor of Law and Vice Dean for the Clinical Programs, is a prominent legal theorist who has made an international reputation by taking a hard look at complex issues of law and by working to secure the rights guaranteed by the Constitution for everyone equally under the law. Professor Ogletree is the author of *All Deliberate Speed: Reflections on the First Half-Century of* Brown v. Board of Education, published in 2004, and was appointed by ABA President Dennis Archer to chair the 50th Anniversary *Brown* commission of the ABA. He is the co-author of the award-winning book, *Beyond the Rodney King Story: An Investigation of Police Conduct in Minority Communities*, and he frequently contributes to many journals, law reviews, and books. Professor Ogletree also serves as the co-chair of the Reparations Coordinating Committee, a group of lawyers and other experts researching a lawsuit based upon a claim of reparations for descendants of African slaves.

Najlah Feanny/CORBIS SABA

Affirmative Action Rally
Students from the University of Michigan demonstrate in support of affirmative action.
(1998)

Reviving *Brown v. Board of Education:* How Courts and Enforcement Agencies Can Produce More Integrated Schools

Gary Orfield and Erica Frankenberg

Even while the American legal profession is celebrating the fiftieth anniversary of *Brown v. Board of Education*, many commentators, courts, and local officials seem to have lost the belief that something—anything—can be done to realize *Brown*'s central vision. Many of those who see the decision as noble nevertheless believe serious integration of American education is impossible. In fact, courts are busily approving plans to terminate successful desegregation orders in favor of returning to intensely segregated and unequal schools. In the federal government's promise to equalize the schools without changing the growing segregation, the No Child Left Behind Act (NCLB) of 2001 requires all schools for all racial groups to perform at high levels or face harsh penalties. Although Rod Paige, the current U.S. Secretary of Education, has praised NCLB as the next logical step to *Brown*,[1] this Act assumes, unlike *Brown v. Board of Education*, that the nation's highly segregated schools will perform equally if pressured by sanctions, something that has never happened on any significant scale in our country's history.

The criticisms of *Brown v. Board of Education* are many: that *Brown* exceeded constitutional logic; that it assumed a judicial power that does not exist; that positive changes would have happened without the Supreme Court's decree and would have been more legitimate; that it weakened the Democratic coalition; that it was really a racial insult to blacks; that nothing really changed; that it diverted attention from the real issues; and that the decision's social science foundations turned out to be wrong. Conservative critics of *Brown* often view what they see as the causes of school segregation—such as segregated housing patterns, white flight to suburbs, and private school choice—as natural forces that the courts cannot or should not challenge. Their general thinking is that the courts tried to do much that went beyond pure legal reasoning, that was not feasible, and that ultimately did more harm than good. *Brown* is celebrated, but the goal of integrated schools is dismissed.

Very few of the critiques contain any serious analysis of what trial judges actually have decided. Desegregation plans are usually developed in an interaction between the parties and the district courts. Although these plans are rarely examined in detail by higher courts, legal theorists typically limit their analyses to the general principles of appellate decisions and often rest conclusions about the effects of judicial decrees either from language in the decisions themselves or from material in the briefs of the opponents of desegregation orders. Such analysis ignores the very rulings that determined the scope and implementation of desegregation in districts across the South and country.

Assumptions that are grounded less in fact than ideology are currently guiding many interpretations of *Brown*, as well as ongoing debates over alternatives such as equalizing segregated schools. The result is to ignore the significant impact that court decisions can and have had on racial patterns within schools. In this article, we examine some of these erroneous assumptions about the courts' role in desegregation. We then discuss research on the realities of desegregation and resegregation and what we have learned from fifty years of experience in hundreds of districts across the nation. We conclude by considering the ways our courts and society could make progress toward achieving *Brown*'s vision.

The commonplace claim that we are little better off than if *Brown* had not been decided is often accepted without analysis or reflection. Yet, to assess *Brown*'s legacy, we must remember what the situation was like before its decree in the seventeen southern states with legally mandated school segregation. Most Americans today were not even alive during this period and many have an inadequate understanding of its history.

Not only did black and white students attend absolutely separate schools—in 1954, only .001 percent of African-American students in the South attended majority white schools[2]—but these separate schools were also far from the *Plessy* mandate of "separate but equal." In 1954, Henry Ashmore's book, *The Negro and the Schools*, summarized the findings of forty-five scholars, the culmination of a Ford Foundation-funded project to carefully examine the South's segregated schools. Although this volume deliberately did not address the question of whether schools should be integrated, it found that separate was hardly equal in the Jim Crow South. For example, in Mississippi, per-student expenditures for black schools in 1952 were only 30 percent of those for white schools. In the South as a whole, the efforts to equalize spending in anticipation of the NAACP litigation campaign had been more successful: funding for black students was 70 percent of the white level by 1952. Teacher salaries and even the number of books in the school libraries showed similar disparities.[3] Even if funding had been equalized, of course, making up for a history of unequal facilities, teacher training, curriculum, and other aspects found in black schools would have been a vast task.

Crowded Segregated Classroom (1940s)

It is vital to remember that at the time of *Brown*, only one-fourth of black students were even completing high school. Not only were the achievement gaps huge, but also they represented gaps between the white population and only a selective group of the most fortunate blacks who were attending schools. Further, equalized funding would not have conferred upon blacks the benefits of being on the powerful side of the color line in a color-stratified society. In short, progress toward equalization was triggered by the threat of desegregation, and even then it was extremely partial and belated.[4]

Though the results of *Brown* in the first decade were quite limited, eventually executive branch intervention and a series of firm Supreme Court decisions gave the decision more enforceable contours. The initial *Brown* decisions established a strange kind of right—undefined, subject to local variation, and gradual application. However, the goals and efforts to establish deadlines, and to create effective implementation strategies led to a huge increase in desegregation after the mid-1960s. By 1970, the South had the most integrated schools of any region in the country.[5]

The height of the Civil Rights era witnessed a major reduction in the black-white achievement gap and large increases in high school graduation levels and college enrollment for black students. Yet through the 1970s and 1980s, progress toward integration slowed in the South, and the courts had limited impact on racial patterns outside the South. Since the late 1980s, there have been steady declines in desegregation, and black students are more segregated from white students than they have been in almost three decades.[6] Despite the current resegregation, our schools—and society—are still much more integrated than in the pre-*Brown* era. But the segregation levels in the southern and border states are nowhere near what they were in the 1950s. Only one-eighth of the black students in the South today, for example, are in the 99–100 percent minority schools that dominated the South in those earlier days.

The story for Latinos, who have rarely been the focus of legal or policy desegregation efforts, is very different. Their right to integration was not recognized until *Keyes v. School District No. 1,*

Interior of Near Empty School Bus
Only five students ride from a mostly white elementary school in the San Fernando Valley to a mostly Chicano school in eastern Los Angeles. The bus was to take approximately 80 students, but only these five chose to be bused. (1978)

Denver, Colorado, 413 U.S. 189 (1973). That decision was never enforced by the federal Office for Civil Rights and produced few court orders. As a result of legal inaction and a demographic tidal wave of immigrants, Latino segregation has consistently risen since the late 1960s. The intense segregation of Latinos by race and poverty (and sometimes by language) has gained greater significance at a time when Latino public school students now are almost equal in number to African-Americans, and even more segregated than black students. The disparities are projected to grow dramatically as the Latino population increases.

Since the late 1960s, there has been a growing diversity of public school students. In the late 1960s, four-fifths of all students were white, and most non-white students in southern states where desegregation plans were implemented were black. Thus, most plans concentrated on desegregating black students into majority white schools and systems. There was an explosion of Latino students in the last third of the twentieth century, almost quadrupling in size from 1967 to 2000. The public school enrollment in 2000 was about 15 percent Latino. The Census Bureau projects that in 2050 little more than 40 percent of American school-age population will be white. This is not because of a shift of students to private schools. Non-public schools serve a smaller share of students now than when *Brown* was decided. Instead, much of these changes are due to low white birth rates and continued Latino immigration.

Developing the Law of *Brown*
What Do We Mean by *Brown v. Board of Education*?

Before we assess the impact of *Brown*, we have to define what we mean. In this discussion, it means the law as developed by the Supreme Court in the two decades after the initial decision. For the first fourteen years, that law was developed by the Warren Court, which included several justices who had decided the original *Brown* cases. Vastly more attention has focused on the original 1954 and 1955 rulings than on the Court's four major decisions spelling out specific requirements and deadlines, or on the Court's three decisions of the 1990s limiting and reversing desegregation. These sets of decisions have had far more dramatic short-term impacts than the early decisions, which were quite explicitly defining policies, not writing them into specific enforceable requirements. The subsequent decisions, beginning with *Green v. County School Board of New Kent County* in 1968 and the administrative enforcement of the 1964 Civil Rights Act, transformed the schools of the South into the nation's most integrated educational institutions after 1970. After two decades in which courts defined the meaning of *Brown* there was a period of relative stability of the law for another two decades until 1991.

The Reagan administration strongly argued that desegregation remedies as a result of *Brown* were temporary and that school systems should be permitted to return to segregated schools under neighborhood assignment plans, so long as segregation was not the explicit goal of the policy. That understanding of *Brown* was written into constitutional law beginning in 1991 with *Board of Education of Oklahoma City v. Dowell*. Since that decision by the Supreme Court permitting resegregation of Oklahoma City schools, schools have resegregated at a much faster rate than they desegregated in the first decade after *Brown*.[7] We have not returned to the pre-*Brown* degree of segregation, but we are going consistently backward, and the progress since 1970 has now been lost. Both the cases defining *Brown* and the recent cases limiting and reversing desegregation have had very large impacts.

The Failure of Initial Judicial Restraint

The history of school desegregation shows that, in the face of strong local resistance, judicial restraint failed, and the failure to enforce the law may well have emboldened the opposition. The original 1954 decision sweepingly condemned school segregation but said nothing at all about how to actually change it. Instead, a year later—in a decision that no one celebrates—the 1955 *Brown II* decision left the remedies up to federal district judges, directing them to act with "all deliberate speed." The Court did not specify what was required of school systems until the late 1960s.[8] Although *Brown* had a great deal of symbolic impact on the Civil Rights movement of the 1950s and 1960s, it originally had little influence on the segregated schools it declared unequal. Ninety-eight percent of black students in the South were still attending entirely black schools a decade after *Brown*.[9]

Most district judges in the South, who were themselves products of segregation and appointed by segregationist senators, resisted ordering significant remedial action as long as possible in the absence of clear directives from the Supreme Court, encouraging emphasis on the "deliberate" rather than the "speed" of the Court's 1955 directive.[10] Desegregation crept along an irregular path for the decade it was left up to the courts with no external support, or perhaps more accurately, in the face of significant external resistance. Virtually every major elected official in the South joined the opposition. The result was to make a hard problem much harder, to eliminate any chance for real discussion about how to implement *Brown*, and to create the need for explosive confrontations in order to prevent total defiance of the law.[11]

Defining What Desegregation Requires

The first significant breakthroughs came a decade after *Brown*. One was passage of the 1964 Civil Rights Act, which authorized the Justice Department to enter school desegregation cases on the side of black plaintiffs and civil rights groups. Another was authorization of monetary sanctions by the Elementary and Secondary Education Act in 1965, which increased pressure on school districts to comply with school desegregation as a condition of federal funding.

Fourteen years after *Brown*, the Supreme Court finally began to specify in *Green* and subsequent decisions the scope of a school board's duty, the limits of federal judicial authority, and the goals and objectives to achieve desegregation as required by the Constitution. In *Green*, the Court imposed an affirmative duty on southern school boards that had previously operated a racially segregated, or dual, school system to "take whatever steps might be necessary to convert to a unitary system in which racial discrimination would be eliminated root and branch."[12] The Court also specified six factors to assist district judges in devising desegregation plans: facilities, staff, faculty, extracurricular activities, transportation, and student assignments.[13] These six *Green* factors not only were the first clear description of what the Court intended desegregation to achieve and how the racial identifiability of schools must end, but also later served to measure the effectiveness of a district's constitutional compliance.

Three years later, under a new chief justice appointed by President Richard Nixon, the Court continued to expand the discretion of federal courts to define and enforce school desegregation remedies. To counter school districts' plans that relied on high levels of residential segregation to maintain segregated schools, a unanimous Court authorized judges to use a variety of remedial tools that included establishing racial goals (but not rigid quotas) for student populations in each school; faculty and staff racial ratios; pairing geographically dispersed neighborhoods within the district in order to achieve these goals; and using cross-town busing or other means of transportation to facilitate desegregation.[14] Finally, in *Keyes*, the Court accepted the need for district-wide remedies outside the South and, significantly, extended desegregation rights to Latinos. These decisions were enforced in the face of President Nixon's sustained attack on the courts and on school desegregation orders.

This series of Supreme Court decisions made a substantial impact. By 1968, 23 percent of black students in the South attended majority white schools—a tremendous improvement in only a few years, likely due to the impact of the 1964 Civil Rights Act. This percentage of black students in such schools increased to 36 percent in 1972, following both *Green* and *Swann v. Charlotte-Mecklenburg Board of Education*, and continued to rise until the late 1980s.[15] The percentage of black students in intensely segregated (0–10 percent white) schools in the South fell rapidly and dramatically in this period.

Before the Court had defined the meaning of the law in the South, both the executive branch and some of the lower courts had given content to the *Brown* decisions. The fact that *Green* came at the end of the Warren Court and was supported by all of the justices still serving who had decided *Brown* is a clear sign that the 1968 decision reflected the evolving meaning of its doctrine. By that time, the Court was aided by fourteen years of experience and the development of legal principles from countless local decisions, the wisdom of the experts in the federal education agency, the appellate judges of the South, and the findings of the U.S. Commission of Civil Rights and other experts about the desegregation process.

Children Coming from Bus
White and African American children come up a flight of stairs from the school bus on the first day of school desegregation in Berkeley, California. (1968)

The Court had the basis for creating workable policy, it did so clearly, and the decisions made a large difference for a long time. The cases beginning with *Brown* eventually produced a profound integrationist policy that initially succeeded in ending apartheid in southern schools, thus making the South the most integrated area in the country. The Court also was instrumental in challenging—if not resolving—the still unresolved issues of urban desegregation and the profoundly unequal and segregated educational opportunities available to Latinos. The Civil Rights revolution was greatly aided by the 1964 Civil Rights Act, administrative enforcement, and changes in public attitudes, but the courts played a very important role and many of the resulting changes were deep and durable.

How Does Segregation Harm Students? How Can Integration Help?

Much of the social science relied upon in *Brown* was about the psychological damage produced by segregation. The Court also relied heavily on its earlier higher education decisions, which were about social networks, mutual misunderstanding, and other lifetime effects of imposed racial separation. As the years have passed, social scientists and educators have developed a much broader understanding of segregation's harms and the possible benefits of desegregation.

Contemporary segregation, for example, is not just by race but also by income. Ninety percent of intensely segregated black and Latino schools have concentrated poverty. These conditions of racial and economic isolation are connected with many forms of unequal educational opportunities and results—such as less well-prepared peer groups, less qualified teachers, less advanced curricula, more health and social problems for the school to cope with, and higher student turnover.[16] Adding to schools' burdens are the various examination and accountability structures that blame the children (and their teachers) for their lower test scores, while ignoring the very different conditions of these schools and the resources they actually need.

In addition to preventing the damage that comes from racially separate schools, desegregation is also seen as benefiting students in racially diverse classes. Decades of social science research has shown that racially integrated classrooms result in higher academic achievement for minorities, higher educational and occupational aspirations, greater access to integrated social networks, increased desire to live, work, and attend schools and colleges in multiracial environments, and foster positive social interactions across racial lines.[17] The benefits of integrated schools accrue to both minority and white students in these schools.

Nothing in *Brown* says that desegregated schools will immediately solve all problems or will equalize all results after centuries of discrimination—no reform has accomplished such lofty goals. Rather, the decision holds only that segregated schools are inherently unequal and therefore violate the constitutional rights of black students. Desegregation, as Dr. King recognized, is merely a first step toward the much more profound change of integration—the transformation of an institution into one that is genuinely fair, with equal treatment and respect for all groups.[18] *Brown*, and the integration campaign more generally, represents one part of what must be a broader attack on inequality in the society. The Supreme Court's 1968 *Green* decision spelled out the kind of comprehensive transformation of entire school systems that could facilitate such changes by requiring the desegregation of many different aspects of its operations.[19]

Are There Harms of Desegregation? Claims of White Flight

The impact of white opposition has long been a theme of school desegregation discussions, beginning with the Court's worries about southern backlash to the original *Brown* decisions. Although, as discussed below, comprehensive plans have proven the most likely to produce substantial and long-lasting integration, that is not to deny their role in encouraging at least some white flight. However, if the most wide-reaching plans produce the most positive and stable results, then clearly much of their opponents' criticism is off-target and the policy implications are quite different.

Beginning with a 1975 study by Professor James Coleman, claiming that school desegregation plans were futile because they simply led to white abandonment of schools and a return to segregation,[20] there has been a long battle of researchers and advocates over the claim that desegregation was self-defeating. The basic finding of the Coleman study was that when the proportion of minority students in a predominantly white school rose, the white enrollment was likely to fall at a rate faster than the previous trend. The widely publicized opposition to desegregation argued that this meant that well-intentioned desegregation efforts only sped the loss of white students and families.

Early white-flight research showed that the maximum decline in white enrollment came in desegregation plans that sent white students to traditionally black schools in metropolitan areas where there were overwhelmingly white suburbs nearby. That is, in fact, what Justice Thurgood Marshall predicted in his dissent from the Supreme Court's 1974 decision limiting desegregation to the central cities of metropolitan areas and isolating the suburban rings. Marshall noted that even before desegregation, Detroit was losing white students faster than any other major district, something likely to be accelerated by a plan limited to the city. "Thus," he said, "even if a plan were adopted . . . such a system would, in short order, devolve into an all-Negro system."[21] Many big-city desegregation plans have been rendered largely meaningless over time by the continuing decline in white enrollment.

It is also true, however, that the decline in white enrollment in central cities has been going on for half a century. It happens before, during, and after desegregation plans. It has run its course to an almost total loss of white students in districts that never had desegregation plans, and it has had similar effects in cities that were among the first to abandon them, such as Atlanta and Los Angeles, which decided against desegregation partially due to concerns about white flight.

The most recent major study of this issue, Charles Clotfelter's 2004 book, *After Brown: The Rise and Retreat of School Desegregation*,[22] concludes that white enrollment declines as black enrollment rises, and that the decrease is more rapid after the black enrollment nears 50 percent. There has been survey research of white attitudes by the Gallup Polls since the 1950s that shows whites much more resistant to school integration plans in schools with more than half minority students, and that resistance to such plans has remained high while acceptance of other levels of integration has greatly increased. One could cite this research either to show that high levels of integration prompt opposition, which is true, or that, therefore, nothing can be done without making things worse, which is false.

The most stable plans, in fact, are the kind that the Supreme Court's 5-4 decision made almost impossible—plans where city and suburban schools are simultaneously desegregated in a way that leaves almost all students in a majority white, predominantly middle-class school. Although such plans stir great public resistance when they are proposed, they produce a kind of desegregation which is much more acceptable, has stronger educational benefits, and is far more stable than the limited plans. A 1987 study of white flight prepared for the U.S. Commission on Civil Rights showed that metropolitan plans achieved by far the highest level of desegregation and were the most stable.[23]

Obviously, the basic causes of white flight are outside the schools, especially in the housing markets and subsidized housing policies. For half a century after the black exodus from the South to the urban North began in earnest, there were few stably integrated neighborhoods, and schools often went through rapid racial transitions as the demographics of neighborhoods changed. Neighborhood school patterns can be highly unstable since neighborhood racial boundaries often shift rapidly. But it is also true that the patterns can be accelerated by desegregation plans.

In fact, the school racial change was often far more rapid and complete than the corresponding residential change because minority families moving out from ghettos and barrios tended to be young, have more children, and use public schools at a higher rate than whites. Since the U.S. is a very mobile society, where the average family relocates every six years, the unwillingness of whites to move into neighborhoods with overwhelmingly minority schools can contribute to the rapid ghettoization of a community. Some whites avoid even moderately integrated schools, and many more are reluctant to have their children in schools where most of the children are from minority groups.

If desegregation is an important goal, it seems clear that the best approach for duration and relative stability is to include as much of the housing market area as possible in desegregation plans and to be as equitable as possible in the racial composition of schools. What experience has shown is that white resistance to desegregation experiences is less an absolute opposition to desegregation than an unwillingness to have children in a racially changing or overwhelmingly nonwhite school, the two basic forms of desegregation in central cities after the key Supreme Court decisions.

The courts can play a truly decisive role because the political system is organized in a way that fragments and divides local governments along lines of race and class. In order to do so, it is essential that judges consider the relationships involving the racial identifiability of neighborhoods and schools. In ordering more drastic remedies to create substantial desegregation, Chief Justice Burger, writing for a unanimous Court, noted that "people gravitate toward school facilities . . . the location of schools may thus influence the patterns of residential development of a metropolitan area and have an important impact on composition of inner-city neighborhoods."[24]

Twenty years later, Justice Kennedy's majority opinion in *Freeman v. Pitts* held that "in the absence of a showing that either the school authorities or some other agency of the State has deliberately attempted to fix or alter demographic patterns to affect the racial composition of the schools, further intervention by a district court should not be necessary."[25] This assumption ignores the more nuanced relationship of housing and school segregation acknowledged in *Swann* and *Keyes* and supported by empirical research. In fact, existing patterns of residential segregation could well be due, in part, to the limited nature of school desegregation.

Why are we going backwards?
The Reverses Are Not from Changing Public Desires.

A remarkable fact is that amidst this vacuum of positive leadership on desegregation issues and the succession of court decisions in the 1990s reversing and limiting desegregation requirements, public opinion has not turned against school integration efforts. Many people assume that because large school districts are ending their desegregation plans, it must mean that public opinion has shifted.

Desegregation was not voluntary in the first place and was not something that large districts chose to do: all but one of our major cities had to be forced to desegregate by either a court or a civil rights enforcement agency. However, following desegregation, public resistance declined and public support grew, though white resistance to mandatory student reassignment in urban areas remained high. By 1961, 63 percent of Americans approved of the *Brown* decision, although this differed by region: only 24 percent of southerners approved at the time (yet 76 percent of southerners thought that the South would someday become integrated).[26] Forty years after the *Brown* decision, 87 percent of the public approved of the decision.[27]

Most desegregation plans since 1980 have relied heavily on voluntary choice through magnet schools, which offer special educational options, a method of desegregation that has far more public support than mandatory reassignment. In any case, nearly three in five Americans questioned in 1999 by the Gallup Poll believed that more should be done to integrate the schools. A large majority believed that desegregation improved education for black students, and half of the public said that this was true for whites as well. Additionally, a larger percentage of the public identified the public schools as the institution that could do the most to improve race relations—more than any other institution.[28] Resegregation began in a time when the desegregation issue had been long settled in many communities and there was no public protest movement of any size requesting a return to segregated schools.

Some Major "Failures" of Desegregation Are Actually the Product of Unworkable Principles in Supreme Court Decisions.

Desegregation critics often point to the spread of segregation after court orders as clear evidence that court-ordered desegregation is impossible. Recent studies have found that school segregation is actually on the rise, both for Latino students and, reversing a two-decade trend of increasing desegregation, for African-American students.[29] What critics ignore is that court orders are not inherently failures; rather, the success of school desegregation depends on what kinds of plans are devised. Although there are several contributing factors, Supreme Court decisions from the mid-1970s onward have drastically limited the ability of school systems and federal courts to devise strategies for substantial and lasting integration. Even worse, they have sometimes sped resegregation by creating foreseeably counterproductive plans.

Part of the problem is that the courts often rely on factually erroneous assumptions and that very few legal commentators look systematically at the long-term results of desegregation. Two central decisions of the post-Civil Rights era seem to epitomize this tendency: *Milliken v. Bradley* and *Missouri v. Jenkins*.

In 1974, in *Milliken v. Bradley*, the Court first limited the remedies available in school desegregation cases.[30] A 5-4 majority, including the four Nixon appointees, ruled that suburban areas could not be part of the area incorporated into a city's desegregation plan unless each suburb had contributed directly to segregation within the city. This decision effectively ended the ability to integrate students across metropolitan areas by isolating districts in heavily white suburbs from central city districts that were predominantly minority. In a scathing dissent, Justice Marshall predicted that this was a "giant step backward."[31] The impact of the *Milliken* decision when combined with *San Antonio Independent School District v. Rodriguez*,[32] the decision the previous year against equalizing funding, meant that desegregation would not create substantial integration outside of the South, given the residential and school system patterns in many non-southern metropolitan areas. As a consequence, these central city school districts would become ever more racially and economically isolated.

The *Milliken* decision presumed that the relationship of housing to school segregation could safely be ignored in an area with one of the most intensely segregated housing markets in the nation; that desegregation could somehow be accomplished within the boundaries of a three-fourths black and rapidly changing school district; and that it made no difference if the remedy excluded all the nearby middle-class white schools, which would be an easy refuge for whites who wanted to leave the city.

In fact, the decision ignored the reality that we were a nation of metropolitan areas in which most aspects of life were organized on a metropolitan basis. Nearly four-fifths (77.8 percent) of the U.S. population lived in metropolitan areas in 1990.[33] By 1993, only 10.9 percent of black students and 5.1 percent of Latino students attended non-metropolitan public schools.[34] *Milliken* assumed, in other words, a world that simply did not exist.

The social impact of the *Milliken* decision on segregated education and the irrationality of the assumption by the Supreme Court majority that desegregation could be achieved within the boundaries of the city of Detroit are apparent today, showing Justice Marshall's prescience in his 1974 dissent. In 1992–1993, 70.3 percent of metropolitan Detroit's African-American students attended schools with 0–10 percent whites, a rate surpassed only by metropolitan Chicago. By 2000, white students comprised fewer than 4 percent of the Detroit public school district enrollment. In contrast, a number of southern and border-state metropolitan areas with countywide desegregation plans had 0–2 percent of African-Americans in intensely segregated schools.[35]

In fact, although court decisions had a major impact on the integration of black students in the South by 1970, the integration of their counterparts in the Northeast and Midwest were hampered by later court decisions. Most black students in the Midwest—because of residential segregation and black migration to the biggest labor markets—were in the public schools of just two cities, Detroit and Chicago, and were rendered permanently segregated by the *Milliken* doctrine. It was not an accident that Michigan and Illinois (together with New York) became—and still remain—the most segregated states in the Union for black students throughout the post-*Milliken* period.

In Detroit, despite strong findings of constitutional violations and despite the Supreme Court's order to desegregate within the impoverished, largely black, and increasingly poor school system, none of the federal judges who handled the case thought that more than very limited desegregation was possible; this was a district where whites were a small and rapidly declining minority.

After the Supreme Court rejected the city-suburban desegregation plan that the district court and court of appeals had said was the only feasible remedy, the trial court ordered the state instead to pay for some educational programs intended to repair the "harms of segregation."

In effect, these judges were willing to settle for a version of the *Plessy* doctrine that the Court had rejected almost twenty-five years earlier. The Court's majority implicitly conceded that they were dealing with separate but equal remedies when they supported this decision in *Milliken II* in 1977.[36] After twelve years of reading and other programs, however, the school system was almost all black, there was almost no desegregation, and the courts ended the educational remedies without any evidence that they had cured the inequalities. The presiding district judge said that the money was just too little to make any impact on a school system in very serious decline.[37] By the early 1990s, metropolitan Detroit had the second-most segregated schools in the U.S. Many of those schools that were supposed to have been equalized by the *Milliken II* remedy are now judged to be failing schools under the No Child Left Behind Act.

Following the mandate of *Milliken I* and *II*, a district court judge in Kansas City, Missouri—an area with few white students—devised a remedy to improve the quality of inner-city schools. The goal was to attract students from the suburban white suburbs and private schools. However, when the court agreed that it was important to look at the test scores of the black students to see whether they had been helped by the remedies, the state objected and was eventually sustained by the Supreme Court in 1995.

Writing a generation after *Milliken* with a Court remade by conservative appointees, a majority of the justices held that such voluntary remedies should be temporary and limited and emphasized the importance of state and local control.[38] The "local control" given to Kansas City was the freedom to cut its enrichment programs drastically after the money was withdrawn. In the majority opinion, the new standard for compliance with school desegregation was whether the defendant had complied in good faith with the desegregation order and whether the vestiges of past discrimination had been eliminated to the extent practical.[39] Chief Justice Rehnquist shifted the burden for continued judicial oversight from defendant school boards to plaintiffs to show that continuing racial disparities in the district are related to prior *de jure* actions by the school board. It also gave the district court considerable discretion in determining whether further elimination of segregation is "practicable"—which skeptical judges often conclude is not possible.

Voluntary Desegregation

Voluntary desegregation through choice programs has been important throughout the last half-century. There was actually very little choice in American school assignment until the South responded to *Brown* with plans that permitted a limited number of black students to transfer to white schools under strict conditions. These "freedom of choice" policies were common in thousands of southern school districts in the 1950s and 1960s. The courts initially welcomed this approach as a way to "desegregate" without compelling any disruptive change or requiring any white students or teachers to change schools. Under this policy, black schools remained completely segregated and very small numbers of black students transferred. Much of the reason had to do with the social pressure that was often brought to bear against black families who wanted to transfer; many transferring students experienced isolation and discrimination, even violence, as unwelcome outsiders in predominantly white schools.

By the time the 1964 Civil Rights Act was passed, requiring all institutions receiving federal aid to end discrimination, it was obvious that unrestricted choice would leave segregated systems largely intact. As a result, in the first year of implementing the new law, the School Desegregation Guidelines began to insert major civil rights protections into choice mechanisms, including requirements of adequate transportation, information about choices, and guarantees of choice to all applicants. These requirements, along with more stringent implementation standards, accelerated southern desegregation; however, the policy of "freedom of choice" still left all-black schools virtually untouched. Whites would not willingly choose to transfer to black schools, which usually lacked many of the resources of their white schools, and few white schools had more than very small black enrollments.

The Supreme Court decided in 1968 that choice was not enough to comply with *Brown* and that districts must take all feasible means to actually fully integrate as many schools as possible throughout each district. During the mid-1970s, choice reemerged as a basic principle of urban desegregation planning, usually in the form of magnet schools with many civil rights protections and explicit desegregation standards regulating their enrollment. By the 1980s, almost all new desegregation plans included important elements of choice, and thousands of magnet schools emerged.

The movement of the policy from accepting choice without success (freedom of choice), to conditioning choice on civil rights standards (1964 Civil Rights Act), to saying choice was not enough (*Green*), to accepting kinds of choice as part a of comprehensive education plan (magnet schools) came full circle in the resegregation era of the 1990s. The federal government pumped rapidly growing subsidies into choice programs—charter schools—with no civil rights require-ments and even higher levels of segregation than normal public schools.[40] The final stage of this process was a series of lower court decisions outlawing voluntary magnet school plans with deseg-regation standards, prohibiting intentional desegregation efforts in many districts, and relying on market-based mechanisms of educational choice. The result was to permit resegregation if the market drove toward racial and class stratification, as markets often do. In the districts affected by such decisions, school authorities were being required to adopt a kind of choice system with a strong tendency toward resegregation that had been forbidden in the first school guidelines forty years ago precisely because they perpetuated segregation.

Despite the resegregation trend, many school districts today strongly value their integrated magnet schools (as well as other integrated schools) and wish to continue them. This is an issue on which there is a great deal of empirical evidence both about the efficacy of various forms of choice and about the compelling interest of students of all races in maintaining substantial and lasting school integration. The goal of these magnet schools would seem to be a "compelling inter-est" as defined in the University of Michigan Law School affirmative action case. Writing for the majority, Justice O'Connor affirmed the importance of racially diverse schools in preparing stu-dents for citizenship: "This Court has long recognized that 'education . . . is the very foundation of good citizenship.' *Brown v. Board of Education,* 347 U.S. 483, 493 (1954). For this reason, the dif-fusion of knowledge must be accessible to all individuals regardless of race or ethnicity. Effective participation by members of all racial and ethnic groups in the civic life of our Nation is essential if the dream of one Nation, indivisible, is to be realized."[41] An earlier 2003 decision by the feder-al district court in Lynn, Massachusetts, clearly found such a compelling interest in a choice-driv-en desegregation approach; in the court's view, creating diverse schools was fully compatible with constitutional requirements, even in a district not under a desegregation court order.

Desegregation Depends on the Size and/or Type of Districts

The implications of limiting desegregation to single districts are significant in our metropolitan society with extremely different forms of local government and school districting systems. In fact, the very different structure of school districts in various states has produced a kind of natural experiment. In parts of the South and West, the county is the basic unit of government and school systems. Often a single school district includes what would be elsewhere both the central city and most of the suburban enrollment, as well as most of the regional housing market. Older urban complexes of the West and Midwest tend to include many small independent municipalities and school districts within a metropolitan housing market.

The South and West have many longstanding black or Latino communities that formed well before the metropolitan area expanded to embrace them. In the industrial North, the city boundaries were usually fixed well before the automobile age and modern freeways led to the rapid growth of the metropolitan area, yet the great bulk of the minority community is often concentrated in the central city and its separate school system. Sometimes the deep fragmentation is intensified by large systems of independent charter schools, which tend to be highly segregated. A few central cities even have multiple school districts. Other areas offer a wide variety of combinations of central city, satellite city, and average size school districts.

The fact that the Supreme Court made it relatively easy to win a comprehensive district-wide desegregation order but almost impossible to cross district lines meant that different desegregation experiences occurred in otherwise similar metropolitan regions. Thus, a court order directing a district to desegregate within its own boundaries can produce either a sweeping transformation of school racial composition, relatively evenly, across an entire housing market, or a plan that would combine a very small share of relatively impoverished whites with large minority enrollments, leaving the white suburbs almost totally segregated. In greater Boston, for example, in 2001, the public schools served only 2 percent of the region's white students but about half of the blacks; a plan limited to the city would be totally irrelevant to 98 percent of white students and would provide access for black and Latino students to almost none of the region's excellent high schools, which send students to all of the nation's elite colleges.[42]

In short, experience with various forms of desegregation plans shows that, contrary to critics' concerns, the metro-wide plans produced by far the highest level of desegregation and were far more stable than the city-only plans often favored by the courts.

Exposure of Blacks to Whites in Districts with Various Desegregation Plans[1]						
District	1988	2000		District	1988	2000
Busing within city				**All/Part Plan Dismissed**		
Columbus, OH	47.9	26.0		Los Angeles, CA	11.0	8.0
Cleveland, OH	21.7	9.7		Dallas, TX	11.3	5.1
Minneapolis, MN	51.8	20.9		Norfolk, VA	31.6	24.0
Denver, CO	34.9	19.4		Oklahoma City, OK	33.7	20.6
Boston, MA	20.4	11.2		Austin, TX	32.3	19.3
				Washington, D.C.	1.5	2.1

District	1988	2000	District	1988	2000
Magnet Plans			**City-Suburban**		
Kansas City, KS	19.6	10.4	Indianapolis, IN	46.7	27.2
Milwaukee, WI	29.9	13.1	Broward County, FL	36.1	23.7
Cincinnati, OH	29.1	16.7	Hillsborough County, FL	58.5	39.5
Philadelphia, PA	11.6	8.7	Clark County, FL	64.4	40.2
Chicago, IL	4.8	3.0	Nashville, TN	52.3	41.1
Busing, Magnet, Voluntary Suburban			Duval County, FL	44.1	36.0
St. Louis, MO	14.8	13.2	**Court Rejected City-Suburban**		
No Plan			Detroit, MI	6.0	2.1
New York, NY	9.8	6.6	Houston, TX	10.1	6.3
Atlanta, GA	3.9	3.0	Richmond, VA	9.5	5.5
Baltimore, MD	9.4	5.9			
DeKalb County, GA	23.4	7.4			

¹All classification of desegregation plans are by what type of plan they had in 1988. Many of these districts are no longer operating under any desegregation plan. Source: *Race in American Public Schools: Rapidly Resegregating School Districts*

Interestingly enough, the first court-ordered busing approved by the Supreme Court came in a metro district, Charlotte-Mecklenburg, North Carolina, over three decades ago. Such plans held whites in these districts much better, for example, than urban districts that did nothing to desegregate their schools or that abandoned desegregation plans for neighborhood schools. The consequences of these different approaches are painfully apparent in the destiny of two large school districts directly touched by major Supreme Court decisions—Charlotte in the 1971 *Swann* decision and Detroit in the 1974 *Milliken* decision. The Charlotte district covered all of Mecklenburg County as a result of a merger years before desegregation took place. In more than thirty years under the *Swann* decision, Charlotte never had a black majority and had very few intensely segregated schools in any part of the county. White and black children often spent their entire school careers together in the same feeder system; all their schools were integrated at high levels.

After an initial period of strong local conflict over the court-ordered remedy, a community movement in Charlotte resulted in the redesign of the desegregation plan in a more effective and acceptable mode. In the late 1980s and early 1990s, as courts elsewhere were moving toward ending desegregation plans, Charlotte-Mecklenburg elected officials who continued to support desegregation. When its desegregation plan was challenged in the 1990s, the district took the extraordinary step of admitting its continuing need to equalize opportunity. Unfortunately for the future of desegregation in the region, lower federal courts subsequently ordered the district to end its desegregation plan on the grounds that it was no longer needed. The district then returned to neighborhood schools, which very rapidly produced substantial segregation and has been strongly linked to unequal educational outcomes.[43]

Detroit's school desegregation process was vastly different, as discussed earlier. The experience of these two districts illustrates the very high cost of limiting desegregation to single central-city districts. Black students in Detroit went all the way to the Supreme Court twice, obtained orders that in theory gave them both integration and then educational compensation, but ended up with disastrous levels of segregation and inequality. The Detroit story under *Milliken II*, like the history of nearly four decades of federal preschool and Title I programs, makes clear that compensatory funds have a limited ability to close performance gaps associated with segregation. There is absolutely no reason to think that merely providing more money for a few years will make a substantial difference in a stratified society.

In Charlotte, a single order produced a third of a century of high levels of desegregation and a community commitment to continue the plan, a commitment frustrated only by the intervention of the lower federal courts and the refusal of the Supreme Court to review their decisions. Ironically, the courts are continuing the basic policies applied to Detroit and destroying the partial but very real success achieved in Charlotte. Yet, the basic social science message of these experiences is the opposite: if you want to desegregate, a comprehensive strategy is better; and equalization is a very long process even in a school district which is, comparatively, quite progressive. It seems very clear in both of these cases that the injuries of segregation (whether *de facto* or *de jure*) cannot be cured by limited efforts.

Part of the problem is that, since *Milliken*, the tendency is to take district boundaries as basic, unalterable social facts. This tendency reflects deep social, political, and constitutional traditions of localism in American education. In fact, however, districts are creatures of state law; voters and their elected officials can readily alter educational boundaries.[44] There has been a vast decline in the number of districts in the U.S. since the early twentieth century because of the consolidation movement, which used state pressure and incentives to merge districts that seemed too small to offer quality education. Although at least one state supreme court has found district boundaries to be a violation of the civil rights of minority students, the prevailing approach is to avoid remedies that cross district borders.[45] Even though statistics clearly show that the roots of traditional segregation are segregation between districts, not within them, *Milliken* has virtually ended the discussion of the racially stratifying effects of district boundaries. This self-imposed limitation has had devastating consequences for racial integration, particularly in large metropolitan areas.

The Courts' Role
Courts Not Using Their Capacity to Improve Results

Some frustration with desegregation plans is attributable to poor design, administration, and enforcement. Needless to say, most judges lack relevant expertise and it is unrealistic to expect grossly underfunded and overburdened civil rights attorneys to know what is happening on the ground and to seek corrective action. In fact, courts have the machinery to ensure better results but generally do not use it, instead relying on a traditional adversary system that can rarely do the job.

Legal scholars often differentiate these "public law" proceedings from the standard litigation resolving disputes between private parties, which usually produces a specific remedy, such as monetary damages. Public law litigation, on the other hand, concerns a disagreement about public policy or a violation of constitutional principles. It typically involves numerous parties and potential parties; remedies that are systemic and prospective and often affect many who are not participants in the lawsuit. In such cases, the judge's role is less the passive arbitrator than the active manager of the development of the case and the implementation of the remedy.[46]

How well overburdened trial judges perform this role has been subject to longstanding debate. Many commentaries from conservative, neoconservative, and even Critical Race Studies perspectives claim that little has been accomplished and that little good can be expected.[47] The issues are intractable, the argument goes, and high hopes are bound to be disappointed. Some argue that judicial intervention is futile, even counterproductive.[48] Others have questioned the appropriateness of the judicial branch's new expanded role. Summarizing this literature, Wendy Parker writes, "Opponents of public law litigation . . . questioned the legitimacy of judges taking such an active role in shaping the litigation and deciding policy issues."[49]

In reality, judges in school desegregation cases have a wealth of expertise on which to draw, although they do not always take full advantage of the resources available. Trial courts can appoint experts as special masters, convene advisory or monitoring committees, or can press the involved parties to negotiate or draft initial decrees.[50] Needless to say, a neutral expert or committee can increase the capacity of the court to understand often confusing evidence, obtain independent data, and monitor implementation, results, and possible ways to improve compliance. Judges, however, too often attempt to manage litigation without such assistance; they rely on the parties and their own ability to reach judgments and tend to assume that all is well if no one formally challenges their decisions. Contrary to critics' frequent complaints that judges run school districts, in most long-standing cases, courts rarely, if ever, exercise such authority. Judges generally act, if at all, in more limited roles, such as bringing different parties to the table for negotiation.

In terms of legitimacy, continued judicial oversight of school systems is surely not the most ideal solution, but it is often the only one. Opponents often object that such oversight usurps power that should belong to locally elected school boards, *not* to appointed federal judges. However, this argument assumes that in the absence of judicial intervention the school board would properly protect the rights of students—which, at least at one time, the school board did not do, in violation of students' constitutional rights. If there is a need for judicial oversight, it is because the other branches of government have failed in their constitutional obligations to these students.[51] As one federal judge noted, it would be better if the other branches of government would solve the problems, but when fundamental rights are at stake, the judiciary must discharge its own responsibilities.[52] This is the essence of the rule of law. Courts are generally only too happy to yield to state and local officials if they are making a conscious effort to comply with constitutional requirements.[53] Where courts play no role, in districts that have dismantled formally segregated school systems, there is often a rapid return to separate and unequal institutions with little political will to face or even discuss these issues.[54]

Recognizing the Political Context

Decisions by the Supreme Court are often treated as if they are the inevitable outcome of logic, precedent, and fact. This perspective, however, is hard to sustain in an arena in which the judicial actions and appointments have often been very salient campaign issues in racially polarized elections. When candidates for President attack court decisions, promise to appoint different kinds of judges, explicitly oppose civil rights policies, use racially charged symbolism in their election campaigns, are opposed by an extraordinary nine-tenths of the black electorate, and appoint judges who vote to radically limit civil rights remedies, it is illusory to dismiss the role of politics in interpreting what has happened to school desegregation law.

Rehnquist Court

All of the Supreme Court's decisions on school desegregation had been unanimous for eighteen years until President Nixon was able to appoint four justices. After he named these justices, they constituted four of the five votes against equalizing school funding[55] and against including the suburbs in urban school desegregation.[56] These key decisions have played a central role in creating today's urban school crisis and the most segregated metropolitan school districts in the country.

The Court that reversed desegregation in the l990s had seven justices appointed by presidents who ran against civil rights and received very few black votes. Presidents Ronald Reagan and George H. W. Bush by the mid-1990s had also appointed 60 percent of district court judges and 70 percent of appellate judges.[57] The remaking of the courts is a much more plausible explanation of the change in policy than the discovery of new information or the lack of feasible desegregation strategies. In fact, social scientists have provided a wealth of useful research about the short- and long-term benefits of school desegregation. If one ignores the political reality and simply reasons from the principles in the decisions resulting from this judicial transformation, one may well reach a completely inaccurate understanding of the legal and policy possibilities.

Legal commentary is often weak about both the origins and effects of these decisions; too little effort has been made to connect law with social science, historical and educational policy research. The *Brown* decision made no such mistake; it relied on social science research and the history of segregated schools in concluding that imposed segregation was inherently unequal. The rationale of the higher education decisions preceding *Brown* that struck down segregation in graduate schools was similarly grounded on sociological premises about the effect of segregation on developing career networks, an important component of professional education.[58]

Recent trends in law, a heavily deductive discipline, have relied more heavily on another deductive discipline, economics, which has its own conservative bias against governmental action and in favor of market approaches to efficiency and productivity. But market strategies generally deal poorly with discrimination. Economic models too often treat private decisions that have been constrained by discrimination as if they were free choices, and therefore optimal, or at least entitled to deference. Further, most judges and legal commentators do not show real understanding about the social science research regarding the issues they are deciding. The facts they cite are often highly selective: the impressions of a trial judge or data extracted from the core of the briefs; contrary evidence is ignored or dismissed.

The Role of Judicial Enforcement

State and local officials often claim that courts and bureaucracies should not set policy, yet experience shows that elected officials will rarely respond adequately to unequal educational opportunities, given the risk of racial wedge issues and the political weakness of minorities. Too often there is a short-term gain to be made from assailing the courts and activating fears that are often present in a racially stratified society. A third of a century of political attacks on desegregation plans and orders has changed the public discourse.

Often, for example, the term "forced busing," popularized by Alabama's openly segregationist governor George Wallace, is treated as if it were a neutral term describing urban desegregation, even though it describes the policy in a way that would sound capricious and unfair to most hearers. The last two decades have witnessed little serious political discussion of positive steps toward urban desegregation and a great many attacks by conservative opponents. NAACP President Julian Bond commented at a national conference in September 2003 that in terms of speaking out on civil rights issues, the country had one party that was "shameless" and another that was "spineless."[59]

There has been no serious policy proposal in Congress for three decades to provide substantial aid even for voluntary desegregation. The repeal of the funding for the Emergency School Aid Act, federal desegregation legislation, over two decades ago brought an end to much of the research and discussion about the context in which desegregation created positive outcomes. Only one major city has ever desegregated without a court order (Seattle). Yet, resegregated districts have become increasingly unequal. In these circumstances, the importance of an independent judiciary committed to enforcing equal opportunity becomes readily apparent. All too often, rhetoric about state and local authority and judicial restraint means the loss of minority rights. In a society with unresolved issues of racial inequality running throughout its history and with clear patterns of backward as well as forward movement on racial justice, the realities and the results, not merely the theory of local democracy, demand urgent attention.

Conclusion

Brown was premised on ensuring the rights of all students as guaranteed by the Fourteenth Amendment. Since that decision promising blacks the right to gain an education equal to that of whites, our society has gone through a legal and demographic transformation. It is ironic that at a time in which we continue to learn more about the educational benefits of school desegregation and in what circumstances such benefits can be maximized, we are in a period in which desegregation is becoming more elusive and the focus by policymakers has shifted.

The decision, whose fiftieth anniversary we celebrate, reaffirms the principles upon which our country was founded: the belief that all men (and women) are created equal. *Brown* was a major step toward ensuring that all people have equal opportunities. Although *Brown* initially had little effect, and outside of the South has never had more than a limited impact, we should not construe this as meaning that the courts cannot create change or that the time for school desegregation has passed. Instead of merely celebrating *Brown* as a legal turning point, which in reality is having an increasingly reduced effect on school desegregation, we should seriously consider how we can affirm its principles and make it a reality.

The judiciary has always played an important role in recognizing the rights of minority groups, who are often marginalized by majoritarian branches of our government. When the courts recognized the rights of black students to integrated schools in 1954, and later helped specify the parameters for school desegregation, the South was transformed. Not only did schools become integrated, but *Brown* also gave inspiration to a social movement that created massive change across southern society. After twenty years, the courts began to limit their role in assuring black and Latino students of their rights. By the 1990s, the federal judiciary was signaling that school desegregation had run its course. This was not due to any systematic research evaluating school desegregation or to any major shifts in racial realities; rather, it was primarily due to a change in the ideology of federal judges and the political leaders who appointed them.

The standards that had governed school district desegregation plans for decades and created remarkable progress were exchanged for standards giving overwhelming deference to locally elected school boards. Even though the ideology of "local control" is reverently invoked by politicians and jurists alike, many aspects of education are not locally controlled (e.g., curriculum, teacher qualifications, assessments). The deference to local autonomy begs the question of why it is so essential that school boards regain control of student assignments when such a transition might easily lead to resegregated schools.

While neighborhood schools or parental choice may be advantageous when everything else is equal, in this society everything is *not* equal. As a practical matter, such approaches of local control limit the constitutional rights of children and create schools of racial and economic isolation that are widely agreed to be unequal. In *Brown* and its progeny, the Court repeatedly held that if local control resulted in segregated schools and jeopardized students' rights to equal opportunity, courts should take corrective action.

The need for such action is still pressing today. As we move further from the era of Jim Crow segregation, many school systems have been released from mandatory school desegregation orders and can only voluntarily use race (often as one of several factors) to seek a diverse student body. Even these voluntary efforts have sometimes been invalidated by the courts.[61] Few would deny that race is still a very important factor in our society, and that we have not yet reached a society that is truly color-blind. As even the most conservative circuit court in the nation, the Fourth Circuit, has noted, "to use race consciously in order to be able to teach students that people of all races have a right to equal opportunities, the sad truth is that in today's world is still necessary."[60] Even more recently, the Supreme Court observed in *Grutter,* that in our society, "race unfortunately still matters."[61] Although a variety of race-neutral alternatives have sought to promote diversity, the reality is that if we want to create racially integrated schools, the most effective and most narrowly tailored way to do so is to consider race.

It is essential that research and evidence—not ideology or assumptions—guide the future of our desegregation efforts. Research has shown that if we are to create an equal society, it is not enough to merely adjust a few educational inputs for a few years. Remedies must be comprehensive, and long lasting, and must involve entire metropolitan areas. Desegregation efforts must involve housing as well as schools. We must learn from our failures. We must take into account the reality of today's multiracial society. Finally, we must acknowledge the significance of unequal opportunity in our society. Although many attacks on civil rights policies claim that race-conscious policies prevent us from being a truly color-blind society, these policies are still necessary in a nation with high levels of residential segregation coupled with concentrations of poverty. The rhetoric of a free market color-blind society ignores the remnants of centuries of discrimination. We must recognize this reality if we are to create the society that we one day hope to achieve.

[1]   Secretary of Education Rod Paige, Remarks at the American Enterprise Institute (Jan 7, 2004).

[2]   E. Frankenberg, C. Lee, & G. Orfield, *A Multiracial Society with Segregated Schools: Are We Losing the Dream?*, Cambridge, MA: The Civil Rights Project at Harvard University (2003).

[3]   Harry S. Ashmore, *The Negroes and the Schools*, Chapel Hill, NC: The University of North Carolina Press (1954), tables 8–15.

[4]   Ibid, p. 51.

[5]   Frankenberg, Lee, and Orfield, *supra* note 2.

[6]   Ibid.

[7]   G. Orfield & C. Lee, *Brown at 50: King's Dream or Plessy's Nightmare?*, Cambridge, MA: The Civil Rights Project at Harvard University (January 2004). *Bd. of Educ. of Oklahoma City v. Dowell*, 498 U.S. 237 (1991).

[8]   *Cooper v. Aaron*, 358 U.S. 1 (1958); *Griffin v. County School Board of Prince Edward County*, 377 U.S. 218 (1964) (holding that "the time for mere 'deliberate speed' has run out" but no specifics as to what a district's constitutional obligations were).

[9]   Orfield & Lee, *supra* note 7.

[10] J.W. Peltason, *Fifty-eight Lonely Men: Southern Federal Judges and School Desegregation*, New York: Harcourt, Brace, & World (1961).

[11] Daisy Bates, *The Long Shadow of Little Rock*, New York: David McKay Company (1962); Reed Sarratt, *The Ordeal of Desegregation: The First Decade*. New York: Harper and Row, 1966.

[12] *Green v. County School Board*, 391 U.S. 430, 437-8 (1968).

[13] *Id.*, at 435.

[14] *Swann v. Charlotte-Mecklenburg Bd. of Educ.*, 402 U.S. 1, 22-31 (1971).

[15] Orfield & Lee, *supra* note 7.

[16] *Condition of Education 1997*, Washington, D.C.: National Center for Education Statistics 97-991, 1997.

[17] E.g., J.H. Braddock II, "The Perpetuation of Segregation across Levels of Education: A Behavioral Assessment of the Contact-Hypothesis," *Sociology of Education* 53, (3), 178–186 (1980); J.W. Schofield, "Review of Research on School Desegregation's Impact on Elementary and Secondary School Students," in *Handbook of Research on Multicultural Education*, ed. James Banks and Cherry McGee Banks (New York: Simon & Schuster MacMillan), pp. 597–617 (1995); Kurlaender, M. and Yun, J.T. (2001). "Is Diversity a Compelling Educational Interest? Evidence from Louisville" in Orfield, G. with M. Kurlaender, eds. *Diversity Challenged: Evidence on the Impact of Affirmative Action*. Cambridge, MA: Harvard Educational Publishing Group, 111–141.

[18] "The Ethical Demands for Integration," in James B. Washington, ed., *A Testament of Hope: The Essential Writing and Speeches of Martin Luther King, Jr.*, San Francisco: Harper San Francisco (1991), p. 118.

[19] *Green v. County School Board*, 391 U.S. 430, 435 (1968).

[20] James S. Coleman, Sara D. Kelley and John A. Moore, *Trends in School Segregation*, 1968–1973, Washington: Urban Institute (1975).

[21] *Milliken I*, 418 U.S. 801 (Marshall, J. dissenting).

[22] Charles T. Clotfelter, *After Brown: The Rise and Retreat of School Desegregation*, Princeton: Princeton University Press (2004).

[23] Finis Welch and Audrey Light, *New Evidence on School Desegregation*, Washington: United States Commission on Civil Rights, Unicon Research Corp. (1987).

[24] *Swann*, 402 U.S. at 20-21.

[25] *Freeman v. Pitts*, 503 U.S. 467, 494 (1992).

[26] "School Integration Backed by Public Since 1954 Decision." June 23, 1961, at Gallup.com.

[27] Ray, Julie. "Reflections on the 'Trouble in Little Rock,' Part II." March 4, 2003, at Gallup.com.

[28] 2001 Gallup Social Audit.

[29] Frankenberg, Lee, and Orfield, *supra* note 2; J. Logan & D. Oakley, *The Continuing Legacy of the Brown Decision: Court Action and School Segregation, 1960–2000*, Albany, NY: Lewis Mumford Center for Comparative Urban and Regional Research (January 28, 2004).

[30] *Milliken v. Bradley*, 418 U.S. 717 (1974) (*Milliken I*).

[31] *Milliken I*, 418 U.S. at 782 (Marshall, J. dissenting).

[32] *San Antonio Indep. School Dist. v. Rodriguez*, 411 U.S. 1 (1973).

[33] U.S. Bureau of the Census, *Statistical Abstract of United States* 1992, table 33, p. 29.

[34] U.S. National Center for Education Statistics, *The Condition of Education* 1995, Washington: Government Printing Office, 1995: 120.

[35] Such as in Brevard County, Florida; Hillsborough County, Florida; Jefferson County, Kentucky; and Greenville, South Carolina. G. Orfield & F. Monfort, *Racial Change & Desegregation in Large School Districts: Trends Through the 1986–1987 School Year*, Alexandria, VA: National School Boards Association (1988).

[36] *Milliken v. Bradley*, 433 U.S. 267 (1977) (*Milliken II*).

[37] G. Orfield & S. Eaton, *Dismantling Desegregation: The Quiet Reversal of* Brown v. Board of Education, New York: The New Press (1996), p. 155.

[38] *Missouri v. Jenkins*, 515 U.S. 70 (1995).

[39] *Id.*, at 89.

[40] E. Frankenberg and C. Lee, "Charter Schools and Race: A Lost Opportunity For Integrated Education," Cambridge, MA: The Civil Rights Project at Harvard University (2003).

[41] *Id.*

[42] Chungmei Lee, "Racial Segregation and Educational Outcomes in Metropolitan Boston," Cambridge, MA: The Civil Rights Project at Harvard University (2004).

[43] R. Mickelson, "The Academic Consequences of Desegregation and Segregation: Evidence from the Charlotte-Mecklenburg Schools," 81 *N.C. Law Rev.* 1513 (2003).

[44] In fact, a number of districts in the South that have been among the most integrated, voted to consolidate city and suburban districts to aid school desegregation, including Jefferson County, Kentucky (Louisville) and Wake County, North Carolina (Raleigh).

[45] *Sheff v. O'Neil*, 238 Conn. 1, 678 A.2d 1267 (1996).

[46] Abram Chayes, *The Role of the Judge in Public Law Litigation*, 89 *Harv. L. Rev.* 1281 (1976).

[47] Works by Alexander Bickel, David Kirp, Gerald Rosenberg, Derrick Bell, and by jurists including J. Harvie Wilkinson, III, Richard A. Posner, William Rehnquist, and Clarence Thomas.

[48] Michael J. Klarman, *From Jim Crow to Civil Rights: The Supreme Court and the Struggle for Racial Equality*, New York: Oxford University Press (2004).

[49] W. Parker, *The Decline of Judicial Decision Making: School Desegregation and District Court Judges*, 81 *N.C. Law Rev.* 1623 (2003), p. 1625.

[50] Chayes, *supra* note 46.

[51] Such logic would favor the continuation of school desegregation cases until all vestiges of racial discrimination have dissipated. However, in contrast to similar areas of litigation such as special education litigation, lower courts have been less willing to maintain extended oversight in the area of desegregation and, relying on the "good faith" of the school boards, prefer to return school systems to local control as soon as possible.

[52] *Hobson v. Hansen*, 269 F. Supp 401 (D.C. D.C. 1967).

[53] Frank M. Johnson, Jr., "The Role of the Federal Courts in Institutional Litigation," 32 *Ala. L. Rev.* 271 (1981).

[54] Orfield and Eaton, *supra* note 37.

[55] *San Antonio Indep. School Dist. v. Rodriguez*, 411 U.S. 1 (1973).

[56] *Milliken v. Bradley*, 418 U.S. 717 (1974) (*Milliken I*).

[57] Gary Orfield, "Conservative Activists and the Rush Toward Resegregation," in *Law and School Reform* (Jay Heubert, ed.), New Haven, CT: Yale University Press (1999).

[58] *Sweatt v. Painter*, 339 U.S. 629 (1950); *McLaurin v. Okla. State Regents for Higher Ed.*, 339 U.S. 637 (1950).

[59] Julian Bond, "The Next Racial Justice Revolution," speech at Color Lines Conference, Harvard University, August 30, 2003.

[60] Julie F. Mead, *Conscious Use of Race as a Voluntary Means to Educational Ends in Elementary and Secondary Education: A Legal Argument Derived from Recent Judicial Descisions*, 8 *Mich. J. Race & L.* 63; see *Tuttle v. Arlington County School Bd.*, 195 F.3d 698 (C.A. 4 1999).

[61] *Grutter v. Bollinger*, 123 S.Ct. 2325, 2341 (2003).

Gary Orfield is a professor of education and social policy in the Harvard Graduate School of Education, and founding co-director of Harvard's Civil Rights Project. He has also taught at the University of Chicago, University of Virginia, Princeton University, and the University of Illinois. He is an author of several books and has served on the editorial board of many journals including the *American Journal of Education, Policy Studies Quarterly,* and the *Teachers College Record and Educational Policy Analysis.* Mr. Orfield has been commissioned to produce studies or advise on research and policy issues by the U.S. Congress, as well as several federal, state, and local agencies and legislatures. He serves on advisory boards for organizations including the Harvard University Faculty Committee on Human Rights, Harvard's Native American Program, the Joint Center on Housing, the Du Bois Institute for Afro-American Research, the Rockefeller Center for Latin American Studies, and the Institute on Race and Poverty. Mr. Orfield received his B.A. from the University of Minnesota, summa cum laude, and his M.A. and Ph.D. from the University of Chicago. He has been a recipient of Woodrow Wilson, Danforth, Falk, and Brookings Institution fellowships and a Senior Scholar fellowship from the Spencer Foundation.

Erica Frankenberg is a doctoral student in education policy at the Harvard University Graduate School of Education. She is a research assistant at The Civil Rights Project where she has co-authored a series of reports on public school segregation trends, including "A Multiracial Society with Segregated Schools: Are We Losing the Dream?" with Chungmei Lee and Gary Orfield. She received her Masters in Education at Harvard with a concentration in Administration, Planning, and Social Policy and earned a B.A. in Educational Policy from Dartmouth College, cum laude, where she received high honors for her senior thesis regarding the end of court-mandated desegregation in Mobile, Alabama. Ms. Frankenberg's research interest in school desegregation stems from her experience as a student in desegregated public schools. She presented "The Impact of School Segregation on Residential Housing Patterns: Mobile, AL and Charlotte, NC" at the Resegregation of Southern Schools conference in August 2002.

Credits

Book Design and Photo Research
Karen Gill, Pinckard Gill Creative

Proofreading and Production Management
Carole Palmer, Creative Services

Consulting Editors
Charles J. White, Katie Fraser, Robert D. Yates

Editorial Support
Craig W. Johnson, James H. Landman

Administrative Support
Adrienne P. Barney, Cynthia Hunt, May Nash

Printed by
Chicago Press Corporation

Director, Division for Public Education
Mabel C. McKinney-Browning

Staff Editor, Brown at 50: The Unfinished Legacy
Charles F. Williams

Cover art
Lawyers and Clients
Jacob Lawrence (1993)

"I deal with the human condition. Lawyers, doctors and ministers have always been very important to the African American Community through history. Great heroes like Thurgood Marshall were strong protectors of our rights."

Andinkra Symbol
Akoma Ntoaso (Joined or united hearts)
Asante people of Ghana
The symbol of togetherness and unity in thought and deed.